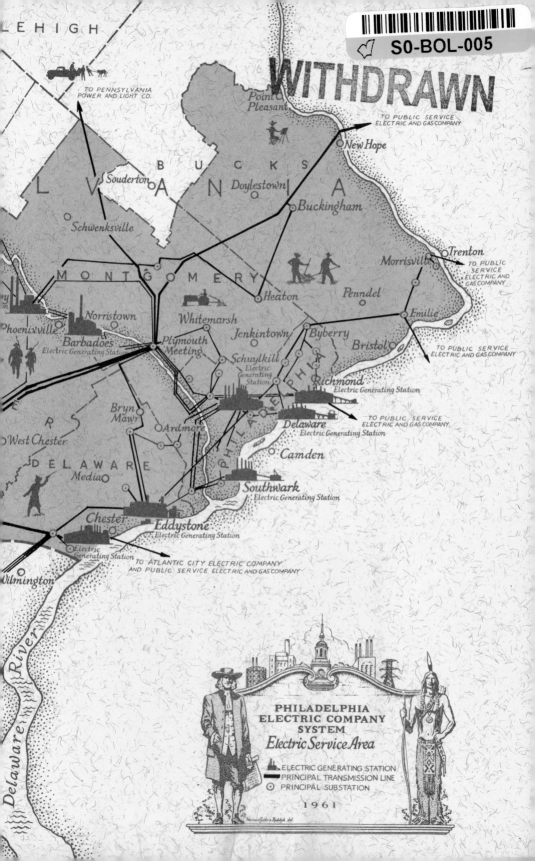

LEHIGH

TO PENNSYLVANIA POWER AND LIGHT CO.

Point Pleasant

TO PUBLIC SERVICE ELECTRIC AND GAS COMPANY

New Hope

B U C K S

Souderton

L V A N I A

Doylestown

Buckingham

Schwenksville

Trenton
TO PUBLIC SERVICE ELECTRIC AND GAS COMPANY

Morrisville

M O N T G O M E R Y

Heaton

Penndel

Emilie

Norristown

Whitemarsh

Jenkintown

Byberry

Bristol

TO PUBLIC SERVICE ELECTRIC AND GAS COMPANY

Phoenixville

Barbadoes
Electric Generating Station

Plymouth Meeting

Schuylkill
Electric Generating Station

Richmond
Electric Generating Station

R S

Bryn Mawr

Ardmore

P H I L A D E L P H I A

Delaware
Electric Generating Station

TO PUBLIC SERVICE ELECTRIC AND GAS COMPANY

West Chester

D E L A W A R E

Media

Camden

Southwark
Electric Generating Station

Chester

Eddystone
Electric Generating Station

Electric Generating Station

TO ATLANTIC CITY ELECTRIC COMPANY AND PUBLIC SERVICE ELECTRIC AND GAS COMPANY

Wilmington

Delaware River

PHILADELPHIA
ELECTRIC COMPANY
SYSTEM
Electric Service Area

⬛ ELECTRIC GENERATING STATION
▬ PRINCIPAL TRANSMISSION LINE
◯ PRINCIPAL SUBSTATION

1961

Norman Gethra Rudolph del.

PHILADELPHIA ELECTRIC
COMPANY

Conowingo

HISTORY

OF THE

PHILADELPHIA ELECTRIC

COMPANY

1881 · 1961

By NICHOLAS B. WAINWRIGHT

PHILADELPHIA 1961

Preface

THOSE OF US associated with Philadelphia Electric, whether as customers, owners of its securities, or
employees, know that the function of the Company is to
provide steam heat in parts of Philadelphia, gas service
in the suburban counties, and electric service throughout
our territory, which extends into Maryland and York
County, Pennsylvania. Few of us, however, have known
much about the Company's background. Few have been
familiar with the major steps by which Philadelphia
Electric grew to its present size. The names of many of
the Company's former leaders who made important contributions have been all but forgotten.

The Philadelphia Electric story, beginning in 1881,
reflects in part the history of Philadelphia itself, and later
the history of the larger territory served by the Company
after 1928. As changes affected our service area, the
Company made necessary adjustments; as population
grew, as industry developed, as invention brought new
conveniences to all of us, in like measure Philadelphia
Electric expanded to meet the demands of a new day.
Thus, to a degree, the history of the Company is the
history of the place in which most of us live.

In May, 1959, the directors of Philadelphia Electric,
believing that the story of the Company was an important
one and should be told, authorized the publication of its

history. This history does not mark an anniversary year. It has been brought out at this time so that the author could have the advantage of meeting a number of senior employees and service annuitants who are familiar with events of long ago, but who may not be here when the Company rounds out its first century.

To write our book we engaged Nicholas B. Wainwright, editor of The Historical Society of Pennsylvania and author of a number of books on Philadelphia. We believe that the account he has produced accurately mirrors our past. With its many side lights on our local development, on personalities and events, this volume should be of value not only to those interested in Philadelphia Electric Company, but in the great metropolitan Philadelphia area as well.

R. G. RINCLIFFE
President

Introduction

The fundamental source for the history of Philadelphia Electric is its collection of minute books, which is complete not only for the Company but also for all the predecessor companies which were eventually merged into the Philadelphia Electric system. Amplifying this source are the executive committee minutes and the informative monthly reports to the board by the president and later by the executive vice-president. In addition, special project reports were consulted, as were the occasional pamphlets issued by the Company, and its publications, the *Bulletin of the Philadelphia Electric Company* (1906–1928) and *Current News* (1909 to date). These printed records were reinforced by the Company's annual reports, the reports of other corporations, notably U.G.I., and trade publications, such as the *Edison Electric Institute Bulletin*.

Interviews with Company directors, employees, and service annuitants constituted an important basis for this study. In this regard, the author owes his thanks to many people, but limits his acknowledgments to those no longer active with the Company: Vice-Presidents Walter E. Long, N. E. Funk, George E. Whitwell, K. M. Irwin, and L. R. Gaty; former Directors Edward Hopkinson, Jr. (of Drexel's) and William W. Bodine (of U.G.I.); and E. G. Boyer, former manager of the gas department.

Several officials who died before the history was undertaken left unpublished memoirs which contain material of vital interest. In 1955, Sidney Shalett conducted a series of tape-recorded interviews with President Horace P. Liversidge. Although Mr. Liversidge's death cut short this fascinating account of his career, the typescript taken from the tape runs to 366 pages. Regional Vice-President Albert R. Granger dictated a lengthy account of his experiences with the Company, "Fifty-Five Strenuous Years, 1892–1947," and John W. Meyer has left a shorter account, "Early Recollections of the Edison Electric Light Company and William D. Marks." Also of interest is an extensive narrative compiled some twenty years ago by William Henry Onken, Jr., on the history of Philadelphia Electric. Such records, together with an impressive amount of supplementary material, are preserved in the Company's excellent library. For data on the local scene, the author depended largely on Philadelphia newspapers, notably the *Public Ledger*, the *Record*, the *North American*, the *Evening Bulletin*, and the *Inquirer*.

Throughout the course of his research, the author was guided to sources of information and introduced to specialists in many phases of the Company's work by Lewis B. Beatty, who acted as co-ordinator of the history project. Deeply interested in its history, Mr. Beatty had served Philadelphia Electric for more than forty-six years at the time of his retirement in 1961, and had been assistant successively to two presidents—Horace P. Liversidge and R. G. Rincliffe. The author is deeply grateful to Mr. Beatty for all his help and also to Miss Lois V. Given of The Historical Society of Pennsylvania for her expert editorial guidance.

N. B. W.

Contents

Illustrations

xi

PHILADELPHIA ELECTRIC COMPANY

CHAPTER 1

The Philadelphia Scene

ONCE CONFINED to a narrow growth which clutched the Delaware River bank and cast its tendrils toward the Schuylkill, the city of Philadelphia by 1880 had long since sprawled across the western river. It had enveloped farm lands to the north and, as its people multiplied and transportation improved, its outskirts expanded steadily with the opening of streets and the building of row upon row of houses.

Second in size to New York, Philadelphia's population in 1880 numbered 847,542, of whom one quarter were foreign-born. It was said to be the largest distinctively manufacturing city in the country, a position won in large measure by its access to coal and iron and by its transportation facilities.

What a contrast this tumultuous center of industry and commerce presented to the Philadelphia of eighty years before! There were still a few old-timers who could recall the year 1800, and who marveled at the changes which had since taken place. The nineteenth-century wave of inventiveness was all the more astounding when contrasted with the paucity of eighteenth-century improvements. From 1700 to 1800, mankind produced no remarkable invention which basically altered Philadelphians' ways of living before the turn of the century. In ocean travel they still depended on the sailing vessel; the

I

horse still carried them or hauled their vehicles over land. In 1800, as in 1700, wood was the fuel used for cooking and heating. Refrigeration remained virtually nonexistent. Illumination was still provided by candles and oil lamps. Water was drawn from private wells all too often contaminated by sewage. No notable advance had been made in sanitation, and medicine had yet to unravel the mystery of yellow fever which plagued the city in the early autumn.

How in one life span, wondered the old Philadelphian of 1880, could anyone again witness so many extraordinary changes as he had seen, so many material improvements. In a bewildering and accelerating rush, man's daily pattern had been projected from the well-nigh medieval to the modern. As early as 1802, a public water system had been created when Schuylkill water was pumped into the city. Soon, hydrants appeared to aid the firemen. In the 1820's, the water supply was vastly improved by the damming of the Schuylkill at Fairmount and the building of the beautiful Fairmount waterworks. An elaborate system of canals which gave access to the hinterland made transportation easier, and in 1832 the city's first railroad, the Philadelphia, Germantown and Norristown, went into operation. Horses pulled the cars in wet weather, for the locomotive, built by Matthias W. Baldwin, was not allowed out in the rain.

Four years after the coming of the railroad, the first gas plant was built, and, before long, most of the buildings and streets were gas-lit. Steam power, early applied to ships and locomotives, came into general use in manufacturing establishments in the 1840's and 1850's and helped create the large factories that symbolized the industrial revolution. Communication was accelerated by the telegraph. Meanwhile, anthracite coal and new coal ranges took over the city's kitchens. The bathroom and the plumber made their simultaneous appearance. Elevators became fairly common after the 1850's, and late in the 1870's came the telephone.

Coal, steam, and gas, through their ability to generate power and light, led to the establishment of many industries and to the rapid accumulation of wealth. In this age of industrialization, Philadelphia became a center of the coal trade and was famed for its machine shops, locomotive works, ironworks, textile mills, sugar refineries, and breweries. By the time of the Civil War, petroleum from Pennsylvania oil fields was flowing into the city, and businessmen were grasping at a whole new range of money-making possibilities. At this time, also, the lumbering, noisy omnibuses that rattled over cobblestone streets carrying people about town gave way to smooth-riding horsecars. Iron rails for horsecar lines were laid down on all the city's major avenues. The demands of commerce gave renewed life to the impressive shipyards at Kensington, Chester, and Camden, whose propeller-driven iron steamships were in demand by the Russian navy and world trade.

Material improvements and scientific advances had certainly altered man's ways of doing many things, and had made his life an easier one. If the octogenarian who had seen so many inventions given practical application believed that the era of change was about to slow down, he was hardly to be blamed. But the younger generation knew better. It knew that the horsecar city with its gaslights was on the verge of another wave of invention that was to outrun the imagination. This wave was to be sparked by electricity.

The city's great wealth enabled it to adopt costly improvements with relative ease. In this laissez-faire, expansive age, business was generally good. The enterprising man found advancement, and with it the leisure to enjoy the recreations which had blossomed in this new day.

The sound of ball on bat was to be heard on many a cricket and baseball field. In and about the city, a number of tracks catered to the devotees of harness racing. Yacht clubs had their regattas on the Delaware, the barges and racing shells of numerous rowing clubs churned the waters of the Schuylkill. Bicycles were coming into popularity, although at first their knickerbocker-clad riders were considered sensationalists, and the vehicle itself was a terror to horses. Before long, however, the new craze was accepted, bicycle meets and races became fashionable, and there was even talk of mounting postmen on tricycles for the quicker delivery of mail.

The city's favorite playground was Fairmount Park. During a June month in the early 1880's, it was visited by half a million pleasure seekers; in addition, more than 5,400 equestrians cantered along its bridle paths, and some 95,000 horse-drawn carriages, including magnificent four-in-hands, paraded on its drives. Escaping from the heat of the city, Philadelphians picnicked in their world-famous park, enjoyed the beauties of nature, and indulged themselves with trips on the Fairmount steamers. These squat little paddle-wheel vessels made regular runs from Fairmount landing, some of them by moonlight, stopping at the Zoo and other points of interest on their way up river to dining and dancing places.

Fairmount Park was considered more refined than Ridgway Park, which was situated on an island in the Delaware near the Walnut Street wharf. Beer was known to be served at Ridgway Park on Sundays in defiance of the law, and the place was occasionally the scene of fights and other disreputable antics. Still, it offered a gala setting for those who behaved themselves. There were swimming, bowling, shooting and scores of other amusements.

4

At night the island was lit by its own gasworks, while Carl Sentz's Military Orchestra performed at the dancing pavilion. A fleet of tiny ferries was kept busy transporting customers back and forth to this popular resort.

One of the diversions at Ridgway Park was watching the comings and goings of the vessels that crowded the Delaware. Six ferry lines connected Philadelphia with opposite points on the Jersey shore, a pleasant ride for three cents. Fishing boats brought in their catches, and, beginning in September, scores of oyster boats from the Maurice River cove and the Western Shore unloaded their thousands of oysters at the Spruce Street wharves. A fleet of two hundred schooners was continually supplying the city with ice from the Kennebec and Penobscot Rivers. They made their return trips freighted with coal.

Excursion steamers took holidaying Philadelphians up to Trenton or down to Cape May. Passenger vessels made regular trips to Wilmington and Baltimore. Ships of the various coasting lines clustered thick along the river front. Freighters loaded Baldwin locomotives consigned to South America, Australia, or the sugar plantations of the Sandwich Islands. Dignified Cunarders sailed for Liverpool; the Red Star Line took on passengers for Antwerp. Full-rigged ships, some of them brand new, still entered the port.

While many Philadelphians took the Cape May steamer for a vacation at the shore, others preferred such inland resorts as Chestnut Hill, or summer places along the Main Line of the Pennsylvania Railroad. It was the railroad that transformed the sleepy little hamlet of White Hall into stylish Bryn Mawr. There, in 1872, a large hotel was opened, and Bryn Mawr became fashionable as a first-class vacation resort. The land nearby was developed by the wealthy for their summer homes. In 1880, publisher George W. Childs built an enormous residence there in the style of a Swiss chalet; not far off, "a college for females" was soon under construction. The railroad was also responsible for a similar development at Devon, where, in the early 1880's, the Devon Inn, a house of many gables and chimneys, supposedly in the seventeenth-century English manner, was erected in park-like grounds of six hundred acres. No sooner did the Pennsylvania Railroad reach Chestnut Hill than the Wissahickon Inn was built, the largest and finest hotel in the suburbs. It, too, was in the prevailingly popular "old English" style.

The Philadelphia of 1880, both city and suburbs, required many services which presented a challenge to a multiplicity of competing enterprises. At this time, for example, it was not true that nearly everyone in Philadelphia read the *Evening Bulletin;* there were seventeen other daily papers to choose from. Whether or not the city needed thirty-six banks, it had them, as well as many trust companies and saving fund societies. The day of consolidation, of the merger, had not yet come, but it was just around the corner. Technological advances could best be achieved by uniting small companies having overlapping functions and heavy overheads into strong, stable corporations. The Philadelphia passenger railway companies were particularly susceptible to such consolidation and were the first local institutions to succumb to the merger movement that swept the country in the latter years of the nineteenth century.

In 1880, there were thirteen separate passenger railways in the city, operating more than 1,200 cars pulled by more than 7,000 horses over 264 miles of track. During the next few years, the track mileage was greatly increased, and it was freely conceded that the extension of the horsecar lines into suburban sections quickened the development of rural farm lands into building lots by bringing those areas within easy access to the center of the city. But while the lines increased their mileage, they themselves declined in number. The move to consolidate the city passenger railways had begun in 1879, and before long was spearheaded by three syndicates, the George F. Work System, the William Wharton, Jr., System, and the Union line, which was eventually to dominate all traction interests.

Horsecars had not been in operation a quarter of a century before farsighted businessmen realized that mechanical power would have to be substituted for the horse. In 1882, the Union line, inspired by the example of San Francisco and Chicago, built a cable road on Columbia Avenue from Twenty-third Street to the east entrance of Fairmount Park. The spokesman for the Union line also requested permission of City Councils to convert its Market Street line to the cable system. "We have examined with great care," he said, "every known system intended to take the place of horses upon passenger railways. After testing many of them, we have come to the conclusion that the cable system, while the most expensive, is the only feasible plan of doing away with horses. Horses are much dearer than they have been for years and it will soon be impossible to run railways with horses [and keep the fares low]. With the cable we can reduce fares; without it we cannot."

The rise and multiplication of the horsecar railways and their eventual consolidation into one great monopolistic system foreshadowed similar consolidations in other utilities. As they evolved in Philadelphia, such consolidations did much to avert rate wars and to achieve standardization and economy in operation.

The situation could have developed differently. The city government, instead of granting franchises to privately owned railway companies, could have built and operated the lines itself. That, however, would have been unfortunate, for the political bosses who controlled City Councils were far more interested in favoring contractors than in protecting the people. They would have seen to it that the railways became a source of graft. The gasworks, for example, was municipally owned, and its operation was a scandal. Service was slipshod and inefficient, and rates were high. In 1880, an investigation disclosed what all knew must be the case—gross mismanagement. Why, for example, did the gasworks pay its suppliers twenty-five per cent more per ton of coal than the going rate? The answer to this and other dubious practices seemed obvious—the Gas Ring headed by the city boss was receiving a million-dollar kickback from suppliers. It was just as well that the political ideologies of the day did not contemplate a broader public ownership of heat, light, and power companies.

The history of the formation of new utilities was similar to that of the horsecar companies. On the invention of the telegraph, and later of the telephone, many companies were incorporated and were granted franchises for identical territories. Unnecessary duplication of services, attended with confusion and waste, ruled for a time. Then the inevitable move for consolidation began.

Philadelphians, while appreciative of the telegraph in 1880, were annoyed by its wires. Dangling from a forest of 4,000 poles which obstructed the city streets, the overhead wires, unsightly and presumably lethal, had already called forth vigorous public protest. The poles carried not only the wires of the telegraph companies, but those of the city's police and fire alarm telegraph and many private lines as well. In 1878, Philadelphia's first telephone directory was published. It contained only forty-seven names, but an industry had been launched and more wires went up.

While the wires were a nuisance and hampered the fire department, they did represent progress. Progress, properly promoted, is profitable, and many people in Philadelphia hoped to establish fortunes by these objectionable lines which snaked from pole to pole along the city streets. Just as in every movement, in every advance, there must be courageous and able leaders, so it was that the rise of electrical utilities in Philadelphia owed much to a small group of men who deserve more than passing mention.

In the last two decades of the nineteenth century, there were in Philadelphia five men who can be singled out for their pre-eminent qualities of business leadership, particularly as it applied to the fields of petroleum, traction, and power and light. Self-made men all, and founders of immense fortunes, their names were Dolan, Widener, Elkins, Maloney, and Warden.

When he died in 1914, Thomas Dolan was said to be one of the five richest men in the city. Born near Philadelphia in 1834, the son of a tollgate keeper, Dolan entered business at an early age. For a time he was a salesman in a knit goods house in Germantown, but when the Civil War came on, he acquired the Keystone Knitting Mills and went into business for himself. In time, as Thomas Dolan and Company, he achieved a virtual monopoly in this line of textiles. Dolan also played a major role in organizing and directing gas and electric companies, and it was under his leadership that The United Gas Improvement Company leased the city gasworks.

Dolan was the perfect corporation-maker, a true captain of industry of his day. Tireless, often hard and ruthless, viewing politics as a mere adjunct to business, working in silence and secrecy, he was outwardly heedless of public clamor, a fast friend and a relentless enemy. His sons are said to have enjoyed spending money more than making it. One of the boys once asked Dolan for an increase to his already princely allowance, but was told by the tycoon that, although he worked as hard as he could all day long, he could not afford to give him more money. Nothing daunted, the son replied, "Well, father, why don't you work nights?"

Dolan was only seventeen days old when P. A. B. Widener was born in Philadelphia. Raised in modest circumstances, the son of a poor brickmaker, Widener was apprenticed to a butcher and rose to the ownership of his own meat shop. A government contract during the Civil War made him a modest fortune which he invested in street railways. Meanwhile, he became active in politics and was a member of that group of Philadelphia politicians known as the All Night Poker Players. Later he served some years as city treasurer, the previous incumbent having been sent to jail. Ready, forceful, and convincing in speech, no one knew better than Widener how to manipulate the city government in favor of his enterprises. He was a close friend of Matthew S. Quay, who controlled Pennsylvania state politics. Quay served as a director of several of Widener's companies and was president of one of them. It was under Widener's leadership that Philadelphia's street railway lines were consolidated. In time, the Widener traction syndicate became the largest in the country, with interests in many cities. On his death in 1915, his fortune of $100,000,000 was probably Philadelphia's largest.

Widener's closest associate and friend was William L. Elkins, whose family moved to Philadelphia from West Virginia in 1840. Elkins made his start in the grocery business, and in 1861 became interested in oil, an interest that won him a Standard Oil partnership fourteen years later. For a time he controlled the Philadelphia oil refinery business, refining oil for illuminating purposes and for gasoline. He also manufactured illuminating gas and bought gasworks. In 1875, he joined with Widener in buying up street railways, and, also with Widener, purchased large tracts of land in the northwestern section of Philadelphia, on which they erected three thousand houses. Dying in 1903, Elkins left a fortune of $30,000,000 and a reputation as one of the most successful and sagacious capitalists in the city. He was a man of brilliant executive ability.

Elkins' refining of gasoline in the early 1870's attracted the attention of Martin Maloney, who had been born in Ireland in 1847 and had been brought to Scranton by his parents in 1854. At the age of twelve he went to work in the anthracite mines, and two years later was apprenticed to learn the trade of plumber and gas fitter. Realizing the possibilities of gasoline as an illuminant, he perfected a gasoline burner. Maloney moved to Philadelphia in 1873 and obtained the contract for lighting the grounds of the Centennial Exposition. Within ten years, through his Penn Globe Gas Light Company, he was supplying street lighting for one hundred and thirty-seven cities and towns. Inevitably, he became a leading figure in gas, water, oil, and electric interests.

William G. Warden was a pioneer oil man. Born in Pittsburgh in 1831, he moved to Philadelphia in 1865 and organized and managed the Petroleum Storage Company. Through Warden, Frew and Company, he built the world's largest refinery. Later, he helped form the International Navigation Company to ship oil across the Atlantic. For twelve years he was president of the Atlantic Refining Company. Warden was also active in real estate speculations and built Philadelphia's first large apartment house, the Gladstone, at Eleventh and Pine Streets.

Mutually bound by a maze of interlocking business interests, it is not surprising to find that Dolan, Widener, Elkins, Maloney, and Warden all backed The United Gas Improvement Company, incorporated in Pennsylvania in 1882 for the initial purpose of introducing the Lowe water gas process, a new method for manufacturing artificial gas. Warden was perhaps the most influential figure in the founding of U.G.I. and served as its president. But Dolan was a director and later became president, Widener was a large stockholder and director, and Elkins, like Warden, was an incorporator of the company and a director. Maloney was also involved in the launching of this new venture which was to prove so successful. From its very start, U.G.I. began a far-flung campaign that was to make it one of the largest gas holding and operating companies in the world. Moreover, it was U.G.I. which brought the Welsbach light to the United States in 1887. This new mantle went into service all over the country and extended the life of gas lighting nearly half a century. It sustained the gas utilities during their unequal struggle with electric lighting and gave them time to discover other productive uses for gas in cooking, heating, and refrigeration.

Absorbed though the founders of U.G.I. were in gas lighting, they were versatile men engaged in many other forms of business. That electric lighting held promise for the future had not escaped their attention. In fact, the year before they organized U.G.I., Dolan, Widener, Elkins, Maloney, and Warden had all entered the electric field by forming Philadelphia's first two electric light companies.

CHAPTER 2

Dawn of the Electric Age

JOHN WANAMAKER, Philadelphia's merchant prince, was so eager to be up to date that he was often ahead of his times, an attribute which was a factor in his great success. Just before Philadelphia staged its spectacular world's fair, the Centennial Exposition of 1876, Wanamaker purchased the Pennsylvania Railroad's former freight station, the Grand Depot, at Thirteenth and Market Streets and converted it into an enormous store. Although everyone but Wanamaker thought the location too far uptown for business, Wanamaker shrewdly believed that the center of the city would move toward his store because it stood next to the new city hall then building on Penn Square.

In his progressive way, he became fascinated with electricity after seeing an experimental light at the Centennial fair. When the Franklin Institute accepted the superiority of the Brush arc lamp over others it tested in 1878, Wanamaker purchased a generating plant to supply twenty-eight Brush lamps for his Grand Depot. Installed in December, 1878, these brilliant lamps made the store's interior almost as light as day and established the practicability of electric lighting in Philadelphia. A few other Philadelphians soon followed Wanamaker's example, notably Thomas Dolan, who lit his mills with Brush equipment.

Philadelphia's interest in electricity extended back to Benjamin Franklin's celebrated experiments. Eighteenth-century philosophers like Franklin delighted in producing electric currents and sparks, though to what use these strange phenomena could be put remained in doubt. In 1800, however, Alessandro Volta invented an electric battery, and in 1813 Sir Humphrey Davy, through the use of a battery, produced an electric arc. This arc was not momentary like the electric spark, but was continuous. Means to supply the arc with sufficient electric power were at last devised by Gramme in 1870, when he invented his dynamo. Six years later, the Russian Paul Jablochkoff perfected his "candles," and the electric lighting industry had the crude fundamentals it needed.

American inventors, led by the incomparable Thomas A. Edison, now entered the electric field to make their contributions. In 1878, the Edison Electric Light Company was formed to finance Edison's invention of an incandescent lighting system and to promote its adoption throughout the world. The arc light inventors, however, had preceded Edison in marketing their equipment. Charles F. Brush, an electrician employed by the Cleveland Telegraph Supply Company, created the first really efficient and complete arc lighting system. In 1878, the Telegraph Supply Company began manufacturing Brush's equipment, and soon changed its name to The Brush Electric Company of Cleveland.

In New York, Hiram S. Maxim, an inventive genius from Maine, was appointed chief engineer of The United States Electric Lighting Company in 1878 and invented the Maxim light. Maxim later went to England and there established his international fame as the inventor of the Maxim machine gun. In Philadelphia, too, there were inventors, the schoolteachers Elihu Thomson and Edwin J. Houston, who produced the Thomson-Houston arc light. Other systems were evolved by other inventors, countless patents were taken out, and before long Americans interested in electric lighting had a bewildering variety of equipment at their disposal.

Despite this progress, Philadelphians were cautious in accepting the new light. San Francisco became the first city in the United States and, as far as is known, the first in the world to have a central generating station for the distribution of electricity to customers. Using Brush equipment, the California Electric Company put its arc lamps into operation in September, 1879. Soon, New York also had its Brush company, but in Philadelphia electric lighting was restricted to "isolated" plants like those owned by Wanamaker and Dolan. In 1880, Philadelphia's Continental Hotel on Chestnut Street, where the Benjamin Franklin Hotel now stands, installed its individual Brush plant. The dynamo was run by the elevator's steam engine. Two large Brush lamps replaced one hundred and forty-four gas burners in the dining room. This light was far too brilliant for bedrooms, being suitable only for large areas.

Some early lighting was extremely dangerous. The Landenberger Mills on Randolph Street were lit with Weston equipment manufactured in Newark, New Jersey. Weston lights had no globes, they flickered badly, and their carbon points frequently threw off sparks. In a fire caused by these unprotected lamps, the mills burned and nine employees were killed. Although electric fires warned people to go slow in accepting the new light, it was found that electricity could be used for other purposes. It was, for instance, applied to bits and spurs for horses. A small battery carried on the saddle and connected by fine wires to the bit and spurs was controlled by pressing buttons. The effect on the horse of this "shocking contrivance" can better be imagined than experienced.

Electricity, however, offered too much to be confined in use to private plants in Philadelphia hotels, stores, and mills, or for bizarre novelty purposes. Impressed with the Brush system he had installed in his factory, Thomas Dolan gathered together a group of wealthy merchants and manufacturers in 1880 and suggested that they form a company. The New York Brush company had just been organized, and late in 1880 was busily engaged in putting up lamps on Broadway. Dolan proposed lighting Chestnut Street.

His plan was taken to City Councils—for $5,000 a year a Philadelphia Brush company would light Chestnut Street from river to river with lamps so strong that newspapers could be read on the street at night. But the city fathers rejected the offer as too expensive. All right, said Dolan, we will light the street at our own expense for one year. Then, if the city liked the light, City Councils could contract for it; if not, Dolan would have the poles and wires removed. It was on this experimental basis that he secured an ordinance permitting The Brush Electric Light Company of Philadelphia to provide free lighting for Chestnut Street.

The company was formed in March, 1881, "for the purpose of carrying on the business of manufacturing, procuring, owning and operating various apparatus used in producing light, heat, or power by electricity or used in lighting buildings." Its initial capital was $200,000, half of which, in the form of stock, was used to buy the necessary patent rights for the Brush equipment. The other $100,000 was equally divided in shares at a par value of one hundred dollars among the ten men who made up the board.

By and large, the directors were simply men who could afford to invest $10,000 in the venture. They included the philanthropist, shy Isaiah V. Williamson. Unable to face the crowd in church, he had left his bride at the altar, but he had made millions in coal and iron and was now an old man. John Wanamaker, who had first introduced the Brush lamp to Philadelphia, was a director, and so was John Lowber Welsh. Aside from Dolan, Welsh, enormously respected for his integrity and financial ability, was the outstanding figure on the board. He was the grandson of the John Welsh who had founded the Philadelphia Bank (Philadelphia National) in 1803, and the son of the John Welsh who had so brilliantly managed the finances of the Centennial Exposition and who had served as United States Minister to England. John Lowber Welsh, one of the wealthy men of the city, had amply proved himself as a financial director of the Reading Railroad and in other important trusts. The dynamic leaders of the community liked to place him at the head of their boards. In 1886, shortly after the first consolidation of the city's electric utilities, it was Welsh who was elected president of the holding company, the Electric Trust. And it was Welsh who was selected to preside over the Union Traction Company in 1895, when the merger of the city's street railway lines at last took place.

The president of The Brush Electric Light Company of Philadelphia from its inception in 1881 until his death in 1886 was Henry Lewis, senior partner in Lewis Brothers and Company, dry goods merchants. Dolan was treasurer, and, as such, chairman of the executive committee charged with the active direction of the company's affairs. It is clear that he ran the company, seldom missing a board meeting and proposing nearly all important measures. When Lewis died, Dolan became president.

It was under Dolan's leadership that property was purchased on Johnson (Ranstead) Street between Twentieth and Twenty-first, just north of Chestnut. There a brick station was erected and equipped with four Babcock and Wilcox boilers from New York, eight Porter-Allen steam engines of 45 horsepower each from the Southwark Foundry & Machine Company, and eight dynamos, lamps of various sizes, 11,000 carbons, and other necessities from The Brush Electric Company of Cleveland. The initial cost of setting up the plant was about $90,000.

Meanwhile, orders for electric lights were received from the West End Hotel, Wanamaker's Grand Depot, the Pennsylvania Railroad's new train shed at Fifteenth Street, Louis Dreka's stationery store, and other business establishments on Chestnut Street. While many welcomed the new service, others had their doubts and cast apprehensive glances at the poles being erected on the Chestnut Street sidewalks. Forty feet high and made of iron, except for two ornamental wooden ones in front of Independence Hall, the poles were painted red. From them hung the powerful Brush arc lamps, and from pole to pole was strung the wire that carried the high-voltage direct current.

The erection of the poles was not accomplished without difficulty. Work had not been under way long before the police put a stop to it, quoting an ordinance passed several months earlier which forbade the further erection of telegraph poles in the city. It took the mayor to convince the police that these were not telegraph poles but electric light poles. When the watchman of the Philadelphia National Bank espied a workman drilling a hole in the bank's sidewalk, he arrested him, and when Stephen B. Fotterall, who lived at 2001 Chestnut Street, looked out a window of his home and saw a wire stretched over his stable, he complained bitterly.

Dolan was kept busy solving problems and soothing feelings. He had to face the fact that many people considered electric light dangerous, or resented it for other

INTERNATIONAL ELECTRICAL EXHIBITION, 1884

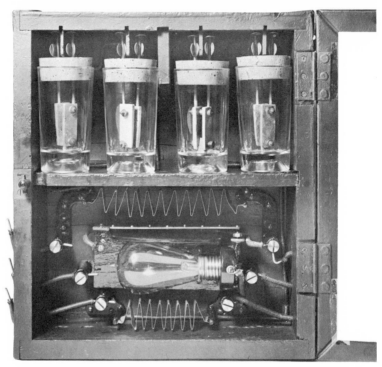

EDISON CHEMICAL METER, 1881

reasons. In a letter to the editor of the *Public Ledger*, a Philadelphian angrily protested: "No resident west of Broad Street desires the electric light. Would any one of the editors or owners of the daily papers like one in front of his private dwelling? Would Mayor King or any member of Councils be delighted with one in front of his sleeping chamber? There is no city in the world where it would be tolerated in a street occupied almost entirely by private residences as West Chestnut Street is. Do you admire the six red poles in each square?"

On December 3, 1881, the Chestnut Street lights, forty-nine of them, were turned on for the first time. Large crowds were attracted, and it was generally agreed that electricity was as superior to gas for street lighting as gas itself was to the oil lamps it had replaced so many years before. The light was not quite as bright as had been expected because the lamps were shaded by globes of ground glass to reduce their dazzling brilliance. Even so, each lamp was equal to three hundred gas jets. A newspaper reported the event in political overtones: "With the combined efforts of the moonlight, electric light, and gaslight, Chestnut Street was better lit upon Saturday and Sunday nights than at any time in its history. The moonlight, being veiled by thin clouds, suffered somewhat; but the gas lamps looked as yellow, dim, and sickly as the Gas Trust itself does before the people, notwithstanding its temporary triumph in getting away from investigation before the Court of Common Pleas."

Dolan and his fellow directors were so much encouraged with their Chestnut Street experiment that they immediately took steps to increase the capital of the company to $1,000,000. At the same time, they elected A. J. DeCamp secretary.

DeCamp was thirty-nine years old and had been with the company, serving without salary, since April 2, 1881.

He knew nothing about electricity, but had had a varied business career and was taken on by Dolan to see what he could do. Before long he had proved his worth. When the first two 40-light dynamos, ordered from the Brush people in Cleveland, did not arrive, Dolan sent DeCamp to get them. In Cleveland, the Philadelphian was told that none would be available for six months, but DeCamp discovered two dynamos that were about to be shipped to Yokohama and pled so eloquently for them that the Brush officials gave in. It was these machines, sent by express to Philadelphia, which provided the current for the lights on Chestnut Street and for the illumination in Wanamaker's basement and the Pennsylvania Railroad shed.

Before the year was out, the demand for lights necessitated the purchase of more machinery and the enlargement of the generating station. To compete with Edison incandescent lighting, now being installed in isolated plants at such places as the Baldwin Locomotive Works, the directors purchased the patent rights of the Swan incandescent lamp for the Philadelphia area, but arc lighting remained the company's essential business. These lights were supplied on a rental basis at rates ranging from fifty cents to seventy cents a lamp per night.

To meet ever-increasing requests for electricity, the company erected pole lines on Market Street, Sansom Street, and elsewhere, thereby greatly increasing the number of overhead wires in the city. The overhead method of conveying wires was extremely unpopular, but Dolan and his colleagues were not yet ready to accept any of the conduit systems, although the company did have an experimental underground line. The matter came to a head in September, 1882, when a public meeting was held to condemn the encroachment of poles and wires on public and private property. At the instance of the Board of Trade, the attorney general of Pennsylvania filed a complaint against the Brush Company for erecting poles and wires on various streets "to the great annoyance, obstruction, and danger of the citizens of the Commonwealth." Embattled, the company successfully defended its practice. Moreover, it won city lighting contracts, including that for Chestnut Street.

While the authorities appeared enthusiastic about the arc lights, they did not turn off the Chestnut Street gaslights, which continued to burn along with the electric ones. This dual lighting may have stemmed from caution, but was, more probably, sheer absent-mindedness on the part of someone who failed to cancel the gas contract.

In 1883, it was again necessary to enlarge the generating plant; indeed, the process of increasing the station's capacity was virtually a continuous one. In 1884, a new boiler house was built and an additional story added to the station. Large lighting contracts from Strawbridge & Clothier and other major enterprises kept business prospects bright. The company was not yet on a dividend-paying basis, for its profits of around $4,000 a month went into its construction program, but at least it was now able to pay its employees. In January, 1883, after nearly two years without pay, DeCamp was given twenty-five shares of the company's stock, par value $2,500, and put on a salary of $2,500 a year.

The profitable operation of electric companies demonstrated that their lighting was becoming more and more accepted because of its efficiency. Philadelphians were now accustomed to electricity to the extent, at least, that virtually everyone in the city had seen an electric light. In September, 1884, their awareness was greatly quickened by the magnificent International Electrical Exhibition. Sponsored by the Franklin Institute and aglow with thousands of lights of every known patent, the exhibition occupied a building large enough to accommodate five thousand visitors at Thirty-second Street and Lancaster Avenue. It contained 1,500 exhibits, and featured the application of electricity to the running of a railroad train, printing presses, sewing machines, and to the playing of pipe organs.

While this distinguished event did much to demonstrate the merits of different lighting systems, it did not help solve the perplexing problem of underground wiring. The year was running out, and telegraph, telephone, and electric light companies were uneasily facing an ordinance which stated that by January 1, 1885, all their poles and wires were to be removed from the streets of Philadelphia. The Brush Company had tried an underground line on Delaware Avenue, but it failed, and the gaslights had to be turned on again. As a result, Dolan naturally felt that underground wiring had not been sufficiently developed to warrant its general adoption.

There was only one company in the city which operated an underground conduit for electric lighting. The Underground Electric Light and Power Company, controlled by the Brush Company, had a cable under Chestnut Street and was supplying customers with incandescent lighting from lamps of the Swan patent. The Underground Company had secured an ordinance permitting it to hang its lamps on the gaslight standards, which at long last had been abandoned. When this privilege was discussed in Select Council, it had met with all sorts of opposition from the representative of the Twenty-fifth Ward. "I may be under the influence of liquor," this gentleman at last confessed. "I fear you are," replied the presiding officer, and amid confusion and violence, the councilman was ejected from the chamber.

The Underground Company's troubles, however, were not over. Its system was nearly destroyed in a series of nighttime disasters. While the audience in the Chestnut Street Opera House was enjoying a show entitled "Mamzelle Nitouche," violent explosions from the underground system threw the house into a panic. On another evening, the audience had just left the Opera House when all the manhole covers blew high in the air, projected on their way by columns of flame. The president of the Underground Company discounted gas seepage as the cause of the trouble. Sabotage, he claimed, had disrupted his system, and he called attention to the fact that the explosions had occurred only a few days before hearings were to take place on putting all wires underground.

The hearings were duly held in November, 1884, and it was agreed by those who could still see manhole covers spinning through the air like poker chips that there was no satisfactory underground system yet available. Among those who testified to this effect was DeCamp of the Brush Company. There simply was no cable he could obtain, said DeCamp, that was effective underground. And so the overhead wires were given a reprieve. But encouragement to do something about them in the future was provided by a tax that was twice as high for overhead wires as it was for those out of sight.

With the danger of having to change all its wiring a thing of the past, the Brush Company's immediate prospects appeared fair enough, but Dolan was skeptical about its future. Other companies were now supplying electric light to Philadelphia, and competition was taking on ridiculous aspects with two or more companies stringing their wires for service on the same streets. At the board meeting of September 11, 1885, it was resolved that Dolan and directors William Wood and John Lowber Welsh be appointed a committee "to devise ways and means to harmonize the company's interests and prevent if possible the depreciation of the company's property." Thus was set up the machinery which nine days later effected the consolidation of The Brush Electric Light Company of Philadelphia with its most pressing rival, The United States Electric Lighting Company of Pennsylvania.

The United States Electric Lighting Company had been founded in Martin Maloney's office in September, 1881, its original name being The Maxim Electric Light and Power Company. It had purchased an exclusive license in Pennsylvania for handling United States and Weston Electric Lighting Company patents, and two years later changed its title to The United States Electric Lighting Company of Pennsylvania to conform to the name of its parent company in New York. Financial backing for the new enterprise could hardly have been stronger. Maloney, its organizer, held a large amount of stock and served as director and general manager. William G. Warden was president, and his brother-in-law and business associate Henry L. Davis was a director. William L. Elkins was vice-president, and his associate P. A. B. Widener was a director. Listed among the early stockholders were John D. Archbold of Standard Oil, Matthew S. Quay, the political boss, A. J. Cassatt, senior vice-president and later president of the Pennsylvania Railroad, Horace Disston of the celebrated saw works, H. H. Houston, the railroad executive and developer of Chestnut Hill, William L. Kemble of the traction syndicate, and Edward T. Stotesbury, a brilliant young partner in the banking house of Drexel & Company.

For a time the Maxim Company restricted itself to setting up isolated plants, using both incandescent and arc lighting, and to the licensing of electric companies in other parts of the state. Its contracts included plants for Philadelphia's new city hall, the post offices in Philadelphia and Pittsburgh, and the Pittsburgh Publishing

Company. Plants were sold to customers in Pottstown, Bethlehem, Wilkes-Barre, Bristol, Lebanon, Allentown, and Reading. Within several years, electric lighting companies licensed by Warden, Maloney, and their fellow directors were in operation at Pittsburgh, Philipsburg, Lancaster, and elsewhere.

On June 21, 1882, The Maxim Electric Light and Power Company, as it was still called, was authorized to erect poles and run wires in Philadelphia. The central city area included in its franchise was nearly the same as that granted by ordinance to the Brush Company. Competition followed, with Maxim winning the city contract for lighting part of Delaware Avenue. About this time, a misunderstanding evidently took place between Widener and Maloney. Both attempted to resign. Elkins persuaded them to stay on, but a few months later Maloney left the board. Thus, he was not on hand in 1885 when Dolan and Warden consolidated the management of their two corporations. Though he missed this initial step to bring the city's electric concerns together, Maloney was to take the leading position ten years later in the move that was to unite every electric light company in Philadelphia.

CHAPTER 3

The Electric Trust

Not long after the Brush and United States companies were organized, a rash of other electric companies appeared in Philadelphia. For the most part, they were small ventures which confined their operations to specific areas in the city, as their names suggest: Germantown Electric Light Company; The Frankford Electric Light and Power Company; The Wissahickon Electrical Light Company; and Southern Electric Light and Power Company, which worked that part of the city below South Street. By 1895, more than twenty electric light companies had been launched to serve Philadelphia.

The multiplicity of these companies was nearly matched by the different electrical systems they operated. Moreover, the current they supplied varied. There was direct current at 100, 220, and 600 volts. Also, there was single-phase, two-phase, and three-phase alternating current at frequencies of 40, 60, 66, 125, and 133 cycles. This chaotic condition resulted in such situations as that of a man moving his household belongings from one side of the street to the other only to discover that his lamps would not light. Or he might find that while his lights would burn, his electric fan or other motors would not operate. It was readily apparent that the growth of the electric industry in Philadelphia could not attain vigor until standardization replaced the prevailing individualistic system—or lack of system—in the distribution of electricity.

The spawning of so many electric companies in the 1880's and 1890's was attended by a certain amount of political midwifery in that peculiarly unwholesome atmosphere that blighted large American cities in those days. According to Lincoln Steffens, while Philadelphia was contented, it was also the most corrupt city in the country. Bosses controlled City Councils and exploited the city for private profit, distributing the "boodle" to their political followers. Public franchises, public works, and public contracts were the principal branches of their business. For years after the Civil War, James McManes, "James I," was the absolute boss of the city and the head of the Gas Ring. In 1889, state boss Quay deposed McManes and replaced him with David Martin. McManes, however, remained a political figure to be reckoned with, a sort of senior statesman. He served on the board of The Penn Electric Light Company, and, as a friend of Widener's, was a director of the principal traction syndicate in the city.

Some electric companies found it expedient to have a politician on their boards to ease their way in political matters and to protect them from the voraciousness of grafters. A number of the principal members of Councils were directors of electric companies, political leaders like Hamilton Disston, Henry Clay, and other lesser lights. When David Martin came into power, he set up a dual control with the contractor Charles A. Porter, and for nine years Martin and Porter ran the city with the support of both the Republican and Democratic organizations. Porter was much interested in electric utilities. In 1890, the Powelton, Suburban, and Diamond electric companies were founded, Porter being an incorporator of the latter two, director of all three, and president of the Diamond. The Manufacturers Electric Company was also founded in 1890, with David Martin an incorporator instead of Porter, but Porter joined as a director in 1893. He was also on the board of The Wissahickon Electrical Light Company. All the electric companies with which Porter was associated enjoyed city contracts.

By the middle of the 1890's, Philadelphia was not only the best lighted city in the nation, but had nearly as many electric street lamps as New York, Chicago, and Boston combined. It also had an annual electric bill approaching $1,000,000. With street lighting the principal business of certain politically controlled companies, reformers vigorously asserted that much of the lighting contracted for by the city was unnecessary. Critics complained about lonely country roads that were kept brilliantly lighted at night. It may well have been so. Porter, as president of The Diamond Electric Company, acknowledged to his stockholders that the company's main dependence in its first years was on public lighting because its territory was principally suburban.

Although many companies were able to keep themselves free of political taint, others had to pay a high price for their franchises. The speculative Penn Electric Light Company, a New Jersey corporation founded in 1886, was given a valuable franchise to lay conduits in the city. This franchise was supposed to be worth $3,000,000, and the appreciative company handed out, so it was said, 90,000 shares, par value one dollar, to be distributed to the politicians. For years, City Councils protected this company by barring competition, even though Penn Electric was hardly in operation.

The distribution of the spoils was kept a dark secret, but an exposure in 1895 revealed a fair example of the process. Shortly after a franchise had been granted to the Mutual Automatic Telephone Company, two councilmen died. It was discovered that each owned six shares, par value fifty dollars, in this concern. An investigation disclosed that the company had issued a large block of stock in a series of six shares each, and another block in a series of twenty shares each. Incredibly, the company claimed it had no record of who owned these shares. But it did have a record of issuing 1,525 shares (valued at $76,250) to David Martin, and 1,525 shares to Charles A. Porter. After taking some time for thought, both Martin and Porter claimed that they had no idea how the stock came to be registered in their names, and every member of Councils swore that none of them owned shares in the unfortunate telephone company.

The political situation just described was a factor with which electric companies had to contend. It is more than doubtful, however, that responsible companies, such as the Brush and United States, whose boards were packed with formidable characters like Dolan and Widener, were held up for plunder by the city bosses. The most important electric company founded in Philadelphia during this era was the Edison, and it was scrupulously correct, a trait which brought it political trouble but a clear conscience. Then, too, many companies were too small to bother macing, and others were founded by politicians and so were safe. Thus, while exposed to municipal corruption, it is not likely that many electric companies were much affected by it.

Theoretically, City Councils rejoiced each time they set their seal of approval on a new electric lighting company. The councilmen believed in competition, and the people of Philadelphia were also convinced that only by having competing companies in the field could rates be kept at a proper level. In its business usage, the term "trust," a word properly signifying integrity, veracity, and justice, was one to shudder at in these times, for it conjured up the specter of rampant monopoly. Consequently, it was a matter of general satisfaction that franchises were freely granted to entrepreneurs seeking to enter the field.

The Philadelphia Electric Lighting Company, chartered in 1882, was an early entry, although it did not actually commence business until 1886. Three of its five founders were partners in a law firm and another was the distinguished Edwin J. Houston. Houston and Elihu Thomson, a fellow professor at Philadelphia's Central High School, had perfected the Thomson-Houston electric lighting system, one which was to become a great success. The company which promoted the Thomson-Houston inventions later acquired control of the Brush Electric Company of Cleveland, and, finally, merged with the Edison General Electric Company to form today's multibillion-dollar General Electric Company.

Another concern using the Thomson-Houston system was formed in 1885—The Northern Electric Light and Power Company. Its first president was Common Councilman George W. Boyer, but the most notable figure on its board was Select Councilman Henry Clay, who ultimately became president. At its first stockholders meeting in September, 1885, the management reported: "We have in our estimation been the most successful company ever started. We have been doing a large business all summer. . . . We have our circuits run on the best streets in the city for the reason of their business being done at night." This company was on a dividend-paying basis from the start, and, increasing rapidly in size, was soon one of the three largest electric lighting ventures in Philadelphia.

The Keystone Light and Power Company, on the other hand, is a study in failure. It represented an effort in 1886 of Henry H. Westinghouse of Pittsburgh to introduce the

Westinghouse system to Philadelphia. A power station was set up, but efforts to control the Westinghouse patents in Philadelphia were unavailing and the Keystone was never fairly established. In 1898, the directors sold the company to Martin Maloney for $25,000, and sadly noted in their minutes, "The business of The Keystone Light and Power Company has not proved commercially successful and its efforts to secure a franchise from the City Government for a more extended territory have proved futile." The Keystone had no one on its board capable of dealing with Councils, a fact which led to the company's demise.

In the early years of electric lighting in Philadelphia, Councils' willingness to grant company after company the right to operate in the same territory made for difficulties, even though it fostered competition. The Brush and the United States companies had virtually identical territories in the heart of the city, an area which was also shared by other electric concerns. It did not seem possible for any one of them to have much future, the danger of rate wars was constant, and the conduct of the electric business was becoming increasingly irritating and difficult.

To improve the situation, the leaders of the Brush and United States lighting companies had agreed to a plan of consolidation in 1885. This plan went into effect in April, 1886, when the Electric Trust was formed. Henry Lewis, president of Brush, was named president of the Trust and on his death six months later was succeeded by another Brush-Electric Trust director, John Lowber Welsh. Thomas Dolan and four other Brush directors also took their seats at the Trust's board, where they were joined by Widener, Warden, and another United States director. The only other trustee was Colonel Charles H. Banes, who had never served with any electric company. He had, however, been director-general of the 1884 Interna-

31

tional Electrical Exhibition and was currently in the key position of chairman of the electric committee of Councils. Colonel Banes, it should be observed, was not a machine politician. Suffering from poor health, he soon retired from the board.

The advantages of consolidating the city's two earliest electric lighting companies were obvious. They were capitalized at the same figure, $1,000,000, and were both furnishing roughly the same arc lighting product to the same area. Fighting each other might well do more harm than good. But Dolan and his friends had bigger plans than the consolidation of two companies. They reached out for others, and were soon in control of The Philadelphia Electric Lighting Company (purchased for $71,554), The Penn Electric Light Company, The Northern Electric Light and Power Company (fifty-one per cent stock ownership), and The Underground Electric Light and Power Company of Pennsylvania. To finance the Trust's two major acquisitions, Trust certificates amounting to $3,000,000 were issued in return for the total stock issues of Brush and United States. The value of the dividend-paying certificates was guaranteed by the stock issues of the operating companies which underlay them. To pick up the other properties and to improve its power stations, an additional half-million dollars worth of Trust certificates changed hands.

The Electric Trust was now in business as a holding company. Its satellite companies could not be merged without violation of charters and ordinances; each had to operate individually. The Trust never courted publicity, and for some years, as far as the public was concerned, its existence was virtually unknown. But, under the leadership of Dolan, Welsh, and Warden, it was active in standardizing procedures and in making economies, such as purchasing supplies for all companies through the central agency. Moreover, all major policy considerations were decided by the Trust. Its trustees dominated the boards of the operating companies, and the general manager of Brush, A. J. DeCamp, was designated general manager of all but one of the companies in the Trust.

It was now possible in an amicable way to consolidate, in effect, the business of the Brush and United States companies by virtually eliminating the weaker of the two through the transfer of business. In the month of December, 1887, scarcely a year after the Trust had been established, Brush earned a net profit of $8,365, while the net profit of United States was only $1,462. The Trust wanted to convert the lighting system used by the United States power station to the Brush system, but was prevented from doing so by the United States contract with its parent company in New York. For a similar reason, it had to retain the Thomson-Houston system at certain stations.

The main purposes of the Trust, which were to minimize competition, standardize rates, and increase the earning power of the operating companies as a whole, were successfully achieved. Two incidents may be cited in which, in one case, the Trust suffered from competition, and, in the other, swamped a competitor. In 1891, the Brush Company lost a city contract for street lighting to a company that was not part of the Trust. The night the new company attempted to turn on its lights for the first time, a little war broke out. Its wires were cut in numerous places and crowds collected to watch the excitement. Blame for the outrage was laid at the door of the Brush Company which stood to regain its contract should the competitor fail to furnish light. It is doubtful, however, that the directors of the Trust were involved in these petty shenanigans.

The other incident points up what can happen when competition assumes its worst aspect and brings on a rate war. In 1888, the Merchants Electric Light Company of North Front Street was formed by businessmen living in that vicinity. Operating with a capital of $200,000, its business was profitable, but its area impinged on that of The Northern Electric Light and Power Company, a powerful Trust member. The Merchants was charging forty cents a night per arc lamp in 1892 when Henry Clay cut his Northern rate to twenty cents. The Merchants naturally lost business, and feelings ran so high that the police were called out to protect the Northern workers when they connected fifteen arc lamps in a clothing store previously lit by the Merchants. From then on, it was just a question of time before Henry Clay secured the entire stock of the Merchants for $50,000 in the stock of his own company and $104,600 in cash. The unfortunate competitor was dissolved in 1894.

That there was such a thing as an electric trust eventually became common knowledge. Because it was secretive, it was feared and misunderstood; because it represented monopoly, it received scathing notice in the newspapers. By 1890, somewhat exaggerated stories were current of a monopoly that was causing the high price of electric light. Rates were exorbitant, crusaders claimed. Actually, if rates were taken in conjunction with the net profits of the Trust, they were not very high. But the profits of the Trust were never made public, and people agreed that there was something sinister about it all. According to the *Philadelphia Record* of November 20, 1890: "The electric light companies of Philadelphia control the Select and Common Councils and many members of both branches are either directly or indirectly interested in those companies. It is folly for any one to talk of competition in electric lighting for the city."

Still, so little known was the Electric Trust that in 1892 Councils, under fire, decided to investigate "the alle-

Thomas Dolan

Martin Maloney

Samuel B. Huey

William D. Marks

EDISON STATION, 908 SANSOM STREET

gations that a combination exists among electric corporations by which the city is overcharged for electric lighting." Nothing came of this investigation, and in the following year the state legislature in its turn launched an equally fruitless inquiry.

For the Trust, however, the handwriting was on the wall. Its unpopularity stemmed from its very name. Its behind-doors management of the operating companies could never bring it good will, and the possibility of getting anywhere in its present guise was hopeless. Moreover, there had arisen in the very heart of the Trust's district a new company of extraordinary strength, The Edison Electric Light Company of Philadelphia. Edison's annual net profit already nearly equaled that of all the Trust's dependent companies combined.

CHAPTER 4

Edison of Philadelphia

It was through the Edison Electric Light Company in New York that the genius of Thomas A. Edison was made available to the world. While maintaining ownership of Edison's patents, the company licensed other firms to conduct the actual business of operating lighting enterprises. Between 1882, when the first Edison central station was constructed in New York, and 1888, one hundred and eighty-five central stations were licensed, twenty-six of them in Pennsylvania cities. Some of these stations furnished arc lights for street service and commercial uses, but that was a side line. Their principal business was to replace gas lighting in the office and home with the inventor's incandescent lamp, which was powered by a low-voltage direct current usually carried by underground conductors.

Philadelphia first became really aware of the Edison light in 1884, when nearly everyone in the city visited the International Electrical Exhibition. Edison's system was featured there and was proved through exhaustive tests to have the best incandescent lamp on the market. Stimulated by its possibilities, a number of businessmen decided that Philadelphia should have this light. Samuel B. Huey, an able lawyer, chairman of the Central High School, and civic-minded citizen, was the leader of this group. Exercising proper legal caution, he moved slowly and deliberately, conferring with experts on the problems involved in setting up an electric plant. Among those called in for advice was Professor William D. Marks.

Professor Marks, and no one took the liberty of addressing him in any other way, taught engineering at the University of Pennsylvania. He was a tall, powerfully built man with a dark mustache pointed at either end from his habit of twirling it when lost in thought. At the age of thirty in 1879, he had written a textbook on steam engineering, *Relative Proportions of the Steam Engine*, and it had gone through four editions. What he may not already have known about electricity he learned as superintendent of the International Electrical Exhibition. For months he had been in charge of the greatest accumulation of electrical equipment in the world, and had tested it thoroughly and scientifically. There is little doubt that Professor Marks was an engineering genius. In addition, he was a leader of men, an excellent businessman, full of determination, and tireless. Unfortunately, he was also opinionated, irascible, and tactless.

Encouraged by Professor Marks, Huey and his friends, after making the necessary arrangements with the parent Edison company, obtained a charter in December, 1886, for The Edison Electric Light Company of Philadelphia. The authorized capital of $100,000 was almost immediately raised to $1,000,000, and Huey was elected president. Professor Marks was engaged as supervising engineer at a salary of $4,500 a year, and was ordered to design a central station to be located on five lots purchased on the south side of Sansom Street near Ninth.

The next phase of Edison's development, building the station and putting it into operation, was one beset with incredible difficulties. In the first place, Huey could not obtain an ordinance from Councils permitting him to lay conduits under the streets. Eighteen times he appeared before City Councils, and eighteen times was met with excuses. The real reason for not granting the privilege was never given—that Councils had recently granted an extensive one for the same purpose to The Penn Electric Light Company and had been rewarded, so it was said, with stock in that venture. The privilege bestowed on the almost penniless Penn Electric was not an exclusive one, but it appears that the councilmen did not wish to invite competition which might endanger their investment.

After trying for more than a year, Huey did succeed in prying an ordinance out of Councils, but the privilege was a minor one. The only way the Edison Company could gain access to the streets was by renting them from Penn Electric, and this rental, it may be observed, constituted virtually the entire revenue that the speculative Penn Electric ever obtained.

Having at last secured access to street conduits, the time had come for Professor Marks to begin construction of the power station. With the company now becoming active, Huey, unable to devote the necessary time to the office, resigned as president but remained with Edison as counsel and later as vice-president. His place at the head of the company was taken by Councilman Thomas M. Thompson, who was paid a salary of $5,000. Thompson's choice may have been designed to win the favor of City Councils, but, if so, it was unavailing. In any case, Thompson was president less than a year when he was rather unceremoniously removed from the board. The cause for this action lay in the necessity of selling eight hundred shares of stock in August, 1888, to raise money needed for the station. The market was not propitious, but Levi D. Brown, a former bank president, offered to place the stock if he was elected president of the Edison Company. His proposition—at least he did not require a salary—was, perforce, accepted, and Thompson departed.

Professor Marks's design for the station was so revolutionary that J. H. Vail, general superintendent of the parent Edison company, disapproved it in no uncertain terms. The New York authorities believed that a station so queerly laid out could not even get into operation. Finally, the matter was referred to Edison himself, and all interested parties met with him at Orange, New Jersey. Professor Marks later recalled, "We were all convened together in his beautiful laboratory there, and the whole matter was taken up with Edison wearing just as judicial an expression on his face as he could get on." The inventor decided that Marks's designs were infinitely better than the New York plans and would yield a profit one-third greater.

Instead of using the customary small machines, Marks had specified that the size of all equipment should be doubled, thus enormously increasing output. Moreover, he planned to crowd this machinery close together, so that within one station he could produce enough electricity to light one hundred thousand 16-candlepower lamps. This sensational capacity was many times that of conventional stations. Marks's plant was to be a massively built structure eight stories high and of unusual arrangement. On the street floor was to be a range of fourteen 500-horsepower Armington and Sims engines; on the second floor, twenty-eight 3,000-light dynamos; on the third floor, the storage battery and ash alleys; on the fourth and sixth floors, 5,000 horsepower in steam boilers; on the fifth floor, ash alleys and blowers; on the seventh and eighth floors, coal storage space, meter room, workshop, and, a professorial touch, a lecture room.

There were a number of highlights in the construction of the station. The contractor who attempted to dig the foundations found it impossible to comply with his agreement and went into bankruptcy to avoid his obligation.

Professor Marks had to supervise the work himself. Then there was the question of water. The city water department asked an exorbitant rental of $2,000, plus two dollars per horsepower used in the plant, or $20,000 more. So the professor, although chided and harassed by city inspectors, dug his own well. In the final stages of this operation, he pumped 1,000,000 gallons of water onto Sansom Street in a single day. While all this was not accomplished without protest from the mayor, the water rent was saved.

Professor Marks had completed the station to the second floor when he had to cap it temporarily with a wooden roof. His board, for financial reasons, had decided to stop there and see what could be made of the plant's operation before committing itself to the entire program. Out of the wooden roof projected iron smokestacks and thirty-six-inch exhaust pipes. The exhaust from these pipes created tremendous atmospheric vibrations which rattled the windows and doors of the nearby Continental Hotel and threatened to demolish the adjacent ramshackle old Irving House where the professor lived. Suits were threatened, and Professor Marks was permitted to build the station to its fourth floor so that the annoying vibrations would be eliminated.

The laying of the conduits was completed with difficulty and under the hostile eye of General Louis Wagner, head of the department of public works. He would not permit the company to open a wide enough ditch in the streets to lay its tubes side by side and, consequently, the tubes had to be laid one on top of the other. Oh, but Wagner was watchful! On one occasion he halted the laying of conduits because he claimed that Penn Electric was not authorized to underlet its franchises. On another occasion, he issued a warrant for the arrest of President Brown for an alleged irregularity in the laying of the conduits. Meanwhile, boiler inspectors were on the verge of condemning the entire station. It seems almost miraculous that the Edison Company survived the scrutiny accorded it by city officials.

On March 5, 1889, the station went into operation when the first machine was thrown on the line, lighting the Union League and Morgan's Drug Store at 1629 Walnut Street. Twenty-eight miles of conduits had been laid and enough machinery installed to supply power for 25,000 lights. The demand for Edison lighting was so enthusiastic from the start that it necessitated the constant increasing of the company's capacity until a 100,000-light output was reached in 1895. Of this output, one third was actually not used for lights but to power electric machines, such as elevators, printing presses, and ventilating fans.

Under Professor Marks's leadership, an intensive advertising campaign was waged. Pamphlets and circulars were industriously distributed and newspaper publicity was courted. Every effort was made to educate the public to the advantages of electricity and to impress upon people that it was no longer a luxury. It cost no more than gas and gave a better light. Moreover, it was safe. The professor delighted in demonstrating to reporters how he could receive through his body the entire current of a dynamo supplying three thousand lights. The full force was only 115 volts, and it took 700 volts to kill a man. Philadelphia Edison, as Marks boasted over and over again, owned the largest station in the world.

At first, people were reluctant if not afraid to permit electricity in their homes. Some thought the light would be injurious to their eyes, others feared that "flooid" would escape and fill their rooms. Fire insurance companies were reluctant to grant coverage to houses wired for electricity. "Death does not lurk in our wires. A complete shock is not even an annoyance," prospective consumers were assured in 1889 in one of Marks's pamphlets entitled *From Cimmerian Darkness to Refulgent Light*. "No heat mind you! There is absolutely no danger." And, on the subject of electric engines, they were so much better than their gas counterparts, many of which "smell like the Philadelphia Gas Works."

Another of Marks's pamphlets was in dialogue form, *A Conversation With a Lady Concerning the Edison Electric Light;* it shows the type of questions his business agents had to answer.

Lady: "Doesn't it explode at times, and blow up the streets and sidewalks?"

Agent: "No, madam. It is the city's gas that explodes."

Lady: "Does it make a room as hot in summer as gas does?"

Agent: "No, madam. The heat from our light is hardly perceptible. One gas jet gives out as much heat as twenty of our lamps."

Lady: "Does it attract gnats and moths?"

Agent: "Madam, it is irresistible to them."

Lady: "How do you light it? With a match?"

Agent: "The electric light requires only the turning of a button to spring at once into brilliant action."

Lady: "Do you blow it out?"

Agent: "You turn out the electric light by merely turning a button, just as you light it."

Lady: "Suppose a draught of air blows it out. Will it fill the room and suffocate the inmates?"

Agent: "As I have said, the lights cannot be blown out."

Lady: "Do your lights ever go up and down at times?"

Agent: "Never!"

It was difficult to expel ignorance. One of the Edison directors had installed electric lights in the library of his

Spruce Street mansion and complained angrily that they did not work. It developed that he expected the lights to go on automatically whenever he entered the room. He had no idea that he was supposed to push the switch!

Not only did the Company try to attract customers by advertising, but, in a further bid for business, it reduced its rate from $1\frac{1}{8}$ cents per lamp hour to $\frac{3}{4}$ of a cent. Later, when business poured in at a greater volume than could be accommodated, Marks sought Edison's advice on the policy of raising the rate. He received the following letter.

April 7, 1891

Friend Marks:

To my mind the raising of the price from $\frac{3}{4}$ to 1¢ per lamp hour is a bid for competition. I am a believer in *Insuring the permanancy of an investment* by keeping prices so low that there is no inducement to others to come in an[d] ruin it. There seems to be a law in commercial things as in nature. If one attempts to obtain more profit than general average he is immediately punished by competitions.

Yours,
Edison

The rate was not raised.

Although it is clear that Professor Marks had little admiration for his unscientific board of directors, its members thought highly of him. In fact, Marks had earned an enviable reputation. When Henry Villard, of Northern Pacific Railroad fame, headed a syndicate of German capitalists in 1889 to consolidate all the Edison electric light companies under the name of the Edison General Electric Light Company, Professor Marks was named chief engineer. On his departure for New York to take up his duties, the directors of Philadelphia Edison eulogized him: "While we congratulate him on his deserved promotion to the highest electrical position in our country, we regret that it deprives us of the constant supervision of the one who has devised our plant and put it in so successful operation. Resolved, that we recognize in Professor Marks a man of masterly powers for constructing both station and machinery and operating them." As it turned out, the consolidation of the Edison companies was never effected, and within a few months the professor was back at his old post. In 1890 he was designated as general manager, and in 1892 was elected president at a salary of $6,500, which was increased to $15,000 by 1895.

During its early years, Philadelphia Edison was in financial straits. The necessity of expanding its plant as quickly as possible called for more funds than it had available. Although the company issued stock worth $1,000,000, it had been paid only $700,000. Thirty per cent of the stock issue had been given to the parent Edison company as a royalty in exchange for its license to use the Edison patents in Philadelphia. Moreover, as part of this contract, five per cent of the cash received on the stock sold, or $35,000, also went to the parent company.

Philadelphia Edison wanted to increase its capital to $2,000,000, but that would have meant turning over to the parent company another $300,000 worth of stock and another $35,000 in cash. The price was too high. As an expedient, the company issued bonds in the amount of $300,000 to finance the enlargement of its plant.

Heavily in debt and unable to consider dividends, the directors were nevertheless optimistic. In their January, 1890, report they stated: "By reason of the unvarying steadiness and brilliancy of our light we have obtained many of the former customers of the stations of other companies. We have made more rapid progress in obtaining customers than any other company. By concentrating great power into a single station and thereby economizing labor, we are enabled to make a profit where lesser plants would meet with a loss." The parent company was not so enthusiastic about the great station. The New Yorkers wanted the Philadelphians to expand by building a second central station, but this the local board would not do. Samuel Insull, vice-president of the Edison General Electric Company, had difficulty in supplying the Sansom Street plant with its new machinery and there were other delays, but gradually the concept of a 100,000-light station became a reality.

The year 1892, when Professor Marks was elected president, was a banner year indeed. Not only was the company making money, but the professor negotiated a new contract with the parent company whereby he saved $250,000 in royalties when the local corporation increased its capital to $2,000,000. The debt was entirely retired, a twenty per cent stock dividend was declared, which represented earnings of previous years applied to increasing the plant, and cash dividends of nine per cent were paid.

Prosperity had crowned the efforts begun six years earlier by Samuel B. Huey, for the company was now on a regular eight per cent dividend basis. On January 18, 1893, directors' fees of five dollars were established, "provided the director reached the meeting within ten minutes of the time appointed." Salaries were raised and Christmas bonuses were declared for the employees. In 1894, eight per cent was paid in dividends and a five per cent stock dividend declared. The next year, the company achieved its maximum capacity, the long-dreamed-of 100,000-light output.

During this time of triumphant attainment, an electrical development of monumental importance had taken place. Widener and his syndicate had introduced the electric trolley, which did away with the horsecars and cable lines. Violent resistance greeted the trolley ordinance when it was presented in 1892 by the renowned lawyer John G. Johnson, who argued the question for the traction company before Councils. A mass meeting of protest was held at the Academy of Music where the perils of the trolley system with its overhead wires were alarmingly presented.

The story is told that two of the senior officials of the traction company attended this meeting and heard themselves violently denounced by the orators. "Well," murmured one of them to the other, "I don't care what they say. My conscience is clear." "It should be," was the rejoinder. "It's been strained often enough." At all events, the traction company triumphed. Councils passed the trolley ordinance, Mayor Edwin S. Stuart vetoed it, and Councils then overrode the veto. In December, 1892, the city's first trolley line went into operation on Catherine and Bainbridge Streets. It was an immense success. People rode the line just for the thrill of it. The trolley ran quicker and smoother than the horsecars. No longer were passengers afflicted with the odor of horse sweat, or of smoky oil lamps. Everything was now done by electricity! In no time, those who had shouted denunciations at the Academy of Music were petitioning for trolley lines, and by 1897 electricity had completely taken over. For the privilege of erecting these lines, the traction companies had to agree to resurface the city streets. The emergence of modern street paving in Philadelphia was due to the trolleys. Widener and his friends created another Philadelphia asset. In 1893, the old Ridgway Park playground was dredged out of sight when Smith's and Windmill Islands were removed. The traction company in 1895 provided a new, beautiful, and elaborate free park at Willow Grove, where one could hear the best music in the world. The park was reached, naturally enough, by trolley.

As the city grew, so grew its Edison Company, and Professor Marks did everything he could to make its operation a brilliant success. A strict disciplinarian, he gathered about him an able staff. Walter H. Johnson was his chief clerk; W. C. L. Eglin was head of the electric department; Joseph D. Israel was superintendent of street work. These department heads, together with other chiefs of sections, constituted a "Board of Control" set up by the professor. It lent guidance in personnel matters, hiring and firing laborers who worked for fifteen cents an hour, and, under the president, ruled on numerous operational problems. Its members were also required to give lectures to subordinate employees. Johnson spoke on "Finances of Electric Lighting"; Eglin explained "Electrical Distribution"; Israel explored the subject of "Underground Conduits and Conductors." These lectures were published by the company in 1895 under the title *A Course of Thirteen Practical Talks to The Working Men of The Edison Electric Light Company of Philadelphia.*

By 1895, Professor Marks had reached the peak of his career as an electric company president. Although he did not know it, disaster lay ahead. He was, however, to contribute one more triumph to his spectacular career with Edison. For three years his company had been struggling with Councils to obtain a franchise to underlay all the central city streets with its conduits. The applications for this privilege were attended by adverse newspaper criticism, and the Edison Company was made to appear an ogre whose appetite battened on the rights of the people.

The professor explained the cause of this situation in his characteristically picturesque way: "If the city councils were paid, nothing would be easier than the passage of a bill in favor of the Edison Company. The newspapers, with a few exceptions, are even more venal than many of the councilmen. The newspapers would not indulge in editorials about snakes and things—the bill would go through. I say this much to you, because you no doubt have been, all of you, very much interested indeed at the horrible character which has been given to the Edison Company in a political way. If it really was what it is represented to be, it would not have any trouble at all. The newspapers would appeal to the councilmen to pass the bill, and it would be passed without a word."

After many words, the bill was at last passed on April 1, 1895, when the company received the privilege of laying conduits under all the city streets between Callowhill and Lombard Streets and the Delaware and Schuylkill Rivers. The business of the other electric companies was protected in the ordinance by a provision that none of the Edison conduits were to be used to transmit current for arc lights. Professor Marks was thus riding the crest of the wave when he learned that Martin Maloney was about to re-enter the electric lighting business in Philadelphia.

CHAPTER 5

Consolidation

THROUGH THE Penn Globe Gas Light Company, Martin Maloney provided the naphtha lamp which lit the streets of so many cities east of the Mississippi. Since 1879, he had been furnishing this light for Philadelphia in ever larger quantities until, by 1895, more than 10,000 of his lamps illuminated the city at an annual cost of a quarter of a million dollars.

Prosperous though this endeavor was, Maloney believed that electricity was the ultimate in street lighting. In 1894 he decided to abandon gasoline. As the organizer and first general manager of Philadelphia's former Maxim Company, Maloney had a good working knowledge of electricity, and he well knew the problems which beset the city's electric companies. These problems, he realized, could not be solved by the Electric Trust which had about reached the end of its usefulness.

The secrecy with which the Trust conducted its affairs had given many people the impression that it existed only to keep rates high. In 1895, its unpopularity reached something of a crescendo. For some years, there had been agitation in the city to break the Trust's rate control by setting up a municipal light and power plant. Just when sentiment in favor of such an experiment was at its highest, the state legislature passed two bills, one of which ordained that if any municipality established its own electric plant it would either have to buy out the local private plants, or else indemnify them against financial loss. The other bill prevented new electric companies from going into territory already occupied by an existing company.

The public was immediately up in arms about these measures, which were believed to have been sponsored by the Electric Trust. The Select Council, on the other hand, came out in favor of the bills. According to Councilman Henry Clay, president of The Northern Electric Light and Power Company, the private companies were entitled to protection. Governor Daniel H. Hastings thought otherwise, and vetoed the measures. The Electric Trust next displayed its lack of understanding, its seeming contempt of public opinion, by permitting General Manager A. J. DeCamp to run for common councilman. His election was greeted by a fresh public outcry against the Trust. Here surely was a conflict of interest. As general manager, DeCamp submitted bids for city lighting, and then as common councilman voted on their acceptance.

Not only was Maloney convinced that new leadership was needed by the city's electric companies, but he was also certain that their diverse systems of electric light and power distribution made for a needlessly awkward situation. The fact was that there were far too many companies operating in Philadelphia. Maloney realized that their unification was inevitable.

As the first step toward bringing such a consolidation about, he obtained a charter in February, 1895, for a corporation called the Pennsylvania Heat, Light and Power Company, capitalized, shortly afterward, at $10,000,000. Next, Maloney purchased control of the Columbia Electric Light Company and obtained title to the abandoned powerhouse of the old Market Street cable railway near Nineteenth. He also took up valuable patent rights of the Siemens & Halske three- and five-

EDISON STATION DYNAMO ROOM
Belt-driven dynamos connect with steam engines on floor below.

EDISON STATION ENGINE ROOM
Note belt drives to dynamos on floor above.

Ogden Mine N.J.

April 7/91

Friend Marks—

To my mind the raising of the price from 3/4 to 1 c per

lamp hour is a bid for competition. I am a beleiver

in _Insuring the permanancy of an investment_ by

Keeping prices so low that there is no inducement to

others to come in an ruin it,

There seems to be a law in commercial things as in

nature,

If one attempts to obtain more profit than general average

he is immediately punished by competition

Yours

Edison

THOMAS A. EDISON TO PROFESSOR WILLIAM D. MARKS

wire distribution system, competitor of the Edison three-wire system, and traveled about Europe inspecting electrical installations.

As a former coal miner, Maloney well remembered the enormous banks of culm, or waste coal, that were thrown up around mine operations. Culm could be purchased at twenty-five cents a ton, and, Maloney believed, could be used in a revolutionary way to generate electricity which could be transmitted to Philadelphia by high-tension wires. This process would make it possible to furnish electric power at half cost, and other companies would thus be forced to purchase it. Professor Marks did not consider Maloney's plan feasible, while Edison, acknowledging that he would not know how to put it into operation himself, supposed it had possibilities, particularly if the culm could be made into briquettes. This scheme for low-cost power, which would force existing companies to turn to him, was probably Maloney's main incentive to return to the electric field. As the Lowe water gas process was to The United Gas Improvement Company, so the use of culm as a fuel would be to the Pennsylvania Heat, Light and Power Company. His chief assistant later said of Maloney's enterprise, "Those of us who were associated in it had some idea of starting what might be called a United Electric Improvement Company of America fashioned after the plans of The United Gas Improvement Company."

The opposition of the city's electric light companies made it extremely difficult for Maloney to obtain a franchise. Many believed that Pennsylvania Heat was not a bona fide business venture, but a stock-jobbing manipulation. Then, too, there were those who feared the effect of a large fish in a pond of small fishes, big business versus little business. But Maloney had his advocates. District Attorney George S. Graham and the reformer

Rudolph Blankenburg spoke in favor of the company. Even so, the controversy over Maloney's ordinance in Councils became so serious that a political split in the dominant party threatened. To avoid such a disaster, David Martin, the city boss, is believed to have called off the opposition, and the ordinance passed, giving Pennsylvania Heat, Light and Power the same territory as Edison.

Naturally enough, this contest had been of the deepest interest to Professor Marks. Several days after the passage of the ordinance, the professor wrote to Maloney to learn his intentions. Noting that Maloney would need steam to provide the heat his company planned to furnish, Professor Marks informed him that his Edison plant was evaporating 1,000,000 pounds of water a day and could sell him steam cheaper than Maloney could make it. A month later, he suggested to Maloney, "This Company, I think, would look favorably upon overtures looking toward a consolidation of our interests." Moreover, he continued, "Should a consolidation of *all* the electric lighting and power interests in the old city proper be contemplated, I should be pleased to lend myself to bring about such a consolidation."

By August, however, the professor was worried. Under the impression that Maloney's group was spreading injurious rumors about the value of Edison stock, in order that they might buy it in cheaply, he circularized a warning to his stockholders. At the same time, hoping to forestall Maloney's steam heat plans, he obtained a charter for the Edison-owned Philadelphia Steam Heating and Power Company.

After preliminary consolidation talks with the Edison people, conversations which Professor Marks had so enticingly invited, Maloney began to lay steam mains from his powerhouse at Nineteenth and Market Streets in

October, 1895. The operation was promptly brought to a halt by the professor, who obtained an injunction against it on the grounds that since the pipes had to pass under the Edison ducts their heat would affect the insulating compound in the Edison tubes. Blocked by this action, Maloney at once offered to lease the Edison Company and terms were soon reached. In return for the lease, Pennsylvania Heat, Light and Power agreed to pay the Edison stockholders an annual dividend of eight per cent for two years and nine per cent thereafter. There would be no changes in the Edison organization, which Professor Marks would continue to head.

In a newspaper interview, the professor explained that both companies had come to the conclusion that this arrangement was far better than ruinous competition. Personally, he considered it advantageous for all who were financially interested in Edison. A stockholders meeting to approve the lease was called for the day after Christmas.

Unfortunately, Professor Marks fell out with his directors before this meeting. Early in December, he testified before City Councils that Edison had been frozen out of competition for city lighting because its ordinance prohibited the company from furnishing current for arc lights. With Edison thus removed from public bidding, the other companies, so he said, were charging the city twice as much as they should. The professor went one step farther; he applied to his board for permission to bid on arc lighting, and not on fair business terms, but at cost. Clearly, his interest in city lighting contracts was not actuated by normal business motives. His directors, who were on the verge of concluding satisfactory negotiations with Maloney, were much embarrassed; Professor Marks's proposals were not only controversial, they were thoroughly inimical to all who operated lighting companies in Philadelphia. Huey told him his suggestion could not be considered while the consolidation decision with Pennsylvania Heat was pending.

Overexcited, the professor interpreted this decision as deference to Maloney. Who was running Edison, he demanded, Marks or Maloney? Frustrated and angry, he turned against the lease and issued circular after circular to the shareholders, urging them to vote against it. In these circulars, he maligned the characters of his directors, ascribed improper motives to their desire for a lease, and called them a useless group of men who should be dismissed. All that the Edison Company had achieved in late years, Marks unequivocally stated, was due entirely to him. Forgetting other newspaper utterances, he informed reporters that he had opposed the consolidation from the first.

Samuel B. Huey and his associates were not to be upset by an election raid, for they had overwhelming stock control in their hands. What they were unable to obtain, however, was the necessary enabling ordinance permitting them to effect a lease. Consequently, at the stockholders meeting the question of the lease was indefinitely postponed. But this was no victory for the professor, who realized that he had lost his fight to keep Edison independent. If Maloney could not obtain control of Edison through a lease, he would gain it by stock ownership. On January 20, 1896, Professor Marks submitted his resignation, and his directors resolved, "That the resignation be accepted and that the remarks regarding this board are utterly uncalled for and without any basis of fact." *

It was a pity that Marks's career as a utility manager terminated so unpleasantly. Having had a free hand in the conduct of Edison's affairs, he could not brook man-

* Re-elected a director at the annual meeting on January 22, 1896, Marks again resigned two days later.

agement interference in his plans, and his temperament was such that he could not bear the censure of his directors for circularizing the shareholders against the lease without the board's permission. Much honor is due him, however, for his accomplishments in leading a pioneer company through its formative stages. After leaving Edison, the professor opened an office as a consulting engineer. His subsequent writings show that he never outlived his prejudice against the unification of Philadelphia's electric companies.

Before the year was out, Pennsylvania Heat, Light and Power had acquired the entire issue of Edison stock. In March, 1896, most of the Edison directors resigned and were replaced by Maloney and his friends. Appropriately enough, among the old directors remaining with Edison was Samuel B. Huey, who stayed on its board for many years until succeeded by his son. Ironically, Professor Marks's function as chief engineer was taken over by J. H. Vail, who had originally opposed the plan for the Edison Station.

The directors of the Pennsylvania Heat, Light and Power Company were exceptionally able men. In addition to Maloney, who served as president, they were District Attorney George S. Graham; George R. Philler, president of the First National Bank; W. W. Gibbs, president of the Electric Storage Battery Company; and William L. Elkins. Later in the year, when Pennsylvania Heat purchased the Electric Trust with all its subsidiary companies, Thomas Dolan and John Lowber Welsh were added to the board.

Maloney's plan to utilize culm as fuel for generating electricity never came to anything. Nor did he ever put into operation the powerhouse he had purchased at Nineteenth and Market Streets. Indeed, he was more interested at first in closing down small stations and en-

55

larging important ones, like the Brush, than in creating completely new facilities. In line with this program, the capacity of the Edison Station was doubled. For office space, Maloney rented a new six-story building on the northeast corner of Tenth and Sansom Streets, and into it were moved the administrative personnel of the Brush and Edison operating companies, as well as the staff of the holding company. Insofar as possible, the purchasing, operating, and sales departments of the different companies were centralized. Maloney also consolidated the engineering staffs into a unified group which alone filled two floors of the Sansom Street building. The offices were lighted throughout with electricity from the nearby Edison plant, which also furnished power for the elevator and steam heat, then a novelty. On the face of the building from the second floor to the roof was a mammoth electric sign that spelled out the holding company's name in varicolored lights. As president, Maloney was in constant attendance, supervising all activities. Impeccably dressed and wearing his customary white vest, he overbalanced one day while looking into a ditch his men had opened in Sansom Street. His appearance when hauled out covered with oozy mud brought laughter from an office boy, whom the furious Maloney fired on the spot. Fortunately for the boy, Albert R. Granger, a department head gave him a job at another station, and he continued with the company for many years, eventually becoming a regional vice-president.

Maloney did as much as he could to standardize electrical distribution in Philadelphia, to improve and modernize it, and to extend it more generally throughout the city. Each year showed an increase in the profits of the operating companies despite his reduction of rates. Maloney's idea of public service, an imperfectly developed concept in the days before regulation of utilities, was expressed in his first annual report. Pennsylvania Heat had acquired control of the Edison and Electric Trust properties, he said, in order to work out what had been uppermost in the management's original plan: "To secure that class of service that would enable the Company to furnish to its patrons electricity under such conditions that they could use it more generally and apply it in many ways that the high prices heretofore prevailing prevented, and to demonstrate to the citizens of Philadelphia that a corporation could work for the benefit of the public and its stockholders at the same time." And again, at the annual meeting of 1897, in announcing another decrease in rates Maloney proudly pointed out that the rates for city lights were much below those paid elsewhere, and that private consumers were also being supplied at less than the average price in large centers. "We are justified in feeling that the city will appreciate our efforts."

Although Pennsylvania Heat's capitalization was not large enough to permit any additional consolidations of major electric properties, the company did acquire the remainder of the Columbia Electric Light Company's stock, a controlling interest in The West End Electric Company of Philadelphia, and ownership of the Delaware Electric Company. This latter concern illustrates how small some of the city's electric lighting enterprises were. Its plant, located near Second and Market Streets, supplied only sixty-two customers and was purchased in 1897 for $4,000.

While Maloney gradually strengthened his position, public interest in electric companies was completely overshadowed by a momentous event in the gas field. For years, Thomas Dolan, president of The United Gas Improvement Company, had been striving to obtain a lease of the municipally owned gasworks. Because of neglect and lack of political support, the gasworks badly needed renovation, improvement, and better management. All this Dolan could furnish through U.G.I., which already supplied the works with nearly forty per cent of the gas it used. In September, 1897, Dolan's lease was at last presented to Councils and referred to a special committee, of which the ubiquitous Henry Clay was chairman.

Once again, the Academy of Music bulged with indignant citizens protesting the "give away" of city property. It mattered not how advantageous the lease was to the city; its people rebelled at the thought of relinquishing control of public property to a private corporation. The principal speaker at the Academy was Wayne MacVeagh, former United States Minister to Italy. One of MacVeagh's principal stock holdings was in U.G.I., and he had nothing but praise for its management. Yet, he was against the lease. In purple language, he called the city's councilmen "the most abandoned and ignorant specimens of humanity God permits to live," and warned that their adoption of the lease would be attributed to bribery and corruption. It is remarkable what little influence protest meetings at the Academy of Music had on current events, and how frequently these meetings were misdirected. All too often they were simply fighting progress in the form of telephone and electric wires, trolleys, or efficient management of the almost hated gasworks. Councils approved Dolan's lease by overwhelming majorities, and Mayor Charles F. Warwick signed it.

While Dolan waged his successful battle, Maloney planned his next big move to consolidate the local electric companies. Arc lighting for the city's streets was an important part of Pennsylvania Heat, Light and Power's business, but it was one in which eight independent companies also shared. Five of these were largely controlled by politician-contractor Charles A. Porter and by William J. Latta, the Pennsylvania Railroad's general agent in Philadelphia.

By this time, David Martin had terminated the dual control he had set up with Porter, and Porter was no longer a figure to reckon with. No longer could he count on help from Martin, because his friend had broken with Quay and was engaged in a political battle royal. Although Martin went on to become secretary of the Commonwealth and then state senator, his power in Philadelphia was gradually to shift to a Quay stalwart, Israel W. Durham. Political preferment in the past had probably brought city business to Porter's electric companies; now, as Porter could plainly see, the future looked black, with his public contracts fair game in a political vendetta.

Whether this consideration played a part or not, Porter and Latta agreed to deliver their five companies to Maloney. To do this, they obtained a charter in December, 1896, for The Hamilton Electric Company, which, early in 1898, acquired stock control of The Manufacturers Electric Company, The Suburban Electric Company, The Diamond Electric Company, The Powelton Electric Company, and The Wissahickon Electrical Light Company.

Maloney, in his turn, obtained a New Jersey charter in February, 1898, for the Pennsylvania Manufacturing Light and Power Company, with an authorized capital of $15,000,000. From Pennsylvania Heat, he detached several officers to head up this new holding company, which immediately took over control of Pennsylvania Heat and Hamilton Electric, together with all their operating companies. It also acquired the remaining shares of The Northern Electric Light and Power Company, as well as those of the West End Company, and it bought the Germantown Electric Light Company from U.G.I. Only two independents now remained to supply the city with electricity—the Kensington and the Southern companies.

In taking over the securities of these several holding and operating utilities, the Pennsylvania Manufacturing Company paid partly in cash and partly in its own bonds. Indicative of Maloney's plans for a day when there would be but one Philadelphia electric company, the bonds did not bear the name of Pennsylvania Manufacturing, but were registered as "Philadelphia Electric Gold Trust Certificates."

The new holding company, which theoretically directed the activities of its numerous operating companies, took space on the third floor of the Tenth and Sansom Streets building. Actual control remained with Pennsylvania Heat, where Maloney and his board of directors remained. Their major problem was coping with the city's rapidly increasing demand for electricity. To provide more current, they leased an abandoned railway power station on the east side of the Schuylkill near the foot of Callowhill Street in June, 1898. This facility was converted into a modern central station capable of generating high-tension alternating current which could be transferred to ease the load at various stations in Maloney's system.

Three hundred and seventy feet above the ground in City Hall tower, a leviathan town clock went into operation on January 1, 1899, its dial illuminated at night by six hundred incandescent lights. Ponderous arms began their circular motions, ticking away the minutes and hours of Martin Maloney's last year in the Philadelphia light and power business.

The year began with the introduction of an alarming, although unsuccessful, bill at Harrisburg. Sponsored by

State Senator Christopher L. Magee, who had street railway interests in Pittsburgh, the bill granted streetcar companies the right to sell their surplus electricity. The effect of the bill was to make traction organizations into heat, light, and power concerns and to put them into direct competition with the electric utilities. David Martin, a political friend of Thomas Dolan's, refused to lend his support to the measure. But Quay, in a bargain with Magee for the support of Allegheny County in his forthcoming campaign for re-election to the United States Senate, came out in favor of the proposal. It amused Quay to do so, for he was not on good terms with Dolan and enjoyed taking a shot at Dolan's utility interests.

Within Maloney's own circle, a controversy arose over the policy of expanding the company's sphere of operations. This was a time of feverish interest in empire building. Every line of endeavor had its "trust." There was a champagne trust, a sewing thread trust, a bicycle trust—in short, a trust for every commodity one could name. Moreover, in line with bigness, gas, electric, and traction companies throughout the country were being brought together into integrated management, with U.G.I. a conspicuous leader in the movement.

Working tentatively in this direction, Maloney acquired options to buy four out-of-state electric light companies. It was at this point that a divergence of opinion took place within his management. The majority of his directors decided not to engage in business outside Philadelphia, but to lend their support toward the founding of an independent holding company which would do so. Accordingly, the options of the four companies were turned over to the Electric Company of America, which was specially chartered for this purpose in January, 1899. U.G.I. held a large interest in this venture, and the stockholders of the Pennsylvania Manufacturing Company were given a favorable opportunity to invest in it. Elkins, Widener, and Dolan served on the board of the new company, which was organized to acquire electric light properties, exclusive of those in the Philadelphia area, and to operate them on a plan similar to that practiced by U.G.I. in securing its gas properties. This corporation later became part of the huge American Electric Power Company.

Upon setting aside the temptation to expand, Maloney's board was instantly threatened with competition at home. In May, 1899, the National Electric Company was chartered with an authorized capital in the appalling, if optimistic, sum of $25,000,000. It entered the Philadelphia market by purchasing the stock of the important Southern Electric Light and Power Company, and of two small companies that had limited rights to operate in Philadelphia areas, The Cheltenham Electric Light, Heat and Power Company and The Overbrook Electric Company. In addition, it acquired lighting companies in Delaware County through the acquisition of the new Beacon Light Company group. Thomas M. Thompson, who had once served briefly as president of the Edison Company and more recently as the city's director of public works, was a member of National's board. Its other directors were not men who had hitherto made their mark in the Philadelphia lighting field.

Maloney's last contribution toward consolidating the city's electric companies was his achievement in persuading National Electric to merge its holdings with his. The two companies were brought together with the formation in October, 1899, of a New Jersey corporation called Philadelphia Electric Company. At this time, the assets of the Pennsylvania Manufacturing Light and Power Company amounted to $16,263,000, and its net annual earnings were $381,000. The amount of the National Electric Company's assets was $3,644,000, with net earnings of $137,000, of which $123,000 was derived from its Southern Company.

With the formation of Philadelphia Electric, only one independent lighting company remained—The Kensington Electric Company. Its territory contained only 378 lamps out of the 7,694 electric street lamps in the city, but, from the point of view of unification, that was 378 too many. Kensington lost its city contract and, unable to exist without it, sold out to Philadelphia Electric in 1901.

During its first year of business, Philadelphia Electric increased its output by nearly thirty-five per cent, and bought a large property at Christian Street on the Schuylkill, where it planned to erect a powerful central station. But the realization of Philadelphia Electric's hopes could not be achieved as long as it had to operate its various companies separately within the territorial limits of each company's ordinance. In 1902, this problem was overcome by an ordinance granted to a new Pennsylvania corporation, one which was entirely owned by Philadelphia Electric Company (of New Jersey), and one which bore an identical name except for the article "The"—The Philadelphia Electric Company. This ordinance gave the Pennsylvania concern the right to erect and maintain an electric system throughout the entire city, and the further right to acquire by purchase or lease the existing light companies within the area. Under the new charter and the provisions of the ordinance, The Philadelphia Electric Company thus leased all the underlying companies and in its own name took over the entire electric light and power business of the city. Before very long, the identities of its component parts, the early operating companies, were forgotten by the public. But these companies were to continue a paper existence for many years.

It was in this way that the modern Philadelphia Electric Company (a later change deleted the article "The") was nurtured by Martin Maloney into an organization capable of providing a truly unified electric service for the city. Its creation was a monument to his enterprise and foresight, but its completion took place after his departure from the utility field in 1899.

The consolidation of the city's electric light and power companies was a tangible fact that all could understand. An intangible factor which helped make the consolidation possible stemmed from the philosophy which Martin Maloney imparted to Philadelphia Electric. Maloney had seen the electric industry surge forward in a catch-as-catch-can era. There was no regulation of rates or of utility practices, and, consequently, every company tried to do the best it could for its owners without due regard for the public. But Maloney had a broader vision. He realized that a public utility needed a solid base of public approval, and he did everything he could to obtain it. By constantly improving electric service and by decreasing rates, he gave Philadelphia an excellent company. There were those who would grumble about monopoly, but that aspect did not disturb the average customer, who was satisfied that he was obtaining good service at a fair rate.

Maloney thus brought about a central management for the city's many electric companies and succeeded in doing so in a way that was satisfactory both to his stockholders and to the public. His major contribution had been of a financial nature. He was the promoter who had negotiated the melding of many stock companies into one ownership. The job of integrating these companies lay ahead. In leaving Philadelphia, Maloney saw to it that a man capable of doing this work was at the helm. His protégé, Joseph B. McCall, was elected president of Philadelphia Electric.

CHAPTER 6

Creating A Unified System

THE PHILADELPHIA ELECTRIC COMPANY (of Pennsylvania) was the instrument by which the older Philadelphia Electric Company (of New Jersey) brought all the city's "neighborhood utilities" into a single operating system. By virtue of the 1902 ordinance granting the Company this right, the Pennsylvania corporation leased the local utilities and by 1904 was operating them under its own name. The Philadelphia Electric Company (of Pennsylvania), however, was owned by Philadelphia Electric (of New Jersey), and control of the city's light and power destinies remained with the New Jersey-chartered concern. That the operating company's existence was merely one of legal convenience is evidenced in its board of directors which was limited to three men, all of whom were employees of the New Jersey corporation. Its executive committee consisted of two of these directors and a third member identified as "a stockholder," Thomas Dolan, the holding company's most powerful leader. The growth of the Philadelphia utility system in the early years of the twentieth century is not, therefore, to be found in the activities of the nominal operating company headed by President Joseph B. McCall. Rather, control of this growth rested with the directors of the holding company, Philadelphia Electric Company (of New Jersey), where Joseph B. McCall also presided.

The members of the holding company's board included McCall, the Company's secretary A. V. R. Coe, William L. Elkins, P. A. B. Widener, Thomas Dolan, and Jeremiah J. Sullivan, a Philadelphia merchant who eventually headed the Union Traction Company. From the National Electric Company came the brilliant physician and medical educator Dr. John V. Shoemaker, John M. Mack, the political contractor, and bank president William F. Harrity, chairman of the Democratic National Committee in 1892 and 1896. When it was later decided that the Company should have a vice-president, Harrity was elected, but this office remained a part-time one for some years. The treasurer of the Company, William P. Conover, Jr., was another one of the early directors.

Having at long last surmounted the difficult legal and financial problems of consolidation, Philadelphia Electric in 1902 was faced with the equally complex technical problems of integrating and modernizing its system. In order to achieve the economies which had been the principal argument for bringing all the local utilities together, the administrative, service, and technical departments had to be thoroughly reorganized. In addition, the system had to be harmonized from an engineering point of view.

The personnel problem is often one of the most difficult faced by those charged with bringing about workable consolidations and mergers. Frequently, no real consolidation takes place for a generation, and during that time the internal operations of the company are kept in turmoil by rival interests. Such a situation could have been severely damaging to Philadelphia Electric, for the Company had to assimilate the officers, foremen, and workmen of numerous companies. These staffs were accustomed to doing things in their individual ways and to operating different types of electrical systems. In most

66

SOUTH BROAD STREET FROM CITY HALL, PHILADELPHIA, 1895

Martin Mahoney, President

§§§§

Heat for your Homes

THE ELECTRICAL AGE
USHERED IN

§§§§

THE consolidation of the different systems of electric supply paves the way for a general use of the subtle fluid in the homes and manufacturing concerns of Philadelphia.

§§§§

Houses heated by Electricity and Cooking done without dirt, dust, gas or odor.

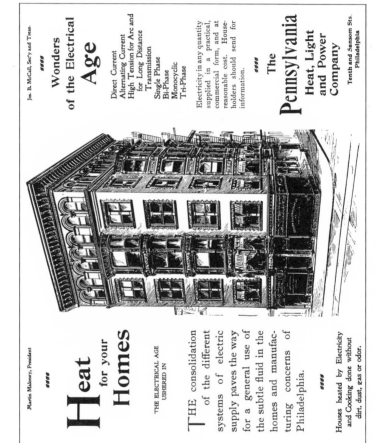

Jos. B. McCall, Sec'y and Treas.

§§§§

Wonders of the Electrical Age

Direct Current
Alternating Current
High Tension for Arc and
for Long Distance
Transmission
Single Phase
Bi-Phase
Monocyclic
Tri-Phase

§§§§

The Pennsylvania Heat, Light and Power Company

Tenth and Sansom Sts.
Philadelphia

Electricity in any quantity supplied in a practical, commercial form, and at reasonable cost. House-holders should send for information.

cases, each staff thought its system was best. But now the systems were to be unified into a single, standardized unit, and many a pet method or theory was to be discarded. This situation created ample room for irritation, suspicion, and antagonism. That these feelings were controlled and abated, that they did not smolder to create serious personnel difficulties, or assert a dangerously disruptive influence on the Company's future, was in large measure due to the personal charm and unfailing tact of the president.

Joseph B. McCall was brought to Philadelphia by his parents not long after his birth in New York City on May 12, 1870. At the age of twelve, he went to work in the shops of the Baldwin Locomotive Works. Three years later, he moved on to a clerkship in the law office of Rufus F. Shapley, where he studied both law and stenography. It was at Shapley's office that Martin Maloney's discerning eye fell on him.

Maloney employed McCall as his confidential secretary, and before long entrusted him with an officership in the Penn Globe Gas Light Company. When the Pennsylvania Heat, Light and Power Company was launched, McCall was elected secretary. Subsequently, he became president of the Pennsylvania Manufacturing Light and Power Company, and in 1899, when only twenty-nine years of age, was chosen president of Philadelphia Electric. He had come through an arduous apprenticeship, a grinding experience which could not have been an altogether happy one. Toward the end of his career, he was to say: "I remember, when I was secretary to a man engaged in the public utility business, that I had a day off in ten years. He planned to go away on a three weeks' trip, and I suggested to him 'Don't you think it is about time that I had a little time off?' 'Well,' he said, 'I don't know about that. The trouble is that when I am here, I want you, and, when I am away, you ought to be here.' I might say incidentally that that kind of executive is not a good leader."

An old story told about the Company puts McCall's elevation to the presidency in rather negative terms. According to this tale, Maloney, after having made a fortune through participation in the various consolidations he had brought about, retired because he could see few money-making possibilities left in Philadelphia Electric. Having squeezed these possibilities dry, he tossed the remains to McCall.

As far as the Company was concerned, Maloney could not have made a better throw. A man of easy, genial humor, with an unfailing fund of anecdotes, McCall's personality was a magnetic and sympathetic one. He was an ideal choice for the difficult task that lay ahead, for he was well versed in corporate matters and was expert in dealing with city and state authorities at a time when the Company's future much depended upon such skill. Under his leadership, the small, disunited, financially insecure utility moved rapidly forward, gaining in strength year by year.

McCall's two chief assistants had both worked under Professor Marks in the Edison Company. Walter H. Johnson had been secretary of Edison and became, more or less, McCall's man Friday, assisting in financial and commercial matters. Inevitably, Johnson came to be recognized as the probable successor to the presidency. He stood well with many important people and interests in the city, and he kept McCall on the go attending meetings and affairs of all sorts. There is reason to believe that the foundation for McCall's ill health, which caught up with him later, was laid in this grueling routine of wining and dining and late hours which he was forced to undergo in fulfilling his manifold obligations.

While many looked on Johnson as the next president, there were those who favored McCall's other right-hand man, W. C. L. Eglin. Ultimately the chief engineer of the Company, Eglin had studied engineering in Glasgow, and on coming to America had joined Professor Marks's Edison Company in 1889. Testy, impulsive, and very sure of himself, Eglin was an aggressive, brilliant worker. To Eglin goes the credit for the engineering work in modernizing and unifying Philadelphia Electric's generating and distribution system.

This work, largely begun in 1902, coincided with the reorganization of the Company's staff, then consisting of 853 people. The engineering group was placed under the immediate direction of the president and under the supervision of the chiefs of the bureaus of arc lighting, incandescent lighting, and steam engineering. The arc lighting engineer, A. H. Manwaring, was responsible for public and commercial arc lights, their installation and maintenance, and aerial line construction and maintenance. The incandescent lighting engineer, Eglin, supervised station construction, underground street work, and all engineering work in conjunction with light and power service for incandescent lighting. He also directed the work of the meter department and the wiring extension department. The mechanical or steam engineer, William H. Norris, had charge of the installation and operation of steam engines, boilers, and all devices used in conjunction with them.

The commercial department was theoretically conducted by Vice-President William F. Harrity, but actually by Walter H. Johnson, who supervised the work of General Agent A. J. DeCamp. Under the general agent were the contract solicitors, the new-business department, and the departments responsible for retention of business, consumer relations, and advertising. This work was subdivided into geographical districts headed by district managers.

The treasurer had charge of the accounting department, which handled billings and collections and the Company's financial business, as well as the work of the purchasing department. Accounts with consumers were under the immediate supervision of the district managers.

Such, in broad outline, was the personnel realignment that McCall brought about to serve the Company's electric properties. In 1902, these properties consisted of many small generating plants equipped with machinery of all sorts, much of which would soon be obsolete and whose total output would soon be insufficient. Some of the plants supplied direct current and some alternating current, those furnishing alternating current having different voltages and frequencies from their neighbors. Such a system had to be standardized in order to establish uniformity in the supply of current. Before any economies could be effected in plant operations, it was necessary to adopt a uniform engineering plan and a single system of electrical distribution for the Company's 12,090 customers, who, in 1902, were using 17,188 arc lights, 440,698 incandescent lamps, and power for 11,868 horsepower in motors.

Philadelphia Electric chose for its standardized distribution system a two-phase, three-wire alternating current at 60 cycles. By 1900 it was generally realized, Thomas A. Edison to the contrary, that alternating current was more adaptable for general transmission and distribution than direct current. However, since direct current as used by the Edison system in the compact, congested area of Philadelphia could still hold its own, it was decided to continue it in the old Edison area but supply alternating current elsewhere. Having determined the voltage and type of current to use, McCall and his engineers were now ready to consolidate serviceable generating stations and shut down the others.

Preliminary steps in this direction had been taken as early as 1898. By that time, the equipment used in the Edison Station practically filled the building, and management was faced with the decision either of building another Edison plant, or of taking what was then considered the radical step of adopting the alternating current system of generation and transmission. Management took the radical course—the manufacture of alternating current at a more convenient location than central city, and its transmission by high-tension underground cables of 2,400 volts to the Edison Station.

To accomplish this, as previously noted, a former traction company powerhouse on the Schuylkill at Callowhill Street was leased, and in August, 1899, it began to supply the Edison Station where rotary converters changed the Callowhill alternating current to the direct current used by Edison. This was a historic step because it not only established the principle of alternating current production and conversion, but it was the first large capacity attempt to utilize a 60-cycle converter which received its energy from a generating source driven by a reciprocating engine. Unfortunately, the switching equipment was entirely inadequate. After nerve-wracking operation for a little over a year, a converter and much of its crude control apparatus blew up in a sheet of flame and wreckage. Before long, two new converters of a slightly improved type were installed, and normal supply of current was restored.

Additions to Callowhill Station soon allowed it to carry the daytime alternating current load of nearly all the stations. Callowhill's four 1,000-kilowatt flywheel generators were driven by cross-compound Corliss engines. All in line, a marvel of shining brass and steel, their operation was a beautiful sight.

A substation, supplied by underground high-tension cables from Callowhill Street, was built in 1899 at 1622 North Eighteenth Street and was tied in with lines to supply alternating current to the Columbia, Wissahickon, Diamond, and West End companies. The steam plant of the Germantown Station was shut down when a high-tension transmission line was extended to it. Thus, steps toward consolidating the system were under way and had proceeded as far as possible before the next move toward unification came with the leasing of all the underlying companies.

The operation of Callowhill Station with its high-tension transmission lines was considered experimental. If it proved advantageous, McCall planned either to enlarge the station, or to replace it with a new one capable of generating all the electricity needed by Philadelphia Electric and of transmitting it to substations.

There were a good many compelling arguments for replacing small generating plants with a central station. By combining the load on one station, the load factor—that is to say, the ratio of the actual output to the possible maximum output for the same period of time—is increased. By generating power in large stations and transmitting it by high-tension current, the cost of electricity is cheaper than if generated locally in smaller plants, provided the station has a good water-front location where it can obtain ample water for condensing purposes and cheap transportation for coal and for ash removal. By 1900, New York, Brooklyn, and Boston had adopted the central station principle with more or less success, retaining their old plants as necessary reserves, particularly for assistance during the peak loads of the winter months.

"I would recommend," McCall informed his directors in January, 1900, "that we first ascertain from the operation of the Callowhill Street Station whether or not the benefits, which appear so numerous from a theoretical standpoint, can be practically obtained." Within two years, all doubts about the practicability of a central station operation had been removed. With the demand upon the Callowhill plant soon exceeding its capacity, the board decided to replace it with a new plant on the Schuylkill at Twenty-eighth and Christian Streets.

The new station, designed by architect John T. Windrim, was to be erected in sections one hundred and sixty feet long, and was planned to be the largest generating station in the world with a capacity of nearly 100,000 kilowatts, a capacity which many people thought the company would never need. Built on a plot of about nine acres, it was serviced by coal barges at its own wharf, and supplied with coal by both the Pennsylvania and Baltimore & Ohio Railroads. The new plant was known as Station A (later, A-1), and was first supervised by Albert R. Cheyney. Its generating units were the largest obtainable at the time. One was a 2,000-kilowatt unit driven by a horizontal tandem-compound Wetherill engine; the other was a huge 5,000-kilowatt Reynolds Corliss engine built by the Allis-Chalmers Company. Both alternators were of the revolving field type, two-phase, 60-cycle machines, wound for 6,000 volts and built by the General Electric Company. The smaller unit was placed in operation September 28, 1903, and three months later the monster 5,000-kilowatt generator, the largest so far installed in Pennsylvania, went into commercial service.

Steam was supplied from boilers of 630 horsepower set in batteries of two and located on two floors of the boiler house. Coal storage was provided above the upper boiler floor, and the ashes from both floors were collected in the basement. All boilers were hand fired.

Changes in the design of powerhouses were taking place extraordinarily fast at this time. While Station A marked the beginning of large base-load stations in Philadelphia and was a great improvement over the Edison Station, it, too, was soon to be outmoded by the much simpler station built as an extension to it. Moreover, the initial equipment placed in the plant had to be discarded long before age had had much effect on it.

The huge slow-speed Corliss machine installed in 1903 was the last reciprocating engine purchased by Philadelphia Electric. A new prime mover had come to the fore, the steam turbine, which in economy of floor space, lubrication, labor, and other features was to outclass the Corliss. When new equipment was needed in January, 1905, McCall reported: "At Station A, Christian Street Station, we desire to install a 5,000-kilowatt steam turbine, which we feel confident has now reached the point of satisfactory service, turbines now being used in Boston, Chicago, and New York, demonstrating fully the ability of steam turbines to meet the requirements of the business." On January 4, 1906, this vertical Curtis turbine went into operation, its steam provided by four new boilers, and its performance promising much in economy. During 1907, two more vertical turbines, each rated at 5,000 kilowatts, were installed, together with sixteen additional boilers. The rating of the station was then 22,000 kilowatts.

The unification of Philadelphia Electric's system with its over-all engineering plan was completed during these years. Stations of the underlying companies located at Oak Lane, Germantown, Second Street and Susquehanna Avenue, Seventeenth and Clearfield Streets, Thirty-first Street and Girard Avenue, Twenty-sixth and Callowhill Streets, Twentieth and Ranstead (formerly Johnson) Streets, Ninth and Sansom Streets, and in West Philadelphia were interconnected through a switching station at Eighteenth Street and Columbia Avenue. By this means, it was possible to supply current to most sections of the city even if one of the stations was disabled. Additional capacity could also be directed to various stations should the local demand become abnormally great. Every effort was thus taken to ensure against the possibility of interruption and to improve reliability of service. Economies achieved through this integration of the system materially reduced the average cost of current and resulted in lower rates to the consumer.

Furnishing a commodity, electricity, was only a part of the Company's function, for it also provided complete service to the consumer, including connection from the supply mains, safety appliances, switches, transformers, and meters. It inspected installations, made minor repairs, and performed many other services without charge. The Company had its own laboratories staffed with specialists and equipped with testing devices. A commercial inspection department gave advice to the consumer on the best arrangement of his lights and the type of light best suited to his needs, whether arc, incandescent, Nernst, or Meridian.

The meter was the foundation of the entire business. It was imperative that the Company know how much electricity a customer was using in order to charge him for it. At the same time, the customer had to be convinced of the reliability of the meter. In 1902, there were less than 6,000 meters in the city, and these were of different types—the Stanley, Slattery, Scheefer, Shellenberger, Duncan, Westinghouse, Thomson, and Edison meters. The Edison type was the most numerous, but, while cheap, was cumbersome to operate and could only be used on direct current circuits. Moreover, it did not register directly the quantity of electricity used. That had to be computed. In substance, the meter consisted of two bottles containing a solution of zinc sulphate, in each of which was immersed two amalgamated zinc plates. Electricity passing from one plate to the other, as in electroplating, deposited the metal from the positive plate on the negative plate. By Faraday's law, the amount of metal thus deposited is exactly proportional to the quantity of electricity consumed.

Each month the meterman came around with his pushcart, replaced the plates with new ones, tagged the used ones, and put them in a rack in his cart. At the end of the day, after pushing his cart around the city and picking up plates, he wheeled them through the dirty streets back to the Edison Station. On an elevator otherwise used for hauling coal, the plates were brought to the meter department on the ninth floor, where they were weighed on scales capable of measuring the weight of an eyelash to calculate the amount of energy the customer had used during the past month.

The Edison meter, as well as all the other meters, was soon replaced with a type that was actually a diminutive electric motor, built with jeweled bearings, like a watch. Its speed varied with the amount of electricity being used, and the output was registered in kilowatt-hours on a dial.

In early years, consumers regarded the meter as an enemy, frequently complaining about high bills and scorning the meter's supposed accuracy. A chief of the meter department wryly observed: "Some write letters asking us to guess again. Others have an idea that the bills are derived by multiplying the number of lamps by the number of dark days in any one month. And when we start to explain the Edison meter, they claim that the meter is only a bluff—that if they don't kick their bills will keep on increasing. They think it advisable to make a complaint about every six weeks!"

In 1899, when the Edison Company had begun replacing chemical meters with rotating watt-hour instruments,

George Ross Green became head of the meter department, assisted by Percy H. Bartlett. Together, they developed into a team of meter specialists. Heading up the meter committee of the National Electric Light Association, they gained national prominence for their research and development in the field of electric measuring devices. Green established what was probably the best meter department in the country, and founded the Philadelphia Electric Society of Metermen, which grew in standing and importance with the years.

It was futile, however, to have accurate meters if the current measured produced little or no light. This frequently occurred because Edison lamps of this period rarely burned out. Instead, they became black with use as the carbon from the filament was deposited on the inside of the glass. Whenever a customer thought he was not getting his money's worth of light from a bulb, he could turn it in at a Company office for a new one. Philadelphia Electric furnished free lamp renewals for the entire city, a policy hitherto confined to the Edison and three suburban companies. It was estimated that the policy of free lamp renewals cost the Company $80,000 in 1905.

"It is important at this time," announced McCall in May of that year, "that we take under consideration a change in our office location. We have entirely outgrown the size of this building." To replace the rented quarters on the northeast corner of Tenth and Sansom, the Company purchased the nearby Assembly Buildings which occupied a lot with a thirty-two-foot frontage on the southwest corner of Tenth and Chestnut Streets, and which extended back 228 feet to Sansom Street. Originally built in 1834 as a place to hold assemblies of all sorts, including schools, exhibitions, and concerts, it had been destroyed by fire in 1851, but had been immediately rebuilt and subsequently enlarged. When acquired by Philadelphia Electric, McCall believed that the Assembly Buildings could be remodeled. But the cost proving too great, the old landmark was replaced with a seven-story fireproof structure designed by John T. Windrim. This handsome edifice was occupied by the Company in the spring of 1907. Steam-heated throughout from the Sansom Street plant, it incorporated every possible use of electricity for lighting and power, including such novel equipment as vacuum cleaners and ice-water machines. Its main entrance, then as now, opened into a dignified and imposing display room where everything that was new in the evolution of electric household appliances was offered for sale.

To a degree, the new building represented the growth of the Company's staff, a group of men and women dedicated to the service ideals which a utility company must represent. There had, to be sure, once been a strike. In May, 1900, some of the linemen and groundmen had walked out, demanding higher wages and recognition of the Union of Electrical Workers. At this time, the linemen were being paid $2.50 for a ten-hour day, and they wanted $2.75 for a nine-hour day. McCall refused to meet the demands and the half-hearted strike quickly collapsed. Annual salaries for the average wage earner working for a private electric lighting company averaged $650 in 1906. This was no fortune, but the salary was in line with the times and was higher than the average annual wage of $576 paid by municipal lighting plants.

Since 1887, a beneficial association, started by the Brush Company, had been in existence. Its operation, however, was somewhat restrictive and only a quarter of the employees were members. In January, 1907, a mutual beneficial association was formed which enlarged the scope of the earlier organization and which was intended to include all employees. Supported by the workers and the Company, the association established a beneficial fund for payments to members for disability from accident and sickness, and life insurance in the event of death.

The growth of the Company's staff stimulated improved "fringe benefits" for their well-being and security, as well as improved offices in which to work. The new quarters in themselves symbolized the importance that the electric company was assuming in the community. From a side street, it had moved its offices to Chestnut Street, one of the city's most fashionable avenues. This move served notice that Philadelphia Electric had reached maturity.

A striking feature of the Company's growth was its method of financing. More than $10,000,000 had gone into new plants, modernization, and the extension of electric service. The money had not come from the banks, or from the sale of bond issues, but was derived entirely from surplus revenues and calls for installments on the stock of Philadelphia Electric (of New Jersey).* The initial financial problems which the Company so successfully overcame were, indeed, as formidable as the engineering and commercial problems.

By the end of 1907, McCall had brought Philadelphia Electric a long way. The underlying companies had been successfully integrated into the system. A standardized engineering plan had been adopted and put into operation. During the busy years 1902 to 1907, when these improvements had been consummated, Philadelphia Electric had grown by leaps and bounds.

* The first assessment on this stock was made in 1899—$2.50 a share. In 1916, the last installment of $2.50 was made and the stock became fully paid up to its par value of $25.00.

CHAPTER 7

Threats of Competition

"NEW THINGS," wrote Professor Marks in his *Finances of Gas and Electric Light and Power Enterprises*, "meet with twice the opposition in Philadelphia that they find elsewhere." Unreconciled to the consolidation of the Edison Company with the other Philadelphia light and power concerns, the professor included in his book a 1900 *North American* article whose caption read: "The Inside Story of a Modern Aladdin, His Electric Lamp, and Gullible Philadelphians. An Account of the Amazing Financiering of Electrical Companies in this City Which Made it Possible for One Promoter and His Associates to Garner Millions—With Nothing Else to Promote Here, Aladdin Vanishes." In this fantasy, Aladdin appeared as a thinly disguised Martin Maloney.

No matter how differently the professor and the Company's officials viewed the consolidation of the city's electric service, they did agree on Philadelphia conservatism. In an appeal to its customers in 1906, Philadelphia Electric informed them: "There are two kinds of conservatism—the ordinary and the Philadelphia kind." Those who sought to sell electricity had much resistance to overcome.

To be sure, the reluctant public was occasionally upset by electrical mishaps or disasters. Imagine the feelings of proper Philadelphians when they read of Neil McCool's horrifying experience of July 30, 1902. McCool, a machinist on his way home from work, stopped in James Browne's saloon at Nineteenth and Callowhill Streets for a drink. He had with him a newly repaired steel-rod umbrella. Demonstrating to a friend how neatly his umbrella had been retipped, he held it up in such a way that it inadvertently touched the metal box of a suspended electric fan. For a moment, everyone in the room was blinded by a dazzling flash; when they recovered, there at their feet lay the unconscious McCool. Simultaneously, there occurred a crackling and sparkling in scores of places nearby. An electric wire in Paul E. Sigmund's saloon blazed up and set fire to his ornamental ceiling. When firemen cut the sputtering wire, another vivid flash scared hundreds of thirsty workmen in saloons throughout the district. Little electricity was sold in those parts for some time to come.

On the other hand, the dangers of operating without electricity were perhaps even greater. A few months before McCool's nasty experience, Denbigh Hall at Bryn Mawr College was destroyed by fire when an oil lamp was upset. During the College's first seventeen years, its campus and buildings had been lighted entirely by oil lamps and candles, but after the Denbigh Hall fire Bryn Mawr switched to electricity.

The most frightful accidents of all took place within the Company's own plants. Their machinery was crude compared to modern equipment. Every now and then something would let go and fatalities would sometimes result. Professor Marks paid high tribute to the bravery of the men who worked in the Edison Station during an extended period of boiler trouble. "It was not such work that happens in the army, where a man is shot and that is the end of him, and where a battle happens occasionally. Day in and day out they stood to this work and did it systematically and coolly, facing the risk of being scalded to death. I do not think you will find braver men anywhere."

Another condition at the Edison Station stemmed from the arrangement of the boilers, which were on the floors above the Armington & Sims engines. From time to time, water would boil over, run down the steam pipes into the engines, and blow out the cylinder heads. Albert R. Granger later recalled one of these accidents: "It was a Christmas night. I had completed my round, and was standing in front of an engine talking with an engineer and the coal weighmaster when the bell in the boiler room rang a warning note. We separated in nothing flat just as the steaming hot water rushed down and knocked out the head of the engine with a resounding smack. The engine head hit the very spot where we had stood! The engineer—I remember him well—was 'Tom' Taggert. He stuck to his post in that blinding steam and finally shut it off. Another man and I pulled him out unconscious and rushed him to the Jefferson Hospital."

During the initial development of electric utilities, ignorance, accident, and faulty equipment all played their parts in industrial tragedies. What happened at Philadelphia Electric happened elsewhere. An indication of the dangers of operating an early light and power system is all that is intended here, that and the idea that the men who worked in the generating plants were often heroic.

Philadelphians, however, were not particularly aware of these problems. They were more interested in Edison's 1903 prophecy that before long all vehicles in the country would be propelled by electric storage batteries. They took sides in the Philadelphia Sabbath Association's campaign to prevent the delivery of ice on Sundays during the summer of 1904. This campaign was hard on the majority of people because they had no proper refrigeration and

CALLOWHILL ALTERNATING CURRENT STATION. CAPACITY, 4,000 KILOWATTS

DUPLICATE.

The Citizens' Electric Light and Power Co., of Delaware Co.

Clifton Heights, Pa., _____ 189_ _189_

Walter Webb M.D hereby agrees to use current to be furnished by **The Citizens' Electric Light and Power Company, of Del. Co.**, at _Sharon Hill_ on _Chester Pike_ for the purpose of supplying Electric Light as specified below, upon the following terms and conditions, viz. :

I. This Company will make the necessary connection between its main line and the building to be lighted if not more than 100 feet distant from said main line, but all other connections and appliances, for the purpose of utilizing the light within the building from that point, shall be at the cost of the subscribers, unless otherwise provided for in this contract, and shall be subject to the approval of the Company's Inspector.

II. The subscriber shall use all due care so as to prevent any waste of light. And that this Company may properly guard its interests, subscriber hereby agrees that this Company shall, at all reasonable times, by its authorized agent, have free access to the premises in which the light is used, to determine if it is being carried, distributed and used in a proper manner, and in accordance with the provisions hereof, and the Company reserves the right to shut off the supply for any of the following reasons : 1st, for repairs; 2d, for want of supply ; 3d, for non-payment of bill when due ; 4th, for fraudulent representations concerning the consumption of light.

III. In case the supply of light should fail from any cause whatsoever, whether natural or accidental, or interference by the State, County or Borough, this Company shall not be liable for damages by reason of such failure, nor shall this contract be thereby cancelled provided a pro rata deduction shall be made from payments then due, for the actual time of said failure, unless such failure be caused by the other party to this contract, when no deduction will be allowed : nor shall this Company be liable in any event for damage to person or property arising, occurring or resulting from the wires, electric equipment or use of the light.

IV. Subscribers are not permitted to use the light for any purpose, or in any place, other than provided for in this contract, without having first obtained the written consent of this Company, and arranged to pay additional compensation therefor.

V. Bills will be rendered monthly, and must be settled at the Office of the Company within ten days thereafter, or a penalty of ten per cent. will be added to the amount of the bill.

VI. Inspectors, agents or any employe of this Company are especially forbidden to demand or accept from subscribers any compensation for services rendered by them.

VII. This contract is not transferable ; and the Company reserves the right to discontinue at once the use of the current and to remove its property from any premises where there has been a change of ownership or tenancy, unless a new contract is made, and any arrearages for the use of the light, by any prior owner or tenant, settled. New occupants using the light without complying herewith, shall be liable for all light supplied until such notice shall have been given and new contract made, when the liability shall commence according to its terms.

VIII. The Company reserves the right to terminate this contract, and to shut off the current, and remove its property from the premises at any time on five days' notice, for failure to pay bills, for any violation of the within contract, or any of the provisions hereto, or rules and regulations of which the consumer has notice. Provided, that this shall in no wise be construed to deprive the Company of the right to recover any amount then due by any form of legal proceeding.

_14_ 16 C. P. Lamps to burn till bedtime.

_1_ 16 C. P. Lamps to burn all night.

_____ 16 C. P. Lamps to burn till store closes.

At contract price, per month, $ _5 00_

_____ 16 C. P. Lamps, on meter, at the rate of _____ per hour, for each lamp burning.

LOCATED AS FOLLOWS:

Parlor	Dining-Room	Hall, 1st floor	Chambers
Library	Kitchen	" 2d "	Bath Room

And I further agree to use not more than _7_ of these lights at one and the same time.

I agree to use these lights during the term of one year, and pay therefor as specified above. This agreement to continue in force after the expiration of the term named, until either party gives to the other ten days' notice of a desire to terminate the same, at the expiration of which term the contract shall be ended.

This contract shall not be binding unless accepted by the Secretary of the Company.

Accepted this _FIRST_ day of _JAN_ , 1898.

THE CITIZENS' ELECTRIC L. & P. CO. OF DEL. CO.

By _Samuel Haigh_

Secretary.

_____ Consumer.

ELECTRIC CONTRACT OF 1898 ISSUED BY A COMPANY WHICH LATER
BECAME A PART OF PHILADELPHIA ELECTRIC

needed daily deliveries. The movement to get rid of over-head wires was revived in 1905 when it was discovered that in Philadelphia there were 17,377 miles of wire (electric, telegraph, telephone) held up by 69,820 poles. But whether one liked it or not, these wires and poles represented progress. Horse racing was temporarily suspended at Point Breeze Track in favor of auto racing, and this also was progress. Scorching around the dirt track in 1907, an amateur driver clocked forty-four miles in a single hour. Queer-looking machines driven by men wearing rubber coats and racing caps tied over their ears and under their chins, their faces horribly distorted by large goggles so that they looked like gnomes, thundered around the oval in a series of explosions from mufflerless engines.

Physical changes were coming to Philadelphia at an increasing tempo by this time, and one of these changes, a change in the transit system, had a direct effect on Philadelphia Electric. In an unguarded moment when Elkins and Widener were abroad in 1901, a group of political manipulators jammed through the legislature and City Councils a series of bills and ordinances which granted thirteen charters and franchises for street railways in Philadelphia. Incalculably valuable rights to the city streets for rapid transit, a new term designating elevated lines and subways, were thus handed out with unseemly haste despite roars of public disapproval. John Wanamaker's offer to pay the city $2,500,000 for the franchises was ignored. Many regarded this franchise grab as a device to force the Union Traction Company to come to terms and to consolidate the new franchises with its own system.

At any rate, that is what happened. The franchise syndicate of 1901 was represented by Robert H. Foerderer, Clarence Wolf, Michael Murphy, and John M.

Mack, the political contractor. Widener and Elkins accepted Mack's proposition in 1902 to lease the Union Traction Company to the Philadelphia Rapid Transit Company. Before long, P.R.T. had started construction of its Market Street subway and West Philadelphia elevated line. Although Widener and Elkins continued to dominate transit affairs, Mack and Murphy joined the P.R.T. board of directors.

Dolan, a long-time director of Union Traction, had been opposed to the lease. Condemning it as a bad financial move, he retired from the traction board. Dolan's action was a dangerous financial setback for the rapid transit project, for his attitude compromised the chances of raising funds to build the subway. As a result of his resignation, several important board changes took place at Philadelphia Electric.

It will be recalled that the National Electric Company had been incorporated in 1899, but that before the year was out it had joined with Maloney's much larger system, thus creating Philadelphia Electric. National Electric controlled only one property of importance, the Southern Electric Light and Power Company of which John M. Mack was president. However, it had announced exciting plans for expansion in the Philadelphia market. To put out this fire, Maloney had been obliged to take over National Electric, a move probably expected by National Electric's founders. This merging of interests was in the identical pattern of Union Traction's consolidation with the thirteen paper franchises. Mack was a leader in both these transactions, and as a result of the consolidations was elevated to the board of Philadelphia Electric as well as to the P.R.T. board.

When Widener learned that Dolan disapproved of the P.R.T. lease, he resigned from the board of Philadelphia Electric where Dolan continued as the most powerful figure. A year later, Mack, his head buzzing with new schemes, also saw fit to resign. Rumors that Widener and Mack planned to undercut Dolan's gas interests had not long been public before Widener left the board of U.G.I. William L. Elkins, however, even though he had subscribed for 50,000 shares of P.R.T. stock, remained friendly with Dolan, but Elkins died in November, 1903, and another of Philadelphia Electric Company's original directors was thus removed.

With transit affairs simmering down, the local utility scene underwent its next trying time when Philadelphia Electric sought to take over a potential rival in 1904. The Keystone Telephone Company, with 15,000 telephones connected, had 10,000,000 duct feet in underground conduits in the city. And who should be president of the Keystone Telephone Company but John M. Mack. Again associated with him were Michael Murphy and Robert H. Foerderer, and while Mack vacationed in Europe his representative was none other than Israel W. Durham, the city's political boss.

Mack and his political friends had been worrying McCall with threats to organize a new electric light company which would use the Keystone conduits and to which would be given the city's million-dollar lighting contract. It was the old game all over again, and Philadelphia Electric had no recourse but to bid for the Keystone system. An agreement was reached between McCall and Durham whereby Philadelphia Electric would purchase the conduits for $2,500,000. Moreover, it was understood that Councils would approve an ordinance prohibiting the further stringing of electric light wires within the districts covered by Keystone's conduits, thereby ensuring the Company's control and safeguarding it from attack by a rival set of politicians and financiers.

Much publicity had been given to this arrangement when Mack returned and repudiated it. He wanted $3,000,000 and McCall would not pay that much. Promising a twenty per cent reduction in electric rates, Mack announced his intention to compete for the city's electric lighting. He reckoned without Durham. Humiliated at the way in which his Philadelphia Electric agreement had been canceled, the irritated political boss vowed that no ordinance giving Mack electric privileges would ever pass.

Still, Mack had a try at it. He sponsored an ordinance permitting the Commonwealth Electric Company, a company in name only, to operate an overhead and underground system for supplying electric light, and permitting that company to take over the Keystone conduits. It was, in fact, given out that Commonwealth had purchased the Keystone system for $3,000,000. But since Commonwealth, despite promise of financial support from W. C. Sheldon and Company of New York, had no money, where could the three millions have come from? Philadelphians remained skeptical of Mack's intention to enter the electric field and anticipated the hopelessness of his struggle with Councils. Nevertheless, his ordinance was introduced and was referred to a committee headed by Mack's enemy and Philadelphia Electric's friend, Henry Clay.

The threat of competition from a company utilizing Keystone's facilities lingered on, but John M. Mack soon departed from that particular scene. Troubles arose within the Keystone Company itself and Mack, according to the *Philadelphia Record* of April 22, 1905, was forced out. He turned his attention to his city contracts, for he was president of the General Asphalt Company and the municipal contracts for street paving were known as "Mack's own." At a later time, Philadelphians became sensitive about the quality of their roads, which seemed to crack up and deteriorate with surprising rapidity. "The streets of Heaven are paved with . . . ," a visitor once began to say, when he was interrupted by a Philadelphian who cried out, "Now, don't say asphalt!"

Merger talk involving Philadelphia Electric was a perennial source of conversation. In 1904, when rumors of its merger with U.G.I. were prevalent, the plan was fully outlined in the *Public Ledger* of April 13. In 1905, a new and more exciting merger possibility came to the fore. A bill had just been passed by the legislature authorizing the consolidation of street railways with electric light and power companies and with hotel, park, and bridge concerns. Gossip was rife that P.R.T., Keystone Telephone, Philadelphia Electric and other corporations would come together in a colossal combine. Newspaper reporters, discovering Widener, Dolan, and McCall lunching together at the new Bellevue-Stratford Hotel, seized on this meeting as significant of consolidation. "That is ridiculous," said Dolan in rebuffing the newsmen. "We did not discuss the matter at all."

Some of the mergers discussed in these days were pretty far-fetched. Nearly all of real importance were referred to John G. Johnson, the Philadelphian who has been acknowledged as one of the greatest corporation lawyers of all time. On one occasion, his opinion was sought while he was traveling in Europe. Johnson cabled back his answer: "Merger possible. Jail certain."

While undoubtedly interested in acquiring Philadelphia Electric for U.G.I., Dolan was entirely occupied in 1905 with his efforts to obtain a renewal of the city gasworks lease. Enormous excitement was created when the public reacted adversely to his proposition. There was the usual monster rally at the Academy of Music, and thousands of buttons were distributed showing a lamp post from which dangled a hangman's noose with the inscription, "Cheaper Gas. The Last Warning."

If U.G.I. should be denied the gasworks lease, who would get it? Who would dare bid against U.G.I.? Any competitor who took the gasworks away from him, Dolan was reported as saying, would face the stiffest fight ever waged in a big city for public and private lighting. According to Dolan in this account, Philadelphia was one of the most profitable gas markets in the country, but only because U.G.I. controlled Philadelphia Electric and was holding back electricity in favor of gas. Should U.G.I. lose control of the gasworks, however, every effort would be bent to make the electric lighting business as profitable as possible, and this would have to be at the expense of the city gas plant.

Wide publicity was given to Dolan's alleged remark that it was immaterial to him whether he made his money in gas or electricity in Philadelphia. But whoever made a better offer than he did for the gasworks would face a battle royal with Philadelphia Electric. A cartoon depicted Dolan, backed up by Durham, barring the way to the City Councils chamber. With a huge electric light bulb labeled "Phila. Electric Company," Dolan is menacing a group of capitalists who have come to bid for the gasworks.

Despite popular outcry, City Councils overwhelmingly approved the lease offered by U.G.I. Mayor John Weaver, more or less to everyone's surprise, then vetoed the measure, and, it being evident that the veto could not be overridden, Dolan abandoned his attempt. Failure to control the councilmen at this critical moment was fatal to Durham's prestige and cost him control of the Philadelphia Republican machine. After all the excitement of 1905, it seems almost anticlimactic to add that U.G.I. obtained the renewal of its lease two years later.

From a public relations point of view, the battle over the municipal gas plant was damaging to Philadelphia Electric. Did Dolan control the Company, and was the extension of electric facilities actually being held back? Dolan was the founder of the electric light and power industry in Philadelphia. In 1905, he was seventy-one years old, while McCall was only thirty-five. Dolan was a member of the executive committee of Philadelphia Electric's board, the other members being President McCall and Vice-President Harrity. It can be surmised that Dolan was in a position to dominate McCall, but did this mean that McCall was forced to curb the electric company?

In his annual report for 1903, McCall had stated: "The demand for the use of electricity is becoming greater every year, and our constant, active efforts are being directed toward increasing and extending the business throughout all sections of the city." The record proves that the Company was going ahead at a rapid rate despite Philadelphia conservatism, and that the Company was not being held back by U.G.I.

Public clamor against U.G.I.'s gas rates in 1905 directed attention to Philadelphia Electric's charges, and they, too, were denounced as unreasonably high. There was much talk of establishing a municipal plant in order to obtain lower rates. Such talk continued for several years and was a favorite topic of municipal reformers. Cognizant of unrest, McCall made a ten per cent reduction in his bid for the 1906 public lighting contract, and also reduced private lighting rates, informing his stockholders: "The continuing growth of the business justified your management in making these reductions, and it is our hope and expectation that the increase in the use of electricity for light and power will be encouraged thereby."

Early in 1906, Philadelphia Electric made drastic rate reductions, up to one third for many sections of the city. There had been a lack of uniformity in rates, principally because different rates had existed at the time the various underlying companies were purchased. In February, 1906, the Company adopted a flat ten cent per kilowatt-hour rate for its entire overhead system. This reduction did not apply to the Edison district where the investment cost for its underground service was six times as high as the cost of the overhead lines. In the Edison district the rate remained at fifteen cents. Acknowledging that the rate change was radical, McCall justified it as equitable, and pointed out that "we have reached that point in the earnings of this Company where we can afford to make the change with justice to both the consumers and the stockholders of the Company."

Although McCall denied that threats of competition and public criticism of electric rates had anything to do with his reductions, that they were simply in line with the established policy of the Company, adverse publicity forced him to take several steps in defending Philadelphia Electric. Much of the criticism with which he had to contend was of an unknowledgeable sort.

For example, in February, 1906, the president of the Trades League in an address discussing Philadelphia Electric concluded: "1. No one will claim that the consolidation of the electric light companies has inured to the benefit of the city or its citizens; 2. Its citizens have been enormously taxed as the result of this consolidation; 3. The city has been compelled to pay an immensely high rate for its lighting, nearly 100 per cent higher than some cities, and 25 per cent higher than any other city of equal importance." The gentleman who made these statements later admitted that they were merely of a general nature and should not be construed as exact statements of fact.

McCall appeared before the League on April 3, 1906, to speak on behalf of his Company's record. After hearing what he had to say, the League decided: "1. The consolidation has resulted in cheaper rates and better service, and to this extent has been a benefit to the citizens of Philadelphia; 2. It is undoubtedly true that since the consolidation there has been a substantial decrease in the cost of public lighting and in the rates charged private consumers; and further that the Philadelphia rates compare favorably with those prevailing in other cities of the first class."

To describe its operations, as well as to promote its business, the Company brought out in March, 1906, its first *Bulletin of the Philadelphia Electric Company*. This attractive pamphlet, issued quarterly, was "published every little while for the information and in the interest of our customers." Filled with helpful hints about the uses of electricity, it explained much about the running of an electric light and power company. It kept consumers up to date on new Philadelphia Electric plants and improvements. It struck out at the fallacy of competition in the electric business, pointed out the dangers of municipal ownership, and deplored the use of private plants for large buildings. The *Bulletin* detailed the Company's victories over isolated plants, such as those in the Jefferson Hospital, the North American Building, and the Philadelphia Record Building, which had been replaced with Philadelphia Electric's more economical central station service.

The *Bulletin* was a valuable public relations instrument, but the most telling document of all was the progress record of the Company since its incorporation late in 1899 until the end of 1907, when no doubt remained about its ability to defend itself and to grow. In 1902, the Company had paid its first dividend and had gone on a five per cent dividend basis. By the end of 1907, the year the Market Street subway and elevated road to Sixty-ninth Street went into operation, business was so good that in January, 1908, the Company declared its first extra dividend, a dollar a share.

In considering Philadelphia Electric Company's growth in the years 1900 through 1907, the story can best be appreciated statistically. Its total connected load had risen from the equivalent of 586,071 lamps of 16 candlepower to 1,489,851.* The Company had expended $10,811,647 for construction and yet had paid $2,618,654 in dividends and had accumulated a surplus of $2,141,934. In aerial construction it had nearly doubled the number of its poles and its miles of wire. Its total number of high-tension transmission cables had been more than tripled to 448,509 feet, and its duct feet of underground conduits had been more than doubled to 6,885,847. Similarly, its miles of underground cable and distributing mains had also been more than doubled to 796. In this period, the number of the Company's customers had risen from 8,145 to 22,973, and its connected load in motor horsepower had increased from 6,291 to 37,319. Its basic kilowatt capacity was now 30,460, with a guaranteed maximum overload capacity of approximately fifty per cent for a two-hour period.

More statistics could be quoted, but they would all add up to the same thing. Under Joseph B. McCall, Philadelphia Electric in its first years had struck out aggressively. It had overcome much popular prejudice against the use of electricity, had combatted public antipathy and misunderstanding about its monopolistic role, and had financed itself without help from anyone into a position of undeniable strength. It had achieved the econ-

---

* It was the custom at this time to report loads in terms of 16-candlepower equivalents.

omies that its founders had hoped for, and it had passed these economies on to the public in the form of lowered rates.

"I give McCall," a later president of the Company was to say, "the credit for having weathered not one financial storm but a multitude of them. Having dealt with the relations of political groups in the area, having dealt with the various franchises and all that went into the deals in those early days, he ultimately succeeded in combining the various companies engaged principally in street lighting or in the supply of alternating current outside of the Edison franchise territory, into one composite group that set the pace or set the stage for the development of what we today [1955] know as the Philadelphia Electric Company."

CHAPTER 8

Before the Storm

By THE END OF 1907, Philadelphia Electric was no longer so much concerned with being snuffed out by competitors as it was preoccupied in keeping abreast of the community's ever-increasing demands for electricity. Its board was still largely composed of those who had been made directors at the Company's inception, or had joined it soon afterward—Thomas Dolan, Jeremiah J. Sullivan, William F. Harrity, Dr. John V. Shoemaker— and the Company's officers, President McCall, Treasurer Conover, and Secretary Coe.

In addition to these men, Charles E. Ingersoll and J. R. McAllister had also been directors for several years. A member of an old and distinguished Philadelphia family, Ingersoll's election to the board was, however, hardly for genealogical reasons. Ingersoll knew something of politics, a valuable attribute, and had held an appointive office during Cleveland's presidency. His successful railroad ventures had won him the admiring respect of the financial community and a directorship with the Pennsylvania Railroad. A very popular man, he was an intimate friend of President McCall.

J. R. McAllister, considered by many to be the city's ablest banker, was president of the large Franklin National Bank and very much the sort of man whose personality would appeal to McCall. To a degree, the same could be said about Edward D. Toland's personality. He was a most attractive man, a stockbroker who was elected to the board after Dr. Shoemaker's death in 1910. When Treasurer William P. Conover, Jr., who had been with the system since joining the Edison Company in 1891, died in 1911, his seat at the board was taken by John T. Windrim, the Company's architect. In 1912, death claimed William F. Harrity. To fill his place, McCall elevated Walter H. Johnson, who had entered the utility field in 1887 when he joined the Edison Company. McCall also designated Johnson as the Company's vice-president.

On June 12, 1914, Thomas Dolan died, his death symbolically closing an era which embraced the founding of electric companies in Philadelphia, their early struggles and accomplishments. Old and in poor health, he had not attended a board meeting in nearly four years. The directors memorialized him as "fertile in suggestion, wise in counsel, clear and firm in decision and action." No one could ever take his place, but at least his vacancy had to be filled. To succeed Dolan, Sidney F. Tyler was chosen. President of the spectacular Fourth Street National Bank from 1886 to 1902, and thereafter chairman of its board, the peppery Tyler represented the interests of the Elkins family and other powerful financial connections. It was with these directors, most of whom had been personally selected by McCall, that Philadelphia Electric surged ahead in the years leading up to World War I.

During this period—that is the years 1908 to 1914—Philadelphia had as its figurehead a mayor representing the Republican machine, John E. Reyburn, and then a mayor who triumphed on a reform ticket, Rudolph Blankenburg. Different as these mayors were, they both suffered the indignity of having their official quarters violated. In 1908, a small animal wandered into City

95

Hall and settled down for a nap in one of the corridors. A janitor took it for a black cat and approached too close before he realized his terrible error. After a sensational chase, the intruder, whose identity had been unmistakably established, took refuge on top of a bookcase in Mayor Reyburn's private office. Max Kauffman, the mayor's able secretary, and Timothy O'Leary, popular assistant superintendent of police, did their valiant best to dislodge the unwelcome visitor, but were badly worsted. When the dejected O'Leary sought to enter an elevator on his way home to bathe, the attendant barred his way. "Don't you recognize me?" demanded the furious officer, producing his card. "I'll recognize you the next time I smell you," replied the elevator man.

The outrage suffered by Mayor Blankenburg in 1912 was less nauseous, but more audacious. During office hours, in broad daylight, a thief entered Blankenburg's reception room, calmly collected all the brass cuspidors and heavy cut-glass inkstands, and vanished with his loot.

This was an era when changing times brought stress on long-established moral values, the world of entertainment and sports frequently running counter to fading Victorian ideals. It was all very well for Houdini, handcuffed and manacled hand and foot, to leap off the Market Street Bridge into the coal blackened waters of the Schuylkill in May, 1908. Twenty thousand Philadelphians watched the daring deed, and it is difficult to judge whether they would have been more thrilled by his nonappearance than by his escape. However, in fifty-seven seconds Houdini arose triumphantly from the deep, holding aloft his handcuffs, and the crowd let out a mighty roar of approval and relief.

Entertainment of this kind did not bother the city fathers. They evidently considered it wholesome. In fact, it was a high-ranking police officer who had manacled

Houdini and had thus co-operatively lent his assistance to a possible suicide or manslaughter. The sort of show that did bother people was Oscar Hammerstein's production of "Salome" at the Philadelphia Opera House in 1909. Several Catholic and Jewish groups, as well as the Christian League, appealed to Mayor Reyburn to prevent the performance, but the mayor would not listen. On the contrary, he purchased tickets and attended the opera himself. Before a sell-out crowd, Mary Garden enacted the "Dance of the Seven Veils" with all its alleged lasciviousness, and, in a horror-inspiring scene, kissed the severed head of John the Baptist. Not a hiss was heard, and, when the opera was over, wild cheering, stamping, and applause broke out. Nevertheless, many went away mildly disappointed that the immoral features of "Salome" were overrated.

City authorities were surprisingly liberal in moral matters. Philadelphia, for example, was one of the few large cities in which movies of the Jeffries-Johnson prize fight of 1910 were permitted to be shown. But there were many in the community who deplored this liberal attitude. In their opinion, prize fights were as immoral as "Salome." Tremendous pressure was brought to bear on theater owners who planned to feature the movie, and some of them suppressed the film. The fifteen hundred enthusiastic fight fans who crowded the new Forrest Theatre were disappointed at the very last minute by the withdrawal of the movie, the proprietors having reluctantly decided that its showing would "degrade the theater."

On the other hand, no one objected to demonstrations of new scientific wonders, foremost among which was the airplane. Since its first feeble flight in 1903, the airplane had developed amazingly. In May, 1910, Glenn H. Curtiss flew from Albany to New York, the longest cross-country flight yet accomplished in America. His speed of fifty-four miles an hour was considered phenomenal. The next month, a round-trip flight between New York and Philadelphia was heralded. On the great day, every fence, housetop, and factory roof for blocks around the big field at Front Street and Erie Avenue, where Charles K. Hamilton was to land, was crowded with observers. Five hundred policemen, later re-enforced by hundreds more, struggled to hold back a crowd of 50,000 which surged about the field itself. Right on schedule, the intrepid aviator brought his Curtiss biplane down on the field, jumped out, and presented a letter from the governor of New York to Governor Edwin S. Stuart of Pennsylvania. Hamilton's return trip was marred by a dirty spark plug which compelled him to land in the marsh flats at South Amboy.

Material progress manifested itself not only in man's domination of the air, but wherever one looked in Philadelphia. In October, 1909, the Chestnut Street section of Wanamaker's huge new store opened. Five years later, construction was begun on another Chestnut Street skyscraper, the Widener Building, designed by Horace Trumbauer to harmonize with nearby Wanamaker's.

Great buildings such as these represented valuable lighting contracts which were aggressively sought by Philadelphia Electric. "If it isn't electric, it isn't modern!" became a Company slogan. To obtain new business, the commercial department spent about $100,000 a year in advertising and soliciting. The managers of the eight districts into which the Company had divided the city sent out agents who followed building operations through architects, builders, and owners. By 1913, about ninety-five per cent of new buildings were being wired for electricity. The assault on isolated plants continued, with consumers like the Cramp shipyards, streetcar manufacturer J. C. Brill & Company, and many others shifting to

Schuylkill Station as it Appeared on Completion in 1903

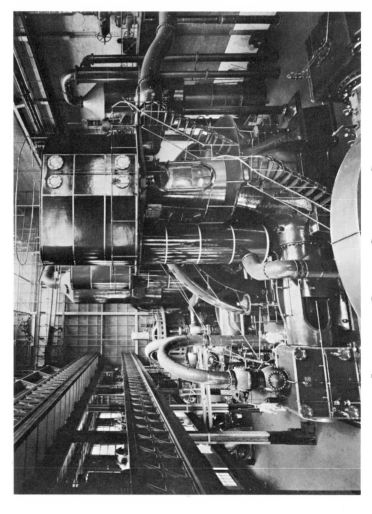

central station service. This shift was advantageous to the city because it meant the gradual disappearance of hundreds of ugly smokestacks that marked the location of isolated plants and disgorged clouds of dirty smoke.

The Company's advertisements convey the flavor of the times and suggest the appearance of new uses for electricity. In 1909, Philadelphia Electric cautioned house renters to be sure the house was wired for electricity: "Modern houses, large and small, are being wired nowadays. You can find them in every section of the city. Hundreds of two-story houses in West Philadelphia are now using electricity." Also in 1909, the Company first promoted electric refrigeration for commercial purposes. Then, in 1910, it announced: "Electric cooking has become something more than an expedient of convenience, as evidenced by Messrs. Horn & Hardart in their new restaurant at 909 Market Street in which they have installed an electric kitchen." By 1911, the domestic electric range had assumed a faintly modern appearance —"Electric ranges can be used precisely in the same way as the coal or gas range and have one to three burners as well as an oven"—but it was to be a long time before Philadelphia Electric was to promote electric ranges with real confidence. Of Philadelphia's eight hundred and fifty churches, five hundred were customers of Philadelphia Electric in 1912, the year that housewives were informed, "The only way to clean the house is to remove the dirt; the only way to remove the dirt is to use a vacuum cleaner."

The Company assiduously promoted the use of electric vehicles, boasting of its own electric fleet in June, 1908: "To maintain our equipment at the highest point of efficiency, and to make our service prompt and reliable, we have a complete automobile service, consisting of cable trucks, service wagons, lamp wagons, and runabouts. These automobiles with their repair crews are kept in readiness day and night." In recommending the purchase in 1912 of "four electric runabouts for use of the right-of-way men," McCall declared that these vehicles would double the men's efficiency. Despite this new equipment, the Company still relied primarily on horses and wagons, and gave little publicity to its ownership of several gasoline cars which were faster for long hauls than the electrics.

Philadelphia Electric was interested in electric vehicles because of its battery-charging service. So highly was this service considered that in 1910 an authority categorically stated, "The best undeveloped prospective load today for central stations is the electrical vehicle." In the several years immediately preceding World War I, electric cars attained considerable popularity in Philadelphia. The fire department, beginning in 1912—not until the end of 1927 was it to retire its final horse-drawn chemical engine—started purchasing electric trucks. Sales points stressed by Philadelphia Electric were the economy of operation of the electrics, their speed and dependability, and the safety of their solid rubber tires. By 1913, Philadelphia had responded to the campaign, having more passenger electric cars than any other city except Chicago, and the largest number of electric trucks except Chicago and New York.

Philadelphia Electric's own fleet had grown to forty-three cars by 1914. The Curtis Publishing Company in that year was using eleven large electric trucks, most of which continue operative, including old Number 3, purchased in 1912 and still impressive as it rolls massively over the city's streets. Curtis, as well as Horn & Hardart, U.G.I., and the Adams Express Company with its one hundred and forty-six cars, all depended on Philadelphia Electric's battery-charging service.

The use of current for lighting purposes remained the Company's principal business. Celebrations helped dramatize the use of electricity, for the illumination of the city at night was a feature of local festivals. It is not surprising that Philadelphia Electric officials co-operated heartily with any anniversary-minded group. In the fall of 1908, Founder's Week, commemorating William Penn and the establishment of his great city, was observed. During this banner week, a notable feature was the "Industrial Parade," a procession of floats provided by various businesses. Philadelphia Electric was represented by six floats on which were demonstrated the uses of electricity. City Hall glowed with 300,000 incandescent lights during this gala time, and all commercial houses and private residences were requested to be illuminated every evening. Such demonstrations were good for business.

Naturally, Philadelphia Electric took the leading part in any major electrical show in the city. In February, 1910, it sponsored an outstanding exhibition at the First Regiment Armory. Thousands of people paid to visit this display, where they saw the application of electricity to such domestic functions as cooking, heating, washing, ironing, and cleaning. The newspapers reported, "Never in the history of Philadelphia has such a bewildering scene of sparkling brilliance been presented indoors." The night the show opened, Mayor Reyburn, Henry Clay, who was now Reyburn's director of public safety, President Joseph B. McCall, and Chief Electrical Engineer W. C. L. Eglin dined together before attending the event.

Reyburn and Clay, spurred on by the various merchants' associations and by members of Councils, were anxious to provide additional lighting for the city's central business district. They wanted to make it the best-lighted area in the world. The first step toward accomplishing this aim was celebrated at midnight on New Year's Eve, 1909, when Mayor Reyburn, attended by Clay and President McCall, threw the switch which turned on Market Street's new lighting east of City Hall. An immense crowd jammed the street at this wonderful moment, and the appropriate airs sung by the German Singing Society of Philadelphia were lost in the din of thousands of firing revolvers and the pandemonium of giant fireworks.

The dazzling new illumination was so successful that Councils passed an ordinance calling for nearly a thousand additional arc lights. The size of the contract necessitated a rearrangement within Philadelphia Electric's system. The old Brush Station was demolished and in its place was erected a one-story building which housed forty 125-arc light machines supplied with current from Christian Street. Ornamental iron poles were erected on Market, Chestnut, Walnut, Arch, and Broad Streets, and from each pole were hung two lights of 2,000-candle-power brilliance. These lamps were turned on by Mayor Reyburn at a ceremony on September 15, when he enthusiastically discussed a plan to illuminate every alley and court in the city. The municipal electric bill, despite periodic lowering of rates by Philadelphia Electric, of course went up, and reformers began to question it.

McCall and his assistants, when not actively engaged in promoting and running Philadelphia Electric, took a leading part in the National Electric Light Association. Philadelphia Electric men held offices in this organization and read papers at its meetings. W. C. L. Eglin had served as its president. In 1914, when McCall was president, he succeeded in bringing the Association's convention of some 3,000 representatives to Philadelphia. "We worked hard to get them here," said McCall remembering that for the past twenty-seven years the convention had by-passed the city. Later in the year, McCall presided over another convention, that of the Electric Vehicle Association of America, which met at the Bellevue-Stratford in October.

By maintaining close touch with state and national electric associations, McCall was able to keep his Company abreast of current changes in the industry. As an example, he was influenced by a pension plan under consideration in 1911 by the public policy committee of the National Electric Light Association, and, through the expert work of Philadelphia Electric's paymaster, B. Frank Day, saw to it that the Company adopted a service annuity plan in advance of the industry's recommendations on the subject.

For five or six years, McCall had carefully watched the progress of the Company's beneficial association. It was a pronounced success, caring for illnesses and making payments in the event of death to the ninety per cent of the staff who had joined it. But it did not provide pensions. "I believe," McCall informed his directors in March, 1911, "that we cannot too strongly recognize the strong asset of our loyal organization; that the human element of the business should be given the same thought that we give the mechanical, that some reward should be given to those who have served, and will continue to serve the Company, through all kinds of conditions, to cover their natural depreciation and help them when they are unfit to continue in the service." On the board's recommendation, the stockholders at their annual meeting in April, 1911, approved a Company-financed service annuity plan, which provided for the retirement of women employees at the age of sixty and men at the age of sixty-five, with a minimum annuity, based on years of service, of twenty-five per cent of their salary, and a maximum of fifty per cent.

If not always a leader in personnel matters, Philadelphia Electric was sensitive to changes which affected working conditions. By 1913, many industries had shortened the working day to eight or nine hours, but the Company's station employees continued the traditional twelve-hour shift. In order to maintain a strong working organization, McCall brought Philadelphia Electric into line by reorganizing its operating department into shorter shifts.

A good deal of thought was given to recreation, and in 1908 the Athletic Association was founded. The various departments had their baseball teams and played in a park provided by the Company. In 1910, the versatile McCall pitched a victorious game for the "Executives" against the "District Managers." Many sports flourished under this program; other talents were catered to by musical and dramatic groups. To all such extracurricular activities the Company lent moral and financial support. It was particularly interested in furthering the professional education of its employees. In 1909, it encouraged the publication of *Current News*. At first, this journal went only to those who had joined the Philadelphia Electric Company Section (later the Philadelphia Electric Employees Association) of the National Electric Light Association. *Current News* served primarily as a publication medium for papers read at the section meetings. Secondarily, this highly scientific journal served as a house organ and endeavored to foster "a spirit of the fullest harmony and co-partnership among the employees." That the magazine was also willing to serve as a clearinghouse for staff news was evidenced in its very first issue: "The Yanigans, Station 'A,' at the present time are looking for a first baseman, they being minus one owing to the appearance of a boil on the throwing arm of the Chief Engineer."

Philadelphia Electric's extraordinary growth in prewar years can be measured by the number of people it employed. In 1907, the staff consisted of 1,282 employees; by 1914, this number had nearly doubled to 2,497. The decline in wages in this period was indicative that conditions were not generally prosperous throughout the nation. The average wage received by a Philadelphia Electric employee in 1907 was $71 a month. This fell off to $66 a month in 1910, and remained at that figure until 1914 when it advanced one dollar.

Since architect Windrim had not counted on the sharp increase in the size of the staff, the Company soon outgrew its new building at Tenth and Chestnut Streets. To furnish temporary relief, its former home at the northeast corner of Tenth and Sansom was once again occupied in 1914, and the property adjoining the Chestnut Street headquarters was purchased. Plans were made to erect on this twenty-five-foot frontage a building which would conform in every respect to Windrim's original structure, and which would serve as an enlargement of it.

Another measure of the Company's growth is reflected in the rating of Christian Street Station, which was nearly quadrupled from 22,000 kilowatts in 1907 to 81,000 in 1913. Its original equipment was all replaced by powerful new generating units. Old "Number 2," the 5,000-kilowatt Allis-Chalmers horizontal-vertical compound Corliss unit installed in 1903, was the largest 60-cycle unit of its kind ever built. Because of its balkiness, it had taxed the patience of engineers to the breaking point. This great, cumbersome unit ignominiously ended its short and hectic career on the scrap heap, being replaced in 1913 by two 15,000-kilowatt units occupying the space from which it had been removed. Even "Number 3," the 5,000-kilowatt turbine of which the Company had been so proud when it was installed in 1906, lasted only four years. The steam end of this unit had been so liberally designed that it could produce much more than 5,000 kilowatts. So, "Number 3" generator was replaced by a 12,000-kilowatt unit which was able to match the capacity of its prime mover. Christian Street Station was enlarged to house new machinery, the other generating stations were also increased in power, and new substations were erected as required throughout the system.

In addition to increasing the Company's electrical output, close attention was paid to improving and modernizing the details of its operation. A notable example of this in 1909 was the installation of automatic Taylor stokers in some of the boilers at Christian Street at a cost of $80,000. Among the advantages of the stokers was the saving in labor, a fifteen per cent economy in the use of coal, the reduction of smoke nuisance, and a reduction in the cost of repairs. It was estimated that the stokers would effect a saving of $50,000 a year.

The purchase of new equipment and the extension of service were expensive. Every year the Company poured large sums of money into its construction program. In 1913, $3,382,000 was spent for this purpose. While some of this money came from operating income, a substantial part was raised by calls on the stockholders. By the end of 1914, Philadelphia Electric's 1,000,000 shares of stock, par value twenty-five dollars, was twenty-two dollars and fifty cents paid up, and the end of financing through calls on the stock was in sight.

The system's growth reflected not only the increasing demand for electric service in areas already supplied, but, to a lesser extent, its extension into new areas. In 1909, the Associated Gas and Electric Company of New York purchased four small companies in Delaware County, forming them into the Delaware County Electric Company. It was contrary to McCall's policy to operate outside Philadelphia County, but he was willing to supply current to outlying operating companies and contracted to do so for Delaware County Electric. The following year, he was forced to purchase the company to protect the bills it owed Philadelphia Electric. McCall proposed to rehabilitate his unwelcome acquisition and then sell it, but was dissuaded from this course by members of his staff who realized the potential value of the Delaware County territory. Advisers also prevented him from selling the Beacon Light Company in Chester. This property had come into the system in 1899. For years, McCall had been anxious to dispose of it and to concentrate all activities in Philadelphia, but at long last he became convinced that it would be a mistake to relinquish the great industrial Chester area.

One of the bright features in the ownership of suburban plants was the contracts they were beginning to receive from traction companies. In 1910, Philadelphia Electric engaged with P.R.T. to supply power to its lines at Media and Chester, a move which was the forerunner of P.R.T.'s great changeover from generating its own current to purchasing it from the electric company.

Since its founding, P.R.T. had been in difficulties. Its record was marred by strikes and poor public relations, and the company was regarded by many as a huge political football. In 1909, its unpopularity reached a crescendo when its directors abolished the "strip ticket" of six fares for twenty-five cents and established the flat rate of five cents a fare. Twelve thousand angry citizens converged on the Academy of Music, which could accommodate but three thousand, for a violent protest meeting. After Clarence Wolf, the city's representative on the transit board, resigned under fire for having approved the rate increase, the P.R.T. board reaffirmed its faith in Wolf by not only re-electing him, but making him first vice-president. In a play for support, the company raised the pay of its motormen and conductors one cent an hour, from twenty cents to twenty-one cents. The raise did little good, for within a month the men were out on strike demanding twenty-five cents. Rioting and property damage occurred. The next year, the carmen went out on a strike which lasted more than a month, and which at one time gave promise of turning into a general strike of all the trade-unions in Philadelphia. By this time, the city was thoroughly disgusted with P.R.T. management and aware that the transit company was on the verge of bankruptcy.

The break came in October, 1910, when Wolf resigned his position at P.R.T. and the company's directors petitioned banker Edward T. Stotesbury to take control and rehabilitate the corporation. Stotesbury called in Thomas E. Mitten, the Chicago street railway expert and adviser in such matters to J. P. Morgan. In June, 1911, management of P.R.T. passed to Stotesbury, and all the old directors, including P. A. B. Widener, resigned. Charles E. Ingersoll, a Philadelphia Electric director, banker Horatio G. Lloyd, who later came on the board of Philadelphia Electric, and Thomas E. Mitten were among the new directors selected to run P.R.T. Mitten served as managing director until 1914 when he became president, and it was largely through his efforts that the giant traction system fought its way back to profitable operation.

A month after he had come into power, Mitten signed a contract with Philadelphia Electric for 8,000 kilowatts of current to be delivered on November 1, 1911. This contract followed the form of the one negotiated between the Commonwealth Edison Company of Chicago and the Chicago street railway, even to the point of accepting the Chicago rate.

Philadelphia Electric had less than four months in which to meet the terms of this agreement. A substation was erected on the Christian Street property and two frequency changers, one of 6,000- and the other of 3,000-kilowatt capacity, were ordered from General Electric, the larger machine being the biggest of its type ever built. These machines were necessary to convert Philadelphia Electric's standard 60-cycle current to the transit company's 25 cycles. Time was so short that the machinery was shipped without having been assembled or tested. By working day and night, the Company's engineers had the 9,000-kilowatt station in operation within four months as scheduled, probably a record for the completion of a station anywhere near that size.

McCall viewed the 8,000-kilowatt contract as basically a trial service in obtaining larger contracts, and early in 1912 ordered an extension of Christian Street Station in which to install a 15,000-kilowatt 25-cycle turbogenerator. It was well that he did so, for in March, 1912, new contracts were signed between Philadelphia Electric and P.R.T. To improve streetcar service and to provide more power for increased rolling stock, Stotesbury and Mitten had decided to abandon some of P.R.T.'s suburban generating stations and to replace their power with Philadelphia Electric current. By November 15, 1912, P.R.T. needed an increase in the 8,000-kilowatt load to 15,000 kilowatts, with additional increases in the following year raising the total to 26,200 kilowatts. Among the areas to be supplied were Neshaminy, Willow Grove, Ogontz, and Chestnut Hill. It was this need for increased power that led to the scrapping of the great Allis-Chalmers engine in 1913 and its replacement with two 15,000-kilowatt vertical turbines, one a 60-cycle machine, the other a 25-cycle unit. Station J, Tacony, received a 9,375-kilowatt turbine to assist it in supplying a substantial P.R.T. load. Pole lines were run to P.R.T.'s former stations where rotary converters were installed.

The P.R.T. contracts served as an introduction to the Pennsylvania Railroad's proposed electrification program. In June, 1913, the railroad opened negotiations with Philadelphia Electric for power to be supplied to its suburban lines from Broad Street Station to Paoli and to Chestnut Hill. McCall's engineers calculated that the railroad would require a minimum of 21,000 kilowatts within five years and an ultimate maximum of 60,000.

Aside from this potentially enormous demand, Philadelphia Electric had to consider the ever-increasing requirements for current from the community at large. In 1913, this load was principally supplied by three stations. The 81,000-kilowatt Christian Street Station fed the central section of the city; the northern district with its industrial load was supplied from the 17,500-kilowatt plant at Tacony; and the territory around Chester by Beacon Station of 8,500-kilowatt capacity. The combined output of these stations would soon be inadequate to meet normal growth, to say nothing of the abnormal growth with which Philadelphia Electric was faced.

To provide for future requirements, steps were taken in September, 1913, toward the erection of another great generating plant which was to be built adjacent to the Schuylkill River Christian Street A-1 Station, and which was to be designated as A-2. Orders were placed with General Electric for turbines to be housed in A-2; each of these turbines was to be of greater capacity than the total station output of Philadelphia Electric ten years earlier. Looking even farther ahead, McCall purchased the Neafie & Levy shipyard in Kensington, thereby securing about eight and a half acres with a 450-foot frontage on the Delaware River. On this site, at some unspecified future time, he planned to erect yet another central station.

Plant construction was a relatively simple matter compared with the perplexities of furnishing current to the Pennsylvania Railroad. The railroad had elected not to use the direct current produced in its own plants, a system then in limited use by one or two railroads, but had decided instead on single-phase, 11,000-volt alternating service purchased from Philadelphia Electric. The wisdom of this step from the standpoint of economy and dependability was to be proved in the coming years and was to lead to Philadelphia Electric's assuming the largest railroad electrification load in the world.

Initially, however, there seemed to be insurmountable difficulties in providing the current. The railroad wanted single-phase energy in large amounts, and this could not be produced by the three-phase generators with which the Company planned to supply the power. For eighteen months, the engineers struggled to devise some means to spread the single-phase load automatically and equally on all three phases. Finally, the Company's two top engineers, W. C. L. Eglin and Horace P. Liversidge, went to the General Electric factory at Schenectady, where a noted scientist, Ernst F. W. Alexanderson, explained to them a patent for a phase-balancing machine, admitting that it had never been tried and that he did not know whether it would work as it theoretically should.

To settle the question, Dr. Charles P. Steinmetz, General Electric's consulting engineer, was called in. The foremost authority in the world on the theory and design of electrical apparatus and distribution systems, Dr. Steinmetz was a man of unprepossessing appearance who did not normally come to the plant because of its rule against smoking. He nearly always had a cigar in his mouth, rarely smoking it, just chewing on it; this process helped him think. When Dr. Steinmetz arrived, he was informed of the problem and given the fundamental equation of the phase-balancer theory. Writing down the mathematical formula involved, he filled a page and a half with calculus computations, and then, with complete assurance in his voice, announced, "Yes, it will work." Two great, complicated phase-balancers were the result. They were shipped to Philadelphia without being tested, and were installed in Schuylkill Station where they operated to perfection.

Before this near-miracle was accomplished, U.G.I. had made another of its periodic efforts to absorb Philadelphia Electric. In February, 1913, Samuel T. Bodine, who had succeeded Dolan as president of U.G.I. in 1912, proposed a ninety-nine-year lease, in return for which U.G.I. would guarantee Philadelphia Electric Company's stockholders an annual eight per cent dividend. At this time, the Company was paying a dividend of six per cent. A committee consisting of President McCall and Directors Sullivan and Toland studied the offer and reported favorably on it, but the board voted it down 4 to 2. The two directors voting for the lease were Sullivan and Toland. As presiding officer at the meeting, McCall did not vote, and his opinion in the matter is not on record.

To placate shareholders disappointed at not obtaining the eight per cent dividend, the Company raised its annual rate to seven per cent, and in the following year negotiated a lease of its own to secure the unused ducts of the Keystone Telephone Company. This lease was obtained on favorable terms, unaccompanied by the excitement that had marked earlier dealings with Keystone. Although the actual consummation of the lease was held up for several years by public authorities, the way was opened for an extension of Philadelphia Electric's underground system.

By this time, however, there were those who were not anxious to see Philadelphia Electric increase its hold on the community; a distaste for monopoly had not died out. The background for this antagonism lay in recent political changes. Durham had died in 1909 after a brief political comeback, and State Senator "Sunny Jim" (James P.) McNichol, a Boies Penrose stalwart, was in control of the Republican machine. His control, however, was not as absolute as that of several previous bosses, because he had to contend with the Vare brothers, who had strong support in South Philadelphia. In 1911, William S. Vare, the garbage contractor, had had the effrontery to run for mayor, claiming that he was the choice of the "plain people." Vare was readily defeated in the primary by the Penrose-McNichol candidate, George H. Earle, Jr. Meanwhile, mounting resentment against the rule of political contractors brought another Republican, Rudolph Blankenburg, into the field on an independent ticket. Earle, a man of great ability, would probably have defeated Blankenburg had he refrained from making campaign speeches, in one of which he alienated the Vares, who failed to support him on election day. The heavily bearded Blankenburg, affectionately known as the "War Horse of Reform" and as "Old Dutch Cleanser," won by the narrow margin of 4,000 votes.

To the office of director of public works, Blankenburg appointed a controversial figure in engineering and liberal political circles, Morris Llewellyn Cooke, and the fur began to fly. Former Director of Public Safety Henry Clay was hauled into court on charges of conspiring to defraud the city through a contracting firm. The rates of the Welsbach Street Lighting Company, a U.G.I. subsidiary, were attacked, and then Cooke turned on U.G.I. itself. At his insistence, the Department of Justice undertook an investigation to determine whether U.G.I. was violating the Sherman Antitrust Law. Cooke wrested the garbage contract away from Vare and gave it to the Penn

Reduction Company for half of what Vare had been charging. His triumph over this economy was changed to embarrassment when he learned that the reason for Penn's cheap rate was its garbage disposal method: it simply dumped the garbage into the Schuylkill! Vare got the contract back, and the city's 39,000 pigs, which had fattened on the garbage he hauled, ate again.

Cooke was convinced that Philadelphia Electric and U.G.I. systematically "mulcted and fleeced" the people, a point of view he stressed in picturesque language. His activities and accusations were followed with sardonic interest by professional politicians, who refused to support any of his campaigns.

The passage of a public service act by the legislature in 1913, setting up a public service commission, gave Cooke his opportunity. He proposed to fight Philadelphia Electric's rates before that body. But when he asked Councils for $5,000 for the purpose, they not only refused him but cut the salary of his gas bureau chief in half. Cooke then brought suit against Philadelphia Electric as a private citizen, charging that its rates were exorbitant, that it was badly managed, and that its system was run down.

With respect to rates, from the Philadelphia Electric viewpoint the Company had been providing ever-cheaper electricity while the cost of everything else was going up. Witness the price of milk. It had advanced one cent a quart to nine cents in 1909! Year by year, the Company had lowered the cost of the public lighting contract. In 1912, it had made a sweeping twenty per cent rate reduction in its underground system area, and had lowered rates for churches, hospitals, and charitable institutions, but the new director of public works was far from satisfied.

His charge that the system was run down, that its equipment was old and inefficient, was not valid. From

Employed by ___Edison___ Co.

Name ___Horace P. Liversidge___ Age _1879_ _21_ Married _No_
VICE PRESIDENT AND GENL MANAGER

Address ___54 54 Pine St. Phila___ Ward _3 r._

Position ___Mining Inspector of Rotary___ Department _____
Asst to Supterinten tender Using Current "Rider 5"
Recommended by ___A. A. Schulz___ Notify Motor Dept. when he Leaves Service.

Date Employed ___May 25/98___ Dismissed _____

Temporary or permanent   Increase } in pay roll
                         Decrease }

Date of change in rate		Nov 4/98	Jan 2/99	10/1/99	10/13/99	1/1/1900	6/1/01	4/1/
Rate per hour					.15	.17		.20
Rate per day							1.53	1.80
Rate per month 7/1/18	20.00	25.00	30.00	35.00	36.21	37.01	46.25	60
Hours per day								
Where previously employed								
Approved			225	250.00	300.00	330 Superintendent	75.00 mo
Approved					10/1/00	675 Engineering Dept.	4/1/03
Approved				4/1/04	7/1/06	7/1/09 Secretary	85.00
				100.00	112.50	125.00 / 150.00

Remarks—Cause of Change, Etc.

Transferred from Mining Inspector to Rotary tender Oct 13 1899.

12/1/01 Transferred to Sta. B. as supt @ 65.00 mo.

2/15/04 " " Christian St Sta—

5/1/05 from Sta " Foreman in D B Dept
See Bulletin #39—Addition #1—Authorizing H.P.L. as

Supt of Sta "A" 6/1/14

7/1/17 Inc 66.47 prmo.

Transferred to Executive Pay Roll 7/1/24

3/3/28 Vice President and Gen'l Manager

ORIGINAL SERVICE RECORD OF HORACE P. LIVERSIDGE

Office Building, 1000 Chestnut Street,
after Completion of 1919 Addition

the standpoint of modern construction, electrical and generating installation and operation, Philadelphia Electric represented a high type of efficiency. Had its service not been reliable, could it have recently acquired the business of the other great local utilities, P.R.T., the Pennsylvania Railroad, and the Bell Telephone Company?

To defend the Company from Cooke's attacks, as well as to develop a concept of its future requirements and organization, McCall hired a firm of experts to make an analysis. The country had been in a depression for several years, but McCall, anticipating better times that would bring a new impetus to business, had under consideration a plan for Philadelphia Electric, as he cryptically informed the stockholders in his annual report for 1914, which would further "unify its Philadelphia companies." To streamline administrative procedure and to aid in future financing, he wanted to wind up the affairs of the numerous electric concerns integrated within the system and do away with their paper existence. The stock of Philadelphia Electric (of New Jersey) was nearly paid up, and that holding company had about fulfilled its purpose and could soon be dissolved. McCall ordered a complete inventory and appraisal of all Philadelphia Electric's property.

Meanwhile, far away at the town of Sarajevo in Bosnia, the Archduke Francis Ferdinand and his Duchess were shot to death in June, 1914. Philadelphians expressed their customary shock at such an event, but it was not an unusual tragedy. Since the turn of the century, at least one head of state had been assassinated each year, including a President of the United States. In 1913, just the year before, both the President of Mexico and the King of Greece had been killed. But the 1914 assassination, unlike the others, meant war. By early August, Europe was in flames.

CHAPTER 9

Rates and Reorganization

W<small>HILE THE</small> great war raged in Europe, Philadelphia Electric engaged at home in a private war with Morris Llewellyn Cooke. At first, McCall seemed to have regarded Cooke's indictment of the Company before the Public Service Commission as merely a political nuisance in a new guise. But, as the case progressed, he came to realize the fundamental practical value that the Commission represented. The Commission wanted to know whether Philadelphia Electric's rates were just and fair. Very well, so did McCall.

Cooke had charged that Philadelphia Electric was overcapitalized and that its "bloated" financial structure was responsible for its "excessive" rates. An examination of the Company's financial history and current value had, therefore, to be made. To this end, McCall employed Dugald C. Jackson, a college professor and member of the well-known Boston engineering firm of D. C. & Wm. B. Jackson. From July, 1914, until October, 1915, Professor Jackson labored on a complete inventory and appraisal of the Company's property, assisted at times by as many as sixty-one men. In his eventual report, which cost more than $150,000 and filled 368 volumes, he announced that Philadelphia Electric represented a value of exactly $51,562,045. In its major headings, his appraisal was broken down as follows:

1. Overhead lines	$4,017,200
2. Lamps and lamp suspensions	511,900
3. Underground lines	6,247,800
4. Land	2,356,400
5. Buildings	2,867,600
6. Station equipment	7,851,900
7. Equipment on customers' premises	1,669,400
8. Horses and vehicles	203,400
9. Furniture, fixtures, supplies on hand	1,224,900
10. Commercial steam heating and power piping	29,800
11. Work in process	5,089,439
12. Added cost due to construction during operation of plant and to piecemeal work	3,500,000
13. Working capital	1,116,800
14. General contractors' profit	1,067,092
15. Corporate organization, bonus payable to the state on issue of capital stock, annual state taxes during construction, administrative and legal expenses	2,201,200
16. Brokerage, discount, and commissions	1,997,741
17. Patents and patent rights	4,609,473
18. Going concern value, historical development, and cost of establishing the business	5,000,000
	$51,562,045

The case was argued before Public Service Commissioner John Monaghan, sitting in City Hall. William Draper Lewis, former dean of the University of Pennsylvania Law School, represented Cooke, and had as his principal witnesses Dr. Ernest M. Patterson of the Wharton School and Frederick W. Ballard of Cleveland. Both Patterson and Ballard attacked Professor Jackson's figures. Ballard, who was connected with a municipally operated power plant in Cleveland, claimed that Jackson's appraisal was fictitious. He could build Philadelphia Electric's system new for a mere $23,583,000. In the past, Philadelphia Electric had often criticized municipally operated light and power plants. Now, a proponent of municipal ownership had a chance to even the score, and Ballard took full advantage of his opportunity. According to him, Philadelphia Electric's rates should be cut in half, its plant was obsolete, most of its equipment was just plain junk, and, as for its officials, they were loafing on the job.

Dr. Patterson had written *A Financial History of The Philadelphia Electric Company*, which had been published by Cooke as part of his 1914 annual report as director of public works. In this pamphlet, Patterson had maintained that the Company, when founded in 1899, was overcapitalized by more than $20,000,000, and, as a consequence, was charging Philadelphians a million dollars a year over and above a fair rate in order to keep up interest and dividend payments. "A radical reduction in rates," asserted Patterson, "is to the interest of the people and the city and is entirely just to the Company."

By March, 1916, sixty-six sessions of the rate case had been held before the commissioner and 8,500 pages of testimony had been recorded. Despite these hearings, it seemed unlikely that an agreement would be reached, for Philadelphia Electric could keep the rate question open indefinitely. Had it fought the case to a conclusion, the attorneys' arguments would not have been finally presented until the fall of 1916. Commissioner Monaghan would have required two months to prepare his report, and the Commission would have taken two months more to render its decision. The Company could than have appealed.

Such delays were not to McCall's liking. Abruptly, he brought the case to an end when he agreed in March to a compromise that was quickly ratified by the Commission. In this compromise, Philadelphia Electric lowered its rates to the city's small consumers by $900,000 a year, and its rates for municipal lighting by $150,000 a year. McCall's solution produced a most favorable reaction.

On behalf of the complainants, William Draper Lewis stated: "The results reached would never have been obtained except after years of further litigation, and perhaps not even then, had it not been for the fact that as the case proceeded week after week, the principal persons connected with the proceedings, the Company's officials, the complainants and their respective attorneys, found themselves working toward the same object, namely the ascertainment of all facts bearing on the solution of the complicated problem of correct electric rates."

The spokesman for Philadelphia Electric was Frederic W. Fleitz, a Scranton lawyer and former deputy attorney general, who for years had been a power in Pennsylvania politics. "In many ways," he said, "this case is by long odds the most important which has come before the Public Service Commission of Pennsylvania since its creation by the law, which we believe to be the most perfect and complete upon the statute books of any state, and with the provisions of which we are in most sincere and hearty accord."

The settlement represented a turning point in the Company's experience and philosophy, observed the *North American* in an editorial on March 15, 1916. Public service corporations, it pointed out, "must realize that the state assumes the right to regulate service and charges, and also permits fair earnings. Thus, their prosperity is to depend not upon the costly, insecure and pernicious promotion of political influence, but upon efficient service, reasonable rates, and honest co-operation with the agencies representing the public interest."

Ironically, the compelling reason why McCall came to terms with his adversaries was simply his desire to make rate reductions, just as he had been doing over the years. The reduction of thirty per cent to residential consumers —the Commission did not require rate reductions for large consumers like P.R.T.—was higher than he would normally have made at this time. But even larger reductions had been made in the past, and McCall believed that lower rates would attract new customers and would not endanger the Company's financial position. Although not required to do so, he extended the Philadelphia rate reductions to the Company's two Delaware County subsidiaries, the Beacon Light Company and the Delaware County Electric Company, and to the Bala and Merion Electric Company in Montgomery County.

The new rate schedule was worked out by Walter E. Long of Philadelphia Electric and Milo R. Maltbie, technical adviser to the Commission, and went into effect on April Fool's Day, 1916. The hope that new business would come in after the reduction was more than fulfilled —the Company was nearly swamped. It is difficult, however, to judge how much of this increase was due to the new rates and how much to the abnormal business activity induced by the European war. In any case, despite its lower rates, Philadelphia Electric netted more in 1916 than in 1915, and the prophecy that these rates would mark the beginning of a new era of prosperity for the Company seemed justified. Unfortunately, inflation, not prosperity, lurked just around the corner. It would soon become apparent that the rates were too low to meet wartime conditions.

McCall had, of course, yielded to pressure in accepting these rates, for Commissioner Monaghan was being advised by Maltbie, with whom McCall was not on speaking terms, and was bound to be influenced by Morris

Llewellyn Cooke and Frederick W. Ballard, the witness from Cleveland. Some degree of the Company's predicament when faced by this array of talent was reflected two years later when Philadelphia Electric was trying to obtain financial aid from the Federal government. A plan to this end was worked out for a Federal agency by none other than Cooke, Maltbie, and Ballard. Their influence perturbed the financial editor of the *North American*, who commented: "There seems to be a good deal of question as to why Morris L. Cooke, M. R. Maltbie, and F. W. Ballard should figure so prominently in the electric power proposition." Neither Cooke "nor the men with whom he is associated in the present case have had any large practical experience, and they are essentially theorists most intent upon reaching ideal conditions."

With the rate case at last behind him, McCall was able to concentrate his energies on a plan to unify the properties over which he presided and to refinance them. These measures had long been uppermost in his mind and had been growing more imperative each month as it became increasingly clear that large amounts of new capital would be necessary if Philadelphia Electric was to fulfill its responsibility and keep abreast of the demand for power and light in its territory.

While the Company frequently turned to the city's banks for short-term loans, it had never applied to them for long-term financing. All new capital had come from operating surplus and calls on the stock of Philadelphia Electric (of New Jersey). But now only one more call for $2,500,000 could be made, for that call would bring the stock to a fully paid-up basis. The time had come when Philadelphia Electric had to apply to outside interests for capital to build new plants and to extend its facilities.

Ever since its founding, bankers had considered Philadelphia Electric financially weak. The assets of nineteen of its twenty-one Philadelphia companies had been pledged as collateral for three bond issues totaling $28,276,500, which had been paid out in return for all the stock of the underlying companies. With its capital structure so encumbered, Philadelphia Electric had no attractive security to offer in return for new capital. It was therefore necessary to refund the bond issues, replacing them with a single issue secured by a first mortgage on the Company's entire Philadelphia property.

McCall took this proposition to Drexel & Company and Brown Brothers & Company. These banking houses, in turn, called for a report by the engineering firm of Stone & Webster. Had its engineers found the Company to be as Ballard had described it several months earlier, McCall would surely have been disappointed in his plans. Stone & Webster, however, estimated the cost of duplicating the Company's property to be more than twice as much as Ballard's estimate, and the bankers agreed to underwrite a bond issue of $35,000,000, providing McCall could secure at least ninety-five per cent of the two larger issues outstanding and one hundred per cent of the $1,994,300 Edison issue.

The refinancing plan, which had been approved by John G. Johnson and Morgan, Lewis & Bockius, was intended to take care not only of the Company's present need for capital, but of future requirements as well. It provided for the creation of a $60,000,000 first mortgage by The Philadelphia Electric Company (of Pennsylvania) on the Philadelphia property, as opposed to the holdings in Delaware County which did not come under the mortgage. Of this mortgage, $35,000,000 was to be marketed initially and used to pay off the $28,276,500 in old bond issues as well as the floating indebtedness to the banks, and to furnish some immediate capital. More money was to be secured by the call of the remaining assessment of $2,500,000 on Philadelphia Electric Company (of New Jersey) stock. Moreover, the authorized stock of The Philadelphia Electric Company (of Pennsylvania) was to be increased from $25,000,000 to $50,000,000. This additional stock could be sold as new capital was required, and it, together with the unissued bonds, could provide an additional $50,000,000 in capital for future use.

Success of the plan depended upon the willingness of holders of the old bonds to surrender their certificates voluntarily. Fortunately, they had little hesitancy in doing so, for they recognized that the security offered by the new issue was greater than that of their present holdings. Several speculators refused to part with bonds which they held for nuisance value, vainly hoping to gouge an enormous price from the Company. Another reaction was that of an elderly lady who refused to relinquish $5,000 worth of bonds, which she insisted on retaining for sentimental reasons, but such recalcitrance or eccentricity was rare. Philadelphia Electric was soon in possession of the requisite amount of the old issues and the refinancing plan went into effect. At the same time, a corporate reorganization, contingent on these financial matters, was approved.

Although Philadelphia Electric represented a consolidation of many companies, all but a few of them had continued an existence of sorts. They retained their charters and franchises; they had their directors and officers; they held annual meetings; they received rental from Philadelphia Electric for their leases and then solemnly passed this money on to their stockholder, which, of course, was Philadelphia Electric. Not only was this arrangement unnecessarily clumsy, it was expensive, for it necessitated paying taxes in New Jersey as well as in Pennsylvania since several of the companies had New Jersey charters.

With the refinancing of the system successfully accomplished, McCall could now put into effect his long-cherished dream of dissolving all these underlying companies. The Philadelphia Electric Company (of Pennsylvania) would take over their property, not by lease as heretofore, but by outright ownership. Philadelphia Electric Company (of New Jersey) was to be dissolved by liquidating its stock on a share-for-share basis for the stock of The Philadelphia Electric Company (of Pennsylvania).

On October 24, 1916, the directors of the New Jersey holding company authorized "the carrying out of the plan for the unification of the properties operating in the City of Philadelphia and controlled through stock ownership by this Company." A year later, on November 19, 1917, its stockholders approved a resolution dissolving their corporation, and, with this action, its board of directors took their places on the board of the operating company. Within a few years, all the old companies were dissolved, and The Philadelphia Electric Company (of Pennsylvania) remained as the single operating company in the city. It was also a holding company for its Delaware County properties, which operated principally in the name of the Delaware County Electric Company.

Thus unified and refinanced, the Company next took care of certain growing pains which needed treatment. With the absorption and then the merger of the numerous companies into the system, many employees occupying important positions had been retained. Their duties were not clearly enough defined and were overlapping in various areas of responsibility. In short, a major reorganization of the staff was essential, particularly so in engineering and operations, where a serious crisis threatened. McCall had hoped that Professor Jackson would solve these problems, but the professor, not knowing the capabilities of the key men in the organization well enough, was reluctant to propose a plan. Consequently, the basis for the reorganization was suggested by one of the Company's own men, Horace P. Liversidge.

Liversidge had had much practical experience in correcting faulty operations. During a varied career with the system, which began in 1898, he had progressed from wiring inspector to rotary inspector, to superintendent of a substation, and then to assistant superintendent of Schuylkill Station. From this position, he had moved on to become general foreman of the station construction department, and in 1906 became assistant superintendent of station design and construction. In June, 1914, he was made superintendent of all station operations at a salary of $200 a month.

When Liversidge took over the superintendency of station operations, he supposed he would have absolute responsibility as far as the plants were concerned. He soon found that this was not so. The roots of his difficulty lay far in the past. In the organization of the typical American electric company, a separation occurred at an early date between those in charge of the electric departments and those in charge of the steam departments, the mechanical engineers. Each group had its top executive, and there was generally violent disagreement between these two chiefs which filtered all the way down into the operating organizations. Such a situation existed at Philadelphia Electric, where the exceptionally able electrical engineer was not on speaking terms with the mechanical engineer, a conservative older man who stood close to President McCall.

When Liversidge tried to break down this antagonism, he, too, came into conflict with the mechanical engineer, who ultimately issued orders which interfered with Liversidge's operation of the plants and which he refused to obey. Liversidge later related the reaction of the offended executive: " 'Well, Mr. Liversidge, if that's the way you feel, I intend to take this matter up immediately with the president.' The sequel was rather surprising and rather interesting as well. He immediately went in, had his conversation with the president of the Company, came back, put on his hat, packed his few belongings and left, never to return. He had been fired." By taking a stand, young Liversidge had broken the back of a serious malfunction in the Company's operations. From then on, electrical and mechanical engineers pulled together as a team.

The new organizational set-up adopted for the entire Company did not go into full effect until the spring of 1918. The president, naturally, headed the chart, with direct responsibility for finance and with the senior counsel, Arthur B. Huey, reporting to him. Under the president came Vice-President Walter H. Johnson, who had over-all supervision of the Company, but who was primarily in charge of the commercial end. In McCall's opinion there was "no man in the United States in the utility business who has a higher standing on the commercial side of this business than our vice-president." Johnson, therefore, was closely concerned with all commercial matters and with the activities of the general commercial manager, Charles J. Russell.

A brilliant man, Russell had been in charge of the system's northern district for years, and superintendent of the plant at Tacony. He was one of the first to realize the importance of the industrial power load. Tremendously successful in attracting industrial business, he had made such a reputation that McCall brought him into the home office and placed him in charge of the contract department, where he supervised salesmen, district managers, commercial engineers, and appliance sales. While engaged in this work, Russell was to make fundamental contributions through the rate structure he developed.

Also under Vice-President Johnson's eye was the comptroller's department headed by Walter E. Long, who had come to Philadelphia Electric in 1904 as a clerk, but who had developed so rapidly that ten years later he had been elected president of the Pennsylvania Electric Association. He was McCall's right-hand man during the rate case and was made comptroller of the Company in 1918.

Secretary A. V. R. Coe supervised real estate in co-operation with the legal department, was responsible for insurance, and kept the Company's records. B. Frank Day, the paymaster, and the managers of the purchasing department, the medical department, claims, and the beneficial and welfare divisions, reported to Treasurer H. C. Lucas.

Chief Engineer W. C. L. Eglin headed up engineering and operations. Recognized as one of the foremost and most progressive engineers in the country, Eglin worked closely on the design and construction of the Company's powerhouses and other buildings, usually in conjunction with director and architect John T. Windrim. Many considered Eglin the outstanding man in McCall's organization, and the man who should succeed to the presidency when McCall retired. These sentiments often came to Eglin's attention and he ended by agreeing with them. When McCall learned of this presidential ambition, he expressed his opinion in December, 1917, by canceling Eglin's appointment as second vice-president.

Supporting Eglin, and very loyal to him, was one of the Company's white hopes, Horace P. Liversidge, who was coming along fast and had now been designated assistant chief engineer in charge of operations. Liversidge, in turn, had his assistant, the very able N. E. Funk, former superintendent of Schuylkill Station.

There were three major divisions under Eglin, each of which had its subsections of design, construction, and operation. The first was responsible for the generating plants and substations and was managed by D. Frederick Schick and later by George Ross Green, former dean of the meter department. Prominent in this division was H. Carl Albrecht, engineer of station electrical design and construction, his assistant Robert A. Hentz, and Robert J. Milligan. In addition, this section contained the mechanical division, which had formerly reported to William H. Norris and Walter Nagel and which was now under Ernest L. Hopping as mechanical engineer and Alex Wilson as construction engineer. Another section was the transmission and distribution department, which supervised everything on or under the streets from the stations to consumers' homes. It was headed by A. H. Manwaring, the Company's specialist on arc lighting who had made his start with The Brush Electric Light Company in 1882. Finally, there was the "Plant on Customers Premises," directed by meter expert Percy H. Bartlett. In this period of expansion, practically all electrical construction was done by the Company's own forces; the total number of men in this division skyrocketed to more than 1,000.

So far, in recalling the years 1915 through 1918, attention has been directed entirely to matters of organization —financial, corporate, and personnel. It should be realized, however, that the vital refunding and recapitalization changes, the setting up of a simplified corporate structure, and the reorganization of operating functions within that structure were overshadowed by the daily events of a period during which the Company experienced the greatest pressure in its history. Providing the power required by the war effort strained the entire system to its very limits.

CHAPTER 10

War Years

In THE EARLY days of the war, its effect on Philadelphia Electric was not particularly disturbing, but in 1915 war industries supplying the Allies began to make heavy calls on the system. These demands were readily cared for because Station A-2 came into partial service with its 30,000-kilowatt turbine in October, and, when the giant 35,000-kilowatt unit went on the lines a few months later, the Company announced that A-2 was the largest and most complete powerhouse of its kind in the world. As an ultramodern feature, it contained an electric kitchen in its cafeteria where the eight hundred men who worked at Schuylkill Station could take meals. In this restaurant there was "a refrigerator, if you please, not an ice chest!" For fifteen cents one could buy an entire dinner.

Hopes that this station would enable the Company to meet all requirements were dampened early in 1916, when the extent of the tremendous war-stimulated industrial development around Chester was realized. At first, McCall thought that Chester could be helped out by high-tension transmission lines to its Beacon Station, or that Beacon Station could be enlarged. Eglin, however, encouraged by Albert R. Granger, insisted on an enormous new waterside plant for that area. While such a station was the most expensive immediate solution for the problem, in the end it would prove not only the most efficient, but absolutely essential. McCall capitulated. Land was purchased, and on September 26, 1916, the board authorized the erection of a 120,000-kilowatt station (initially to contain only two 30,000-kilowatt generators) at a cost of $5,500,000. This plant, fourteen miles from Schuylkill Station, was to be connected to it by steel towers from which would hang two circuits of high-tension lines, each capable of transmitting 30,000 kilowatts of three-phase energy at 66,000 volts. McCall believed that the new station, together with a change in one or two units at Station A-1, would provide enough generating capacity until 1919. In the meantime, however, it would be necessary to draw plans for yet another station in Philadelphia—Delaware Station on the Company's water-front property at Beach and Palmer Streets.

The building of the Chester plant was accomplished with much difficulty, huge additional expenses, and many heartbreaking delays which were only partially compensated for by the earlier completion of the high-tension line for service in the Eddystone and Chester sections. To provide space for coal storage, Eglin located the powerhouse some distance out in the river, beyond low watermark. He was influenced not only by the need for coal storage, but by the desirability of shorter channels to deep water for coal barges, and by lower dredging costs. Accordingly, a cofferdam of interlocking steel piling was hammered in. The enclosed area had just been pumped out preparatory to foundation work when the cofferdam broke and the site was inundated. This disaster alone added several months to the building schedule.

Difficulties arising from the war complicated the project. Labor was scarce and expensive, and so were materials. Money to continue construction seemed always on the verge of running out. Not until October 1, 1918, with

Motor-driven Generators for Arc Lights in the Brush Station, 1919

This station could supply 9,500 lights.

LUDLOW SUBSTATION, 1925

A typical direct current substation equipped with rotary converters
and a motor-generator set

the war almost over, were the engineers able to get the first 30,000-kilowatt unit into operation, and even then the powerhouse was only partially completed. Thanks to Eglin and Windrim, it was architecturally one of the handsomest plants in the United States. Indeed, it was so ornate that it attracted humorous comment. If one could see over the coal piles on the landward side, one might mistake the plant for an enormous public library!

Of the war period, during which Chester Station was built, it may be said that the longer it lasted the greater were its demands on the American economy. Inflation started before the United States entered the conflict in April, 1917. By October, 1916, the price of flour was higher than it had been since the Civil War, and the purchasing power of the housewife's dollar had fallen to seventy-four cents. This brought some families close to the starvation point. Rioting broke out, with women who could not afford bread roughing up grocers and food peddlers. Some companies gave Christmas bonuses to help their people meet rising costs. Philadelphia Electric distributed $25,000 to its employees in $2.50, $5.00, and $10.00 gold pieces. The price of milk continued ever upward—twelve cents, thirteen cents, fourteen cents. Daily papers sold for a penny in 1916; in 1917, the price doubled.

Next came the coal shortage during the winter of 1917–1918. In September, 1917, McCall warned that the outlook was "anything but pleasant." To provide for coal storage, the generating stations having inadequate room for it, a tract of land was purchased on Petty's Island in the Delaware, across from the site of Delaware Station. With the quality of coal declining, Philadelphia Electric saw its consumption double during the war, and also saw the delivered price advance from $2.75 to $5.40 a ton.

By December, many poor people were without coal. Those who had illuminating gas in their homes were using it for heating purposes. Gas consumption went up twenty-five per cent that month, and U.G.I. complained that its plants were overtaxed. January, 1918, came in with a blizzard. Twenty-eight inches of snow fell, and the ice in the rivers threatened to destroy the water system. Across the Delaware in Camden the lights went out, and industry in South Jersey was halted when the state's largest power plant at Burlington shut down for lack of coal.

In this emergency, the Federal Fuel Administrator ordered all manufacturing plants in the East, except those engaged in shipbuilding and fuel production, to close for the five days of January 18 to 22 inclusive, and to do no business on the next nine Mondays. Many restrictions were placed on the use of electricity, for its supply depended upon coal. People were urged to think twice before turning on their lights. Then, in the autumn of 1918 came the tragic influenza scourge. "Don't telephone," proclaimed huge advertisements. So many operators were sick that if the volume of calls did not decrease, Bell Telephone would have to close some of its central offices.

Philadelphia's extraordinary industrial growth during the war threatened to overwhelm the Company. Enormous contracts poured in, huge plants were built, and 200,000 workers flocked to the area. So great was the city's output in guns and munitions that it was called the "Arsenal of America." The new Baldwin Locomotive plant at Eddystone was converted into the largest rifle-making factory in the world, employing 15,500 workers. It turned out 600,000 Enfield rifles for the English army, and then, within a single year, manufactured 1,000,000 Springfield rifles for the American forces.

The development of the industrial area between Philadelphia and Chester was almost unbelievable. Steel plants and arms factories sprang up as if by magic, and along the Delaware the magnitude of shipbuilding enterprises was the most extensive ever known. Without warning, the United States found that it must become the world's carrier and had to develop its merchant marine. So scarce was shipping—and so high were freight charges— that a vessel could earn its entire cost in a single voyage. Square-riggers were resurrected and for a final time appeared on the river. By October, 1916, the Delaware had become the greatest shipbuilding center ever seen. A year later, twelve of its yards were employing 44,000 men and building thirty-six per cent of the nation's merchant ships. But even this was only a beginning.

In September, 1917, the Emergency Fleet Corporation, an agency of the United States Shipping Board, was authorized to spend some $300,000,000 to develop a shipyard at Hog Island and build 180 ships. At this time, Hog Island was simply 860 acres of swamp, but within a year it had been filled in, fifty shipways had been built, a city constructed, and some 32,000 men employed. Hog Island had been transformed into the largest shipyard in the world! The vessels it contracted to build were fabricated ships whose steel plates and other parts were manufactured elsewhere and were hauled in by the railroads. The launching of the first of these ships was a long-heralded event. The great day was to be August 6, 1918, and President and Mrs. Wilson were to attend. The day arrived, the President and his wife were on hand; amid joyous celebration the vessel skidded down the ways to bob up and down on the Delaware. Everyone went home satisfied, little realizing that the ship's riveting was only sixty-five per cent completed, and that it would take five more months to finish her. The officials had permitted the launching just to satisfy public expectation.

Money was a secondary consideration in furthering the war effort. Many war contracts were let on a cost-plus-profit basis, which does not promote economy but can promote speed. Hog Island with its hastily built housing needed P.R.T. transportation. More trolley cars were also required to service the new plants at Essington, Eddystone, and the Sun Shipbuilding Company at Chester. To help P.R.T., the government agreed to lend it $4,250,000 so that it could finance the new lines and purchase 190 more cars.

Although the government spent money freely, it was reluctant to assist the power and light utilities, which labored under a tremendous load in supplying war industries with the current essential to their operations. By the end of 1917, war industries were taking half of Philadelphia Electric's power and were calling for much more. In his annual report for 1917, McCall stated: "The Company is now supplying more current to munitions factories and other war industries than any other utility in the United States, and is second in supplying transportation facilities." The transportation "facilities" included the electrified lines to Paoli and Chestnut Hill, which went into service during the war, and P.R.T. with its heavy increase in power consumption. All told, the power supplied to the trolleys and railroad in 1918 amounted to 35,950 kilowatts, and the Company's total capacity before the first unit at Chester was available in October was only 205,026 kilowatts.

Although Philadelphia Electric did everything it could to increase its generating capacity, it could not keep abreast of the demand. Not compelled by the government to discontinue service to the so-called nonessential industries, the Company was virtually forced to accede to the demands of those that were essential. With a power shortage in sight for the peak loads of 1919–1920, the Federal Fuel Administration in August, 1918, absolved the Company from blame. In a statement, the Fuel Administration pointed out that Philadelphia Electric "foresaw the need for more energy and provided for it, but the accelerated requirements for war purposes outran the facilities required."

When the peak loads were reached during the last two years of the war, the central generating stations needed all the help they could get from the system's five small stations. These stations were outmoded, and their antiquated equipment was normally used only for arc lighting or as stand-by units. While Schuylkill Station A-2 burned only a pound and three quarters of coal per kilowatt-hour, Callowhill Station used nine pounds, and the old Edison Station gobbled up thirteen. Maximum output rather than efficient output was demanded by the exigencies of the times.

Since the load carried by the system was so frequently its maximum, there was no reserve in case of accidents. Anticipating equipment breakdowns, government agents went over the Company's list of consumers, establishing priorities. Consumers with low priorities were informed that they would have to cut off their power if called on to do so. When equipment failed, such users were telephoned to open their switches while emergency repairs were made.

With the system overloaded during the war, the Company's problems were aggravated by the labor situation. "To hold our men," announced President McCall at the end of 1917, "we will be compelled to change the operating force from a seven-day week to a six-day basis and to grant a general increase in all departments of about fifteen per cent." Many were leaving to work at Hog Island, where the government paid high wages. Although a majority of the employees were exempted from the draft because they filled positions essential to the war effort, 715 joined the armed forces, and of these twelve gave their lives. For several years, Philadelphia Electric had been running a cadet school to familiarize well-educated technical men with its property and methods, hoping thereby to supply the organization with promising young engineers. At one time, there were as many as 130 cadets enrolled, but shortly after the outbreak of the war these men went into the service and the school was closed.

Despite personnel losses to other industries and to the Army and Navy, the Company's staff increased from 2,497 in 1914 to 3,566 in 1918, and wages rose on an inflationary wave from an average of $67 a month to $104. Additional office space became necessary, and in 1917 the Company erected a new building adjoining 1000 Chestnut Street. Similar to the old building, except that it was nine stories high—two more floors were added to the original structure—this addition blended so well that the combined buildings appeared as one.

Faced with soaring prices of coal, labor, and supplies, and with taxes rising rapidly, McCall forecast a deficit for 1918 unless the Public Service Commission permitted a rate increase. In response to McCall's pleas, the Commission granted a ten per cent war surcharge for one year on all forms of business except municipal, residential, and steam heat. This increase strengthened the Company's credit, enabled it to obtain a loan from a banking syndicate, and made continuance of its dividend rate possible.

The Public Service Corporation of New Jersey, in which U.G.I. had a thirty-five per cent interest (rumors to the contrary, U.G.I. did not own shares in Philadelphia Electric), was not so fortunate. In 1918, it reduced its dividend. At a time when most businesses were making money hand over fist, the power and light industry was in difficulty. Vital to the war effort as it was, it did not succeed in obtaining public assistance.

The major themes in Philadelphia Electric's war story were the ever-increasing governmental demand for its power and the unending efforts at financing in which McCall engaged. It must be borne in mind that no one knew when the war would end, and the object of planning was to meet the peak loads of 1918 and 1919, when Philadelphia Electric would have to supply at least the full capacity of another central station.

By mid-1917, the Company had stopped soliciting business and would accept large new contracts only with the distinct understanding that such additional customers would not be serviced during peak periods. No one demurred; all were glad to get power on any terms. In September, referring to the "extraordinary and unprecedented growth of our business," which would take up all the reserve capacity during the coming peak load, McCall told his board that energetic measures must be taken immediately to forestall a power shortage in 1918. To provide the generating capacity necessary for the next two years, construction of Delaware Station had to be started at once so that it would be ready by November, 1918. The directors approved the president's plans, which called for the expenditure of $18,000,000 beyond the $6,500,000 already authorized.

Whether or not there was to be a power shortage hung on the fate of Delaware Station. Work on its foundation was promptly begun according to blueprints worked out by Eglin and Windrim, but within two months the project was brought to a halt. McCall could not finance it; indeed, he was in straits to find the money to complete Chester Station and to pay off a $2,500,000 loan due Drexel & Company. The potential capital so recently provided for was all but useless. As McCall said on the last day of 1917, "The present state of the money market makes it impossible for us to utilize our plans for future

137

financing at this time." Meanwhile, the Company was declining almost daily requests from manufacturers with war contracts.

Just when the financial situation was at its worst, McCall succeeded in persuading Harris, Forbes & Company of New York to underwrite a $7,500,000 issue of two-year 6% notes, the net amount to Philadelphia Electric to be 94¼ or $7,068,275. Harris, Forbes brought Drexel & Company and Brown Brothers in to participate in this issue. With the money from the notes, McCall paid off the Drexel loan and completed Chester Station. The fate of Delaware Station remained in the air. Pressing needs for money necessitated a loan of $1,500,000 on expensive terms from Harris, Forbes in June, 1918, and, late in the year, a $5,000,000 stock allotment was offered to the shareholders.

Failure to raise money required for Delaware Station made its need no less urgent. The cost of the station would be immense, completely abnormal because of war conditions, and yet it was those very war conditions that necessitated the plant. Under these circumstances, McCall insisted that the government should provide help. Philadelphia Electric would later return that part of the government loan which represented such additional cost over its own contribution as would equal the arbitrated value of the plant when the war was over. Having paid high for the Chester plant, McCall could not afford to build another station at a time of exorbitant prices without a government subsidy.

In 1918, McCall exhausted much of his energy dashing between the Public Service Commission in Harrisburg, the bankers in New York, and the War Industries Board and other agencies in Washington. Investigating engineers from Washington came to Philadelphia to examine the power situation, and, on their return, recommended to the War Industries Board that assistance be granted Philadelphia Electric to complete its plants. Nothing came of this, and McCall opened negotiations with the Emergency Fleet Corporation, which was demanding an enlargement of Chester Station and the immediate building of Delaware Station.

While these negotiations were in progress, the city buzzed with rumors. The government was going to build huge plants in the Pennsylvania coal fields, thereby saving freight charges for fuel. Power would be transmitted by high-tension lines to Philadelphia Electric and to Public Service of New Jersey. In July, 1918, a bill—"The Pennsylvania Plan"—was introduced into Congress providing for the expenditure of $200,000,000 to build power stations in the coal centers. This was Martin Maloney's idea of 1895 all over again. There was only one flaw in it: there was not enough water available in the coal fields to run steam plants of the size contemplated.

On the heels of the Pennsylvania Plan came word that Hog Island would build its own plant to avoid the imminent power shortage. Unless a government plant was erected at Hog Island, its manager asserted, there would be a 90,000-kilowatt shortage by the spring of 1919. But still nothing happened. Then, in August, it was learned that the government might take over control of the power plants in Philadelphia and other industrial centers, and operate them as it was already operating the railroads. A bill to this effect was introduced into Congress by the War Industries Board. Just what advantage government operation would have was not well understood locally.

Finally, it was unimpeachably recorded that sufficient electric power for Philadelphia homes and war industries was assured because Philadelphia Electric had closed a contract whereby the Emergency Fleet Corporation would put up $5,800,000 toward the $14,500,000 needed to build Delaware Station. The Company's share, roughly $9,000,000, was to come from a syndicate of four banking houses—Brown Brothers, Drexel & Company, Harris, Forbes, and The National City Company of New York. This plan, the successor to one rejected in September by the Secretaries of the Army and Navy and the chairman of the United States Shipping Board, was pending when the war ended and the government lost all interest in the proposition.

The day the Kaiser fled to Holland, the Philadelphia Electric system, having held up for so long, suffered a major failure. With the 30,000-kilowatt unit at A-2 temporarily off the lines and largely dismantled, its larger running mate broke down. Two thousand consumers lost their power for several days, and industries were rationed according to their essential, semiessential, or nonessential ratings.

For McCall, the breakdown brought to a focus all the difficulties under which Philadelphia Electric had operated for the past year, and he issued a statement to the Company's customers.

1. We knew that the excessive power demands for war work had deprived us of spare capacity essential for proper operation of this great property.

2. We gave the most positive warning of this fact.

3. We did all that was humanly possible to obtain the funds necessary to install capacity which we had been forehanded enough to order in advance.

4. Our budgets, prepared several years in advance and based on accurate estimates of the normal growth in our business, covered ample generating and distributing capacity for more than normal needs.

McCall had no need to apologize for Philadelphia Electric's performance during the war. The Company had provided immediate current to the new shipyards, which would otherwise have been delayed a year in building their own power plants. Without the utility's light and power, the Delaware would not have merited its wartime title, the "Clyde of America," nor would Philadelphia as a manufacturing center have earned itself the designation of the "Workshop of the World." While isolated electric plants were still numerous, the great bulk of the current necessary for Philadelphia's extensive manufacturing enterprises was furnished by Philadelphia Electric. Its contribution to the national effort was profound.

The individual contributions of its staff during the trying war period cannot be detailed. Long hours and heavy responsibilities took their toll. One of the plant superintendents, who was living on aspirin at this time, his nerves frayed to bits, broke down and cried when a contractor submitted routine plans for service to a new customer. Like many others, the superintendent was enduring high-tension days followed by nearly sleepless nights.

The end of the war brought untold relief. November 11, 1918, was a perfect day. Gathered on the roof of the Company's newly enlarged Chestnut Street office building was an emotional throng of employees. From below rose the din of shrieking whistles and the joyous ringing of bells. President McCall officiated at a flag-raising ceremony and, after the singing of "America" and the "Star Spangled Banner," complimented everyone for the devoted service they had given during the great emergency.

For most people, the end of the war was a time for rejoicing and gaiety, but it was not so for President McCall. His son Howard, after an outstanding athletic career at the University of Pennsylvania, had taken his law degree at the University's Law School and had then joined the legal department of Philadelphia Electric. When the war broke out, young McCall earned a captain's commission and went overseas in command of an infantry company. He was killed in action on July 20, 1918, at Château-Thierry. Although President McCall maintained an appearance of calm and resignation, those who knew him intimately were aware that he had suffered a blow from which he would not recover.

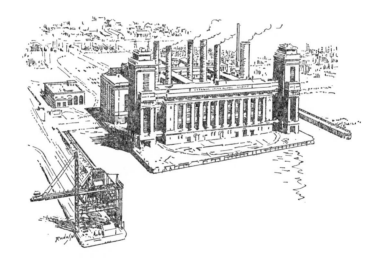

CHAPTER 11

Peacetime Readjustment

The years which followed the war were awkward ones of readjustment. Although times were good at first, the boom soon dwindled and a severe business recession set in. Wartime inflation had thoroughly upset the labor market. Unions struck for higher wages, shorter hours, and for recognition, while management, fighting these demands, tried to maintain the principle of the open shop. Strikes became the order of the day, with the public suffering from the crippling results of major walkouts in the steel, railroad, and coal industries. Americans, disturbed by talk of socialism and bolshevism, were apprehensive of anarchy itself. In Boston, the police went on strike and hoodlums took over the city. In Camden, the militia was mobilized to protect the transit system from rioters, but failed to prevent the burning of the trolley terminal. Steel workers and state police clashed in Pittsburgh. Federal troops were ordered into the coal fields of West Virginia. All this in 1919.

In January, 1920, the cohorts of sobriety celebrated the inauguration of that "noble experiment," prohibition. While vast machinery was readied to enforce this measure, William Jennings Bryan proclaimed, "I am expecting the whole world to profit by our nation's example." Unfortunately, the only people who profited were the bootleggers. Their business was immensely lucrative, for no agency regulated the prices of their illicit goods.

The utilities, on the other hand, were regulated, and for them the problems of postwar readjustment were particularly trying. All utilities pleaded for higher rates to meet inflationary costs, and many, like Public Service Corporation of New Jersey which passed its fourth quarter dividend in 1919, had difficulty in bridging the gap. Old alliances were severed by the stress of the times. In P.R.T., a bitter quarrel flared up between Stotesbury and Mitten over the way in which fares were to be raised. When Mitten won, Stotesbury and his partner Horatio G. Lloyd resigned from the transit board. Mitten, who knew how to play up to the public, let it be known that he had "beaten the bankers." Despite his victory, Mitten nursed an enmity toward Stotesbury that was to break out later and embarrass Philadelphia Electric. Meanwhile, U.G.I.'s city gasworks plum had turned sour. President Bodine complained that the city contract was archaic. In 1920, U.G.I., losing more than $2,500,000 on its Philadelphia utility service, cut its dividend in half. The next year, the Pennsylvania Railroad lowered its dividend; the stock market suffered a major break; there was a general building trades strike in Philadelphia.

Gloomy times, however, were not destined to remain long, and much transpired which gave promise of renewed industrial activity, or was, at least, of interest to the public. In 1920, a merger brought forth the Pennsylvania Power & Light Company, operating in eastern Pennsylvania near Philadelphia Electric territory. Glamor was provided by Stotesbury, who gave a housewarming in 1921 to celebrate his occupancy of Whitemarsh Hall, the most palatial private residence ever erected by a Philadelphian. In 1922, work was begun on the Delaware River Bridge, and a wave of optimism hit northeast

Philadelphia with the opening of the Frankford elevated line. By then, the hard times of the postwar years had been conquered and the country was prepared to surge ahead, prosperity-bound. Women bobbed their hair, and men turned to the sports section of the morning paper to read about the latest exploits of Big Bill Tilden, Babe Ruth, Bobby Jones, and Jack Dempsey. Financiers noted with satisfaction that industry and business had made tremendous progress in 1922, outstripping the losses of the postwar readjustment period and working into a position of normal profits. Yes, the country had returned to "normalcy." But before this happy state of affairs came about, Philadelphia Electric had much with which to contend.

To no small extent it was able to weather the storm because of revolutionary new procedures instituted by its operating engineer. When Horace P. Liversidge took charge of the generating stations, they were virtually isolated—little systems unto themselves at Chester, Schuylkill, and Tacony. Control over each station was exercised by personnel located in the station and in close contact with the station switchboard. According to the experts, that was where the control should be—in the station, where everyone could know exactly what was going on.

Liversidge disagreed. How could these men keep their wits about them and do the right things when explosive trouble broke out at the station? Moreover, knowing that the time would come when there would be a number of huge power plants in Philadelphia, Liversidge wanted a system that could handle all their operations. Centralized control of this system had to be at 1000 Chestnut Street. Disregarding the obvious intention of his superiors to keep him at Schuylkill Station A-2, where fine quarters were being prepared for him, Liversidge moved to a cubbyhole in the Chestnut Street office building. In this little space he installed a load dispatcher's board. For a time it worked in parallel with the load dispatcher at the main generating station. When his men were sufficiently trained, Liversidge dismantled the dispatch board at Schuylkill Station and concentrated the load dispatching system at 1000 Chestnut Street. The experts threw up their hands in horror.

As other stations were erected, or were tied in by transmission lines, they, too, came under this central control. Thus, the load dispatcher at 1000 Chestnut Street became responsible for the supply of power to all parts of the system, and scheduled the amount of load which each station was to carry, those stations having the lowest operating cost receiving the largest share. No station apparatus upon which the load was in any way dependent could be taken out of service to be worked on without the permission of the load dispatcher.

Before long, those experts who had so violently disagreed with Liversidge about central load dispatching began to appreciate the need of such a control point. Today, no one would attempt to operate a large system in any other way.

Having centralized control over power generation, Liversidge set up a coal bureau to handle all coal operations from the time the coal was received from the shippers until it was delivered into the bunkers of the power plants. Before this system was adopted, coal was channeled to the stations according to the demands of station superintendents, the superintendent who raised the most fuss, or who had the most influence, receiving preferential treatment. From now on, coal would go to the stations according to their needs as appraised from an over-all point of view. Liversidge also set up a central maintenance system for the generating stations, thus putting at

Joseph B. McCall
President 1899–1924
Chairman of the Board 1924–1926

the command of the station superintendents a force of skilled mechanics who could diagnose equipment trouble and repair it in a manner calculated to prevent its reoccurrence. Philadelphia Electric soon enjoyed one of the finest and most efficient maintenance units in the industry, thanks largely to William F. Oberhuber, who was appointed general superintendent of all maintenance.

The changes Liversidge instituted were thought to be unsound by leaders in the industry, but they soon proved their worth under arduous tests. During the ticklish coal situation of the early 1920's, the coal bureau jockeyed the Company through the fuel shortage. With the numerous mechanical breakdowns and failures of the period, the central load dispatcher and the centralized maintenance system were superior aids in overcoming problems that might otherwise have shut down a part of the system for an extended time.

Strengthened in its operating procedures, the Company entered the postwar period with confidence. An independent view of Philadelphia Electric at this time is of interest. In the month the war ended, David C. Johnson, an adviser to a New York investment house, noted a number of the Company's strong features in an elaborate analysis. He found that Philadelphia Electric was one of the largest and best-established utilities in the country; its management was excellent, and its employees exceptionally loyal; the territory served was good; the large generating stations were well located, excellently designed, and of high efficiency; the property was in fine operating condition; there was substantial equity over the bonded debt; public opinion was favorable.

Despite all these good features, Johnson felt that Philadelphia Electric had not adequately developed its territory. Nearly 2,000,000 people lived in the area served by the Company, and of these only 102,464 were customers by the end of the war—a ratio of about 1 to 20. Commonwealth Edison's ratio was about 1 to 7, and Detroit Edison's about 1 to 6. Clearly, Philadelphia had not had the electrical development to which it was entitled. How much of this lag was due to Philadelphia conservatism and how much to the Company is impossible to determine. At any rate, times had changed, and when the Company once again began to solicit new business, it found that Philadelphians were more than willing to accept electricity.

The difficulties of operating isolated plants, which had furnished one third of the power used by Philadelphia war industries, had convinced many manufacturers that they should shift to central station service. Operators of isolated plants had been sorely tried during the war by the problem of replacing trained men and by the near impossibility of obtaining equipment to increase their generating capacity. Many were now ready to buy their current from Philadelphia Electric.

Another result of the war was a domestic revolution which increased the demand for electricity. Wages of servants had risen so high that thousands of housewives who had formerly enjoyed at least part-time help were now doing all their own work. In accepting this change, they insisted on the aid of labor-saving devices—washing machines, cleaners, irons—most of which were electrical. Their need for this kind of equipment stimulated the wiring of old houses. While nearly all new houses were wired for electricity, old houses represented an enormous source of business for utility companies. Of the nation's 21,000,000 homes in 1921, only about 6,250,000 had been wired.

Through the leadership of Charles J. Russell, Philadelphia Electric's commercial manager, a "Wire Your Home" campaign had been started back in 1916. An organization of contractors was formed to undertake this work, but the project had to be abandoned in 1917 after 6,000 properties had been wired. The war then proceeded to shake Philadelphians out of their sequestered ways. The city's population, congested by a heavy increase in its labor force, created an unprecedented demand for housing, bringing on a sharp rise in property values and wholesale changes in ownership. This condition of flux stimulated increased requests for electric service. People who liked to use an electric washer would not rent an unwired house, and landlords were faced with the necessity of modernizing their properties.

Realizing that people were much more receptive to electric service, the Company embarked on a number of successful house wiring campaigns after 1918. To benefit from the Company's plan, a house had to be adjacent to the Company's lines, and its occupant had to be its owner. Under these circumstances, Philadelphia Electric would finance the wiring, giving the owner eighteen months in which to repay, but requiring him also to purchase an electric washer and an electric iron. In September, 1923, the Company announced that 79,000 old houses in Philadelphia had been wired for electricity during the preceding two and a half years.

The rise of appliance sales during this time was little short of phenomenal. People purchased electric toasters, cleaners, washers, ranges, refrigerators, and a host of other devices. Residential business had long been thought of as merely electric lighting business, but with the application of so much current for other purposes it became known as "electric service in the home." Philadelphia Electric expanded its retail appliance trade and permitted customers to make their purchases on a deferred payment plan. According to the electrical wizard Dr. Charles P. Steinmetz in 1920, "We are absolutely dependent on electricity today, although we have only begun to use it. The time will come, and before long, when all labor in the house will be done by electricity." And so the demands on Philadelphia Electric multiplied. The Company had 103,015 customers at the end of 1918; by the end of 1923, this number had risen to 305,644, with 64,258 added in that year alone.

One of the features of the Company's increasing load was its enlarged contracts with the Pennsylvania Railroad and with other utilities. Not long after P.R.T. suffered a bad power failure in 1919, it applied to the Company for an additional 12,000 kilowatts. This raised the P.R.T. load to about 40,000 kilowatts in Philadelphia and made it the Company's largest customer. From time to time, P.R.T. asked for more power, as it did in 1922 when current to run the new Frankford elevated was needed. At this time also, a large contract was closed with Public Service Corporation of New Jersey. Rather than build a big powerhouse at Gloucester, Public Service decided to purchase Philadelphia Electric current. Through this contract, McCall observed, "we get the advantage of all the increased business in Camden and vicinity that will be brought about by the building of the bridge." It was recognized, however, that the Public Service contract was only a temporary arrangement. When the demand in Camden increased to the point where it would be economical for Public Service to build its own station in that area, it would do so.

At the end of the war, the Company's generating capacity, including both new units at Chester Station, was estimated to be 8,000 kilowatts greater than the peak load requirement for 1919. To provide for 1920, however, it would be necessary to resume the construction of Delaware Station, which was situated two miles northeast of City Hall and adjacent to Penn Treaty Park where, in 1683, William Penn had negotiated a famous pact of friendship with the Indians. Stone & Webster were the general contractors for the construction of the plant, which was successfully erected despite a building trades strike in 1920. Demands for wage increases during this crisis exceeded fifty per cent, and, while by no means met, substantially increased the cost of Delaware Station. For a while, building operations had to be suspended. When resumed, Stone & Webster were successful in maintaining an open shop, except for their recognition of the carpenters' union. Before the year was out, both 30,000-kilowatt generators installed in the first unit of the station were in use.

No increase in the Company's capacity was made during the recession year of 1921, but in January, 1922, in recognition of the fact that the system had no reserve, a third 30,000-kilowatt unit was ordered for Delaware Station. Charles J. Russell estimated that the peak load for 1922 would be 240,000 kilowatts, but business so far outstripped his prediction that on December 14, 1922, a load of 260,355 kilowatts was reached. McCall ordered the erection of the second part of Delaware Station, where two more 30,000-kilowatt units were installed in 1923. Even with these additions, Philadelphia Electric had to face its 1923 peak without adequate reserves. The demands on the system were growing faster than McCall could build new capacity into it.

In the summer of 1923, a final 30,000-kilowatt unit was ordered for Delaware Station and the final two units for Chester. With the installation of these turbines, all the room in the system's three central stations would be filled, and yet it was obvious, so rapid was the rate of growth, that two or three more generators would have to be available for the peak loads of 1925. To meet this requirement another station would be needed. Sixty-four acres of ground between Lewis Street and Erie Avenue on the Delaware River were purchased in 1923 as the site for a new plant.

The construction program required millions of dollars, which were raised, often through the agency of Drexel & Company, by the sale of stocks and bonds. In 1920, the authorized capital stock was increased from 2,000,000 shares (par value twenty-five dollars) to 2,600,000, the increase being in 8% preferred stock, most of which the owners soon converted to common. To provide a flexible method of financing, a first lien and refunding mortgage was created in 1922, through which the sale of bond issues could be made from time to time. The Company's debt limit of $60,000,000 was then increased to $150,000,000, and the authorized capital stock was again raised, from 2,600,000 shares to 4,000,000, the entire increase being in common stock. The connection with Drexel's in marketing immense quantities of securities became so important that a Drexel partner, Horatio G. Lloyd, was elected to the board in 1922. William A. Law, a banker who was about to assume the presidency of the Penn Mutual Life Insurance Company, was also elected a director at this time. Mitten, who had purged his board of bankers, observed these elections with unfriendly interest.

Dangers of a raid on management by Mitten were little thought of during the years immediately following the war when McCall struggled with many exasperating problems, not the least of which was the procurement of coal to keep his steam plants in operation. Coal represented forty per cent—the biggest single expense—of the manufacturing costs of electricity. All Philadelphia Electric plants, except the anthracite-burning Edison Station, used bituminous coal, about a million tons annually. Mined in the Clearfield district of central Pennsylvania, this coal was shipped to the Port Richmond piers of the Philadelphia and Reading Railroad and to the Greenwich piers of the Pennsylvania Railroad. At these points it was dumped into barges for delivery at Philadelphia Electric's waterside stations, or for storage on Petty's Island. The Company had lighterage contracts by which seventeen coal barges of a thousand-ton capacity each were kept in continuous operation between the piers and the stations. Seven tugs were employed in this service. Any interruption to the methodical day-by-day delivery of coal from the shippers created hazardous problems which the Company guarded against by its reserve supply on Petty's Island. But this reserve was insufficient to care for any major interruptions in coal deliveries, and such interruptions haunted the postwar years.

On November 1, 1919, the bituminous miners, led by John L. Lewis, struck for a sixty per cent pay boost, a six-hour day, and a five-day week. Within a month, Philadelphia felt the pinch. According to the fuel administrator, who barred the use of electric signs in an effort to conserve coal, "The seriousness of the situation cannot be overestimated." P.R.T. cut off the heat in its trolleys; the railroads planned sweeping reductions in train service in and out of Philadelphia. By December 9, nearly all the drastic restrictions on lighting and heating that had been in effect during the coal shortage of 1917–1918 were restored. Manufacturing plants were put on a one-day week. Lightless nights were ordered. And then the coal union settled for a fourteen per cent pay raise.

Harassed by complicating factors, Philadelphia Electric did not recover from the strike for several months. Coal did not arrive in adequate quantities, being held up by blizzards in the coal regions and by a shortage of coal cars. When it did begin to come in, a railroad strike interfered with deliveries; then the tugboat crews and coal handlers at the piers walked out. At this point, in February, 1920, there was only a twenty-four-hour supply of fuel at the generating plants, and the health of the city was in jeopardy. Philadelphia Electric volunteers manned the piers and loaded the barges to save the Company from shutting down. Pocahontas coal, shipped by barge from Hampton Roads, arrived in time to help.

The strikes at the Greenwich and Port Richmond piers continued during 1920, and these difficulties, together with the coal car shortage, kept the fuel supply on a hand-to-mouth basis. By June, the Company had used all the reserve supply it had accumulated for the coming winter. To a great extent, the inability to get coal to Philadelphia stemmed from the inadequate number of coal cars available for the task. During the war, when the government operated the railroads, practically no additions were made to the already depleted coal-carrying rolling stock. Early in 1920, the railroads were returned to their owners with the coal cars reduced by wear and tear. Moreover, the government had pooled these cars and scattered them to the four corners of the country, thereby crippling the principal coal-carrying railroads. Although cars were allotted to the utilities by the Interstate Commerce Commission to see them through the emergency, it was not until October that Philadelphia Electric was able to recoup its reserve supply.

The coal situation remained a troublesome one, with frequent shortages. On April 1, 1922, the union again ordered a walkout which shut the mines in twenty states. McCall had built up a reserve supply of 160,000 tons and, more shipments being on the way, was ready for the strike. Should his reserves become depleted, he had made arrangements to procure coal from nonunion mines in West Virginia, but when that time came a strike on the Norfolk & Western Railroad shut off the supply. Orders were immediately placed in England, and five freighters were chartered to bring the coal across the Atlantic. Of inferior grade and expensive to unload since the freighters could not get in to the station docks, the coal arrived in August, sorely needed, although the strike had just ended. The fuel shortage, strike or no strike, continued to be a menace. On December 26, 1922, the directors were informed: "The car shortage is more acute than ever. Some weeks, between all the railroads, we have only received two thirds of our burn. To avoid touching coal in storage we have been buying in the open market." Perhaps it was because of the efficient management of its coal bureau that Philadelphia Electric, unlike some other utilities, was not forced to place any restrictions on the use of its current during this difficult time.

With the price of coal soaring, Philadelphia Electric's operating expenses were greatly increased. Moreover, labor costs were much higher, and supplies of all sorts were at a premium. In 1920, a rate rise for railroad freight was estimated by Company officials to add a million dollars to operating costs. The war surcharge of ten per cent on certain electric rates had been continued for a second and then a third year by the Public Service Commission, but this was only a temporary measure. In 1920, it became apparent that the surcharge, even if continued, could not produce sufficient revenue. A new rate schedule was, therefore, put into effect on January 1, 1921. No changes were made in residential or municipal rates, but the others were adjusted to absorb the ten per cent surcharge, and a fuel adjustment clause—a coal clause—was added to the wholesale light and power rates. When he filed this new tariff, McCall explained: "It is, of course, manifest that the electric light and power industry has not been free from the burden of cost imposed upon general industry by the enormous increases in the price of all materials and labor, and we have endeavored to carry the whole amount of them. But the increasing cost of coal, which is the largest single item of our expense, together with additional cost of freight charges, which we are now obliged to meet, have so added to our costs that we deem this application for relief necessary."

It is significant of the Company's standing in the community that there was no protest against the new rates. Other utilities did not enjoy so healthy a state of public relations. When Philadelphia Suburban Gas & Electric Company, a subsidiary of the American Gas Company which cared for a large part of the area encircling Philadelphia Electric's territory, raised its rates in 1921, its customers were infuriated. Mass meetings and rallies were held at nearly every suburban town and village, and a torrent of angry oratory was unleashed.

Helped by its new schedule of rates and with business increasing rapidly, the Company's affairs took a decidedly prosperous turn. Gross earnings and net income before dividends tell the story of Philadelphia Electric's progress in the postwar years.

	1919	*1921*	*1923*
Gross earnings	$16,279,239	$21,445,651	$27,609,189
Net before dividends	2,639,037	4,093,908	6,805,259

As profits went up, McCall voluntarily revised rates. On May 1, 1922, a rate reduction saving the Company's customers $1,200,000 annually was made, and on May 1, 1923, another rate reduction of $1,000,000 was put into effect. These reductions were in line with the Company's established policy of sharing with its customers benefits resulting from increased business, for it was the greater volume of business which made possible the cheaper unit production of electricity. The Company also shared its profits with its shareholders, raising the dividend rate in mid-1922 from seven to eight per cent.

It was during these years that Charles J. Russell perfected the Company's system of rates. This is a subject too complex for description here, but some appreciation of Russell's achievement can be gathered from a statement made by a Company spokesman in 1955: "Due to him Philadelphia Electric developed in those early days a structure that was not only accurate but consistent with regard to every classification of business that we were supplying. It was so sound in its basic elements that to this day there have been no major changes made in the formulas that were developed and have been in operation over all these years. I will go further and say that while many companies have tried to pattern after our basic formula a number of them waited too long to put in these systems. In fact, it would have required major upsets in the rate structures to have done it. Therefore, today they are operating under rates that are in no way comparable with the results that we have had over all these years. I can't say enough about the contributions that Charlie Russell made to our Company and made to the utilities throughout this country by his absolute intelligence and basic establishment of our rate structure."

Profitable operations did not depend on rates alone, but rested in large measure on the interest and ingenuity of the employees who were ever alert to find ways of improving procedures and lowering operating costs. McCall felt that Philadelphia Electric's prosperity should be shared by the staff, since, to a degree, a margin of the Company's profits resulted from economies innovated by its employees. Since 1910, they had been responding through a suggestion system for this purpose.

In 1922, McCall put through a "wage dividend" plan as a means of recognizing the loyalty and efficiency of the Company's workers. In part, he was motivated by a desire to counter labor unrest and to attract the caliber of worker that he wanted. Other utilities in the area paid time and a half for overtime, and double time for Sundays and holidays, whereas Philadelphia Electric did not. Moreover, the extensive building operations then under way in the city made the labor market a highly competitive one. But McCall also had other thoughts in mind in promoting the wage dividend idea. "I believe," he said, "that the work done by the capable and loyal employee may not always be entirely recompensed in the yearly wage and that, under certain conditions, he is entitled to a proportionate share of such prosperity as may result from increased efficiencies which are not alone due to painstaking and intelligent supervision, but are equally brought about by the individual who, regardless of position, is giving the best that is in him for his employer and, above all, for public service."

The wage dividend plan provided that after the Company had paid all its fixed charges and dividends, and had provided a reasonable credit to surplus, employees would receive from the net profit remaining a percentage of their salaries based on length of service and ranging up to a maximum of eight per cent. The actual over-all payment for 1922 amounted to a little more than five per cent of the annual payroll.

McCall's interest in the welfare of his employees was well known and was, in large measure, the reason for the happy relationship that existed, and still exists, between the Company's management and its workers. On the outbreak of the war, Philadelphia Electric had been one of the first utilities to announce that any of its employees who entered the service could have their jobs back when the war ended. The Company had taken an advanced position in personnel management by its early pension plan and by its support of the beneficial association, which provided disability and death payments. Shortly after the war, the Company increased the recreation facilities at its athletic park. At Howard McCall Field, as the park was then named, there was a clubhouse, a golf course, tennis courts, a baseball field, and many other attractions. Tilden and other stars gave exhibitions on the courts before large gatherings of employees and their families. A feeling permeated Philadelphia Electric that no other corporation in the city did so much for its employees. Their interest and faith in their Company is illustrated by the fact that in 1923 a third of them owned Philadelphia Electric stock, which had been made available to them on a generous time-payment basis.

In 1918, it will be recalled, David C. Johnson reported that Philadelphia Electric workers were exceptionally loyal. They were also personally devoted to their tremendously popular president. McCall not only succeeded in inspiring his staff with the ideals of service and good will, but he enjoyed the absolute confidence of the stockholders and won for the Company the respect of its customers and the community at large. Their high regard for the Company was well illustrated by their forbearance and patience during a dreadful period of mechanical failures.

The first few months of 1920 were a nightmare for McCall. He was later to characterize this time as one filled with more trouble for the Company than the entire twenty-five years he had been with it. Within a single three-week period, the 35,000-kilowatt unit at A-2 broke down and went off the lines for six weeks, a 12,000- and a 20,000-kilowatt unit, both at A-1, developed trouble and were put out of commission, and a generator and a rotary converter at the Edison Station short-circuited. "These accidents," McCall explained, "are largely the result of the wear and tear and the excessive strain on them during past years."

In January, 1920, a breakdown at Chester shut off power at Hog Island and idled 20,000 workers. On March 24, a fire destroyed feed cables and threw downtown Philadelphia into darkness. McCall gamely ventured out to the Forrest Theatre to see a musical comedy entitled "Listen Lester," starring Ada Mae Weeks. A small light on either side of the stage hooked up to a storage battery furnished light of sorts, but the performers in an act billed as a shadow dance were something less than shadows—they were invisible.

On April 1, part of the city was again thrown into darkness and elevators were stalled when another failure took place. This was followed by three more failures in the next week. A Friday concert by the Philadelphia Orchestra at the Academy of Music was halted until oil lamps were procured. Factories were closed down. Candles were at a premium. There was another bad failure in May. At times, when no failure occurred, lights would dim when peak loads overtaxed the generating plants.

Failures of generating units were troublesome, but repairs to the machinery could generally be made quickly. There was one serious breakdown, however, that put a major unit out of operation for an entire year. On September 3, 1921, the 30,000-kilowatt turbine at Schuylkill Station A-2, which supplied most of the railway load, halted with frightful damage to its moving parts and with its exciter armature flung thirty feet into the air. Philadelphia Electric was extremely fortunate that no one was hurt and that the station was not damaged. This accident was not an isolated one. All over the country the standard single-shaft 30,000-kilowatt generators were experiencing such disastrous failures that the electric industry was appalled. When these $2,000,000 machines tore loose, they sometimes destroyed power stations and killed workers. Philadelphia Electric engineers were the ones who located the malfunction, which the manufacturer then corrected.

The mechanical difficulties that disturbed McCall shortly after the war were particularly prevalent in downtown Philadelphia, the old Edison direct current district. It became shockingly apparent that the Company was short in capacity and failing in reliability in the most important area of its territory. The Edison Station was not only outmoded, but at times had to be operated in excess of its safe capacity. Moreover, the cables leading from the station were so crowded in some manholes that the slightest trouble on one was liable to pass to the others.

Horace P. Liversidge, the operating engineer, decided that a new substation would have to be built at the corner of Ninth and Sansom Streets to strengthen the Edison system. The old Edison Station simply could not hold the converter equipment necessary for transforming alternating current into direct current. As Liversidge began to develop his plans, he became dissatisfied. Why, he asked himself, should the Company bring in alternating current just to convert it at large expense and inconvenience to direct current, sustaining losses of about twenty-five per cent of the electric energy. Looking ahead, he could see that the expansion of the direct current system would involve staggering costs and greater complications in operation. More substations to house converter equipment would have to be built and be provided with costly heavy-duty electric storage batteries. It would be far better to do away with the direct current system altogether. His preliminary studies on this revolutionary idea indicated that the changeover would cost $9,000,000 and take ten years to accomplish.

Liversidge took his plan to McCall, but failed to interest the president in it. Continuing power failures in the

Edison district, however, forced McCall to reconsider. Liversidge now played his trump card. He pointed out that it would cost nearly as much to strengthen the direct current system as to replace it with alternating current, which was much cheaper to operate. Without even consulting his board of directors, McCall said "go ahead." But that was easier said than done. An enormously complicated task lay ahead, and many special studies had to be made. To help in the planning, Philip H. Chase, an expert in transmission and distribution, was employed in 1921. Chase undertook to devise a system just as good as Edison's, but one which would use alternating current.

In New York one day to attend a meeting of utility executives, McCall casually told a few of them about the changeover on which Liversidge was working. Their reaction was almost violent. Samuel Insull of Chicago declared that Liversidge must be crazy. Backing McCall into a corner, Insull, the greatest utility leader of the day, addressed the Philadelphian in the following vein: "Didn't Thomas Edison originate this electric lighting system? Didn't he design everything from his dynamos through the switchboard to the distribution system, including even junction boxes and manholes, right on through to the lamp? He's the man who designed all this and now along comes an upstart, a man who is prepared to tell you that Edison was all right in his day but here's a plan and here's a program that's much better than Edison's. Can't be. Why, Joe, you don't use any batteries with this alternating current system. How's he going to guarantee continuity of service? There isn't an Edison system in the country that doesn't have to rely on batteries because we are bound to have interruptions to our generating and converting apparatus—bound to have it. Downtown areas in big cities absolutely require one hundred per cent continuity. All the theaters and hos-

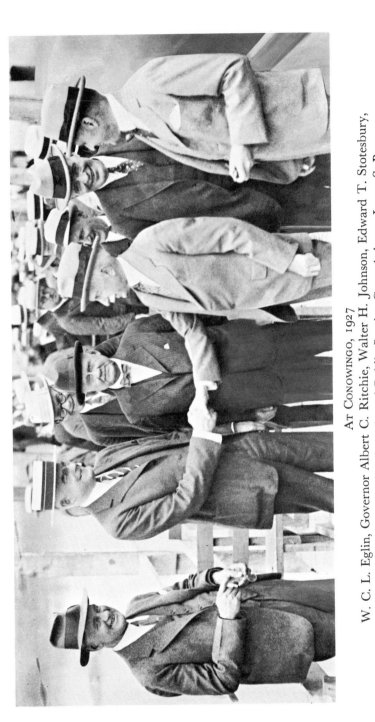

At Conowingo, 1927

W. C. L. Eglin, Governor Albert C. Ritchie, Walter H. Johnson, Edward T. Stotesbury, Former Governor W. C. Sproul, and Public Service Commissioner James S. Benn

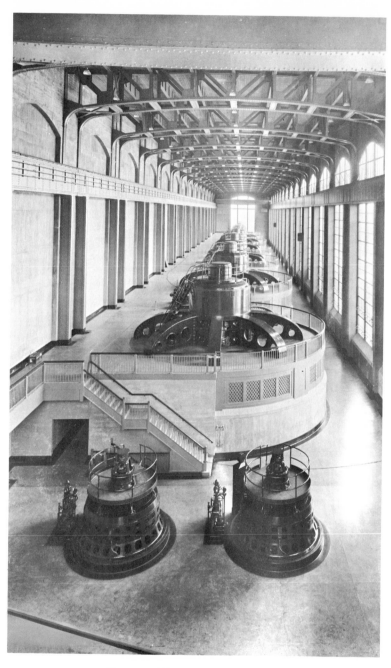

TURBINE HALL AT CONOWINGO
Completed in 1928, it contained seven generators,
each of 36,000 kilowatt capacity.

pitals, all the big stores are there. Would you depend on an alternating current system to supply this important load? It won't work, Joe."

The other executives supported Insull. Alex Dow, president of Detroit Edison, and John W. Lieb, vice-president of New York Edison, were among those who advised McCall that he was wrong to make the change. McCall returned from New York a discouraged man; he called Liversidge into his office and told him to abandon the project.

Continuing failures in the Edison district again forced McCall to reverse himself. By this time, Philadelphia Electric's direct current system was one of the poorest in the country because Liversidge had been systematically refusing to spend money on it. At his wit's end, McCall had the following conversation with Liversidge:

McCall: "I don't care what they say, and I don't care what difficulties you may have. You say you can do it?"

Liversidge: "I know I can, Mr. McCall."

McCall: "Well, go ahead and do it."

Fortunately for Liversidge, Philip H. Chase soon came up with a workable transmission system which, without depending on storage batteries, would provide the continuity that Insull had said was impossible. While the replacement part of the changeover did not begin until 1926, in 1923 a program was initiated for installing a network of 2,300-volt alternating current feeders and secondary mains in the Edison district to relieve the load on the direct current substation and the Edison distributing system. In certain sections, all new business was to be connected to the alternating current distribution system. This limited the extension of the old system and facilitated the eventual changeover.

The start of another major changeover also had its inception in 1923, when Manwaring's broad carbon arc lamps used for street lighting began to be replaced with high candlepower series incandescent lamps. The arc lamp, the pioneer electric light, was expensive to maintain, requiring trimming and the replacement of carbons; its use was doomed by the more economical incandescent light.

The postwar years with their many serious problems had been difficult ones for McCall. Whether it was the strain of these years or because of other factors, in the spring of 1922 his health broke down. One thing was paramount in his mind at this time—he must make sure of the succession to the presidency. During his administration, there had never been any question about who ran Philadelphia Electric, and McCall had no difficulty in dictating who his successor would be. At a board meeting in June, Walter H. Johnson, the Company's only vice-president, was elected senior vice-president, and three new vice-presidents were elected in the following order: Arthur B. Huey, in charge of the legal department; Charles J. Russell, in charge of the commercial department; and W. C. L. Eglin, in charge of the engineering department. McCall had very strong feelings about the order of seniority, so strong that when he learned that one of his most valued assistants had criticized the order, he lost his friendly regard for the man. The president attended the meeting on June 27 when the promotions were made, and then did not preside over another meeting for ten months.

On April 11, 1923, he returned to conduct the annual shareholders meeting. During its recess, he held a reception, shaking hands with scores of directors, stockholders, and employees who pressed forward to congratulate him on his improved health. A noted cricketer in his day, McCall had later turned to golf, and it was he who opened the new golf course at Howard McCall Field on

May 5, 1923, by driving a long straight ball up the first fairway, using the driver his son Howard had used in a number of national championships. The president was well enough on this occasion to play in a foursome with Vice-Presidents Johnson, Huey, and Eglin, but it was clear that his health was not really restored.

Everyone was glad to see McCall back on the job. He received a tremendous ovation at his first appearance before a large gathering of employees. "I wish to express my appreciation of this very, very kind reception," said McCall. "Indeed, it is not necessary for me to say I would be very unhappy without it. I have been so kindly received at such times as I have been brought before you in the past that I have taken it not so much because I was president . . . but just that I am Joe McCall." Responding to a resolution naming him the outstanding executive in the country, McCall humorously observed, "The truth never hurts anyone."

Although it may have been at the expense of his health, McCall had led the Company through the postwar years of readjustment. His pride in the Company as it emerged from that era was justifiable. Its relations with the community were excellent. Its earning power was such that it had recently raised its dividend, had repeatedly lowered rates, had increased salaries and declared wage dividends. The future looked bright. Plans were being drawn for a new generating station which Eglin designed to be the largest steam plant in the world.

Another source of power was also being considered. Eglin was anxious to acquire a hydroelectric site on the Susquehanna River in Maryland and bring its current to Philadelphia Electric by high-tension lines. The hydroelectric site had an Indian name—Conowingo.

CHAPTER 12

Conowingo

Sometimes as a raging torrent, sometimes as a tired and shallow trickle, a broad river flows through the Susquehanna Valley, draining an area on the Atlantic coast second in size only to the St. Lawrence. For centuries this river has played a vital part in man's life, providing him with routes of travel and with food to sustain him. Tarrying on its lower reaches a thousand years ago, an ancient people carved strange designs on boulder-strewn shores. These people disappeared as mysteriously as they had come and were ultimately replaced by the Susquehannocks, who flourished for a while in the seventeenth century before their tragic extermination by disease, war, and massacre. Although they are gone, vestiges of their life remain. Spring ploughing still turns up the arrowheads they fashioned, and deeper in the ground are yet to be found funeral pits containing articles of adornment, clay pipes, pottery, weapons, human bones, and pots of food needed by a dead warrior on his passage to another land. The memory of these people survives most actively in the names they gave to localities, names like Conowingo, which means "at the rapids."

At first, the white man used the Susquehanna in much the same way as had the Indian. His farming, his traveling, hunting, and fishing centered about the river. Later, he used its waters in his lumbering operations, built canals along it, and dreamed of harnessing its power. These dreams approached reality in 1884 when the Maryland legislature granted to The Susquehanna Water Power and Paper Company of Harford County authority to acquire any property needed for the development of a dam. The company built a small wing dam to furnish power to its paper mill at Conowingo, and was later sold to another corporation which became known as the Susquehanna Power Company. In 1905, this enterprise decided to build a hydroelectric plant, and, while in the development phase of the project, came into conflict with the Susquehanna Electric Power Company and the McCall Ferry Power Company, which also had hydroelectric rights on the lower Susquehanna. To avoid litigation, the three companies consolidated their interests in 1908 under the leadership of the Susquehanna Power Company, which fell under the control of Bertron, Griscom & Company, investment bankers of New York and Philadelphia.

Unable to finance a development of their own, the stockholders of the Susquehanna Power Company watched with interest while the Pennsylvania Water and Power Company built a dam across the river at Holtwood, Pennsylvania, in 1910, and began to transmit power to Baltimore and York. Bertron, Griscom & Company, encouraged by the success of the Holtwood project, employed engineers to collect data and to study river conditions below the new dam. Serious consideration was given to five potential hydroelectric sites near Conowingo, which was situated three miles south of the Pennsylvania line and ten miles above the Susquehanna's outlet into Chesapeake Bay.

During the war, the Federal government eyed this area in its search for electric power, and in 1918 discussed its possibilities with Philadelphia Electric. Action was set aside, however, because of the expense and the length of time that would be required to develop it. After the war, a period of high construction costs followed by a business depression again deferred consideration of the project. But in 1921, the subject was revived by Morris R. Bockius, Philadelphia Electric's counsel, and Eglin was sent to Washington to obtain the views of the government. Meanwhile, the banker Rodman E. Griscom offered McCall an informal option on the Susquehanna Power Company, whose most tangible assets were 5,424 acres and the control of eight companies owning part of this land—companies like the Conowingo Land Company of Cecil County, and The Proprietors of the Susquehanna Canal, an eighteenth-century venture.

In the spring of 1922, McCall was incapacitated by illness and then went abroad to recuperate, leaving to Eglin leadership in the Conowingo project. From that time on, Eglin spearheaded the undertaking and became its most enthusiastic advocate. During the second half of 1922, he conducted preliminary studies of all sorts. One of his engineers, George P. Roux, arranged a survey party and checked on field conditions. Eventually, an elaborate report was prepared by Eglin and Roux, assisted by Malcolm MacLaren and Lewis B. Beatty, with Morris R. Bockius providing the necessary legal opinions. This report was then checked by the engineering firm of Stone & Webster.

Unfortunately, just at this time matters took an awkward turn. When Griscom presented the option to Philadelphia Electric for the purchase of the Susquehanna Power Company, he insisted on a clause which guaranteed twenty-five per cent of the output of the proposed hydroelectric development to the United Gas and Electric Corporation. The charge to United Gas for this energy he set at a rate which appeared to be below production cost. Protecting United Gas by other clauses which infringed on Philadelphia Electric's freedom of action, Griscom justified these requirements by pointing out that United Gas had just purchased more than fifty per cent of the Susquehanna Power Company's stock and needed power for Lancaster and Harrisburg. Bertron, Griscom's interest in United Gas was natural enough. They had put that company together in 1912, and ten years later it remained under their control to the extent that seven Bertron, Griscom partners were on its board of directors.

At a board meeting in January, 1923, Walter H. Johnson presented Eglin's report and the option to purchase the Susquehanna Power Company, stating that it was economically feasible to erect a dam and power plant capable of generating 237,500 kilowatts. This hydroelectric power could be transmitted to Philadelphia at a lower price than it could be manufactured by the system's steam plants. Johnson estimated the cost of the Conowingo project at $45,000,000 and stressed the importance of protecting the Company's interests should this development take place. If cheap power was to be available, Philadelphia Electric must have its share. If it did not control the project, Johnson warned, antagonistic interests might.

Consideration of this extremely important matter was referred to a committee of directors, all of whom, except Horatio G. Lloyd of Drexel's, were bank presidents or former bank presidents. There were tremendous problems involved in the Conowingo project, some of which had not been completely resolved in Eglin's report. There was, for example, uncertainty as to whether the government would allow the dam to be built. Construction bids rather than estimates were needed. Political questions remained to be determined. The special provisions protecting the United Gas and Electric Corporation were highly objectionable. Most formidable of all was the expense. Swayed by these points, the committee reported against Conowingo, specifically mentioning "the immense amount of money involved." The directors hoped that the hydroelectric project would be underwritten by someone else from whom the Company could buy the current.

Fearful that "certain interests" would step in and take up the option which Philadelphia Electric had rejected, Eglin and Walter E. Long requested Lloyd and his partner Thomas Newhall to protect the Company. Out of this discussion came Drexel's decision to acquire the option for itself. In negotiating for it with Bertron, Griscom & Company, Lloyd succeeded in eliminating all the special clauses in favor of the United Gas and Electric Corporation. Thus, the option passed to Drexel's with whom the officers of Philadelphia Electric had an understanding that the rights under the option could be exercised in favor of the Company. The main question to be determined was whether Philadelphia Electric wanted full control of Conowingo, or whether it would share control with other utilities. Eglin continued to devote virtually his full time to Conowingo studies, and Drexel & Company reinforced his research by employing Stone & Webster to analyze the situation.

The new studies on Conowingo were submitted to McCall in December, 1923. After his chief commercial advisers had reported on them, McCall decided that the Company would be able to absorb all of the project's power, estimated at 1,150,000,000 kilowatt-hours annually. Studies conducted by Walter E. Long and N. E. Funk pointed up distinct economic advantages in taking the hydroelectric development into the Company's system, even though its initial cost was now believed to be $59,000,000. Accordingly, McCall recommended to the board that Philadelphia Electric take over the entire project from Drexel's. McCall summed up the advantages of this step: it would represent a saving in capital investment of $21,000,000 in producing an equivalent amount of power, and would also save in the cost of generating power; by delivering hydroelectric energy on the west side of Philadelphia, the expense and difficulty of building a future power station on the Schuylkill, where water conditions were not ideal, would be avoided; Conowingo would be useful for emergency power, since a 36,000-kilowatt hydro unit could be put in service in one minute, while a similar steam unit took an hour and a half; 18,000 carloads of coal—750,000 tons—would be saved annually; water power supply was most abundant at those times when coal deliveries were most troublesome; water power improved the reliability of service, protecting it against the effect of coal strikes; by bringing hydroelectric power to Philadelphia and thereby joining in the progressive policy of conserving fuel resources, the Company would make a favorable impression on public opinion.

In July, 1924, when $100,000 was authorized for test borings and other preliminary work at Conowingo, the Company notified Drexel's of its desire to acquire Bertron, Griscom & Company's option on the stock of the Susquehanna Power Company, which owned the water power site at Conowingo. Drexel's replied by stating its side of the bargain:

> You will recall, and we believe recognize, the services which we have performed, both before and after the decision of your Company not to directly develop the project; that we have spent many months in bringing the matter to the point where your Company may now realize very great savings, both in capital investment and operating expenses from its development and utiliza-

tion, and that we would expect to co-operate in the development of the enterprise during its construction period, which will require active services on our part over a long period of time. In such projects, as you are aware, it is not unusual for bankers who have thus acted to be compensated by a substantial interest in the common stock of the resulting corporation.

The option which we have developed is one of very great value, entirely apart from its special value to your Company, and this option we are turning over to the enterprise.

Having in mind these various considerations, we believe that our compensation therefor should be fixed at 3% of the amount realized to the project from the sale of bonds, which would be our only compensation in the transaction, other than the usual discount or commission on the bonds or other securities marketed or underwritten by us.

Since $39,000,000 worth of bonds was to be sold, the price set by Drexel's for the option was $1,170,000.

The transaction aroused criticism because Philadelphia Electric had once had the opportunity to acquire the option for nothing. Director Horatio G. Lloyd's activity in the matter was also criticized—he had been on the Philadelphia Electric committee which had rejected the option, had then secured it for Drexel's, and had now sold it at a handsome price to the Company. How this was all brought about, how Drexel's was urged by Eglin and Long to take up the option, has been described, and Drexel's right to make a charge is unquestionable. From first to last, the investment house rendered important help to the Company in the Conowingo business. N. E. Funk has said that, in his estimation, the services of Drexel's were worth the price of the option. Throughout the construction period, control over all expenditures and major engineering problems rested in a supervisory group headed by Thomas Newhall of Drexel's. Everyone had profound respect for Newhall. Calling him "a wonderful character," Liversidge has noted that "during the period in which he was acting as chairman of this group, he made a real contribution."

Since Conowingo lay in Maryland, and since its reservoir would back up into Pennsylvania, it was necessary to obtain approval for the project from the public service commissions of both states. In addition, since the War Department had ruled that the Susquehanna was a navigable river, it was necessary to obtain a license from the Federal Power Commission.

Engineering plans, estimates of costs, every detail to do with financing and the corporate structure set up for the enterprise had to be perfected for presentation to these three commissions. In working out the corporate organization, Philadelphia Electric created the Philadelphia Electric Power Company, a Pennsylvania corporation which was to own the hydroelectric property in Pennsylvania. This property included the major part of the reservoir and the transmission lines up to the point where they entered Philadelphia Electric territory. The new company was to be a subsidiary of Philadelphia Electric and was to own The Susquehanna Power Company, a Maryland corporation in which was to be vested title to the project's property in Maryland—the dam, powerhouse, and portions of the reservoir and transmission lines.

Their plans all in final shape, officials of Philadelphia Electric appeared before a joint hearing of the Pennsylvania and Maryland Public Service Commissions and a representative of the Federal Power Commission on March 6, 1925. Just as the hearing was being called to order in the Supreme Court Room at City Hall, the entire legal staff of P.R.T., headed by Ellis Ames Ballard, filed into the room. William Clarke Mason, attorney for the Company, needed only one look at this array of legal talent to realize that Thomas E. Mitten had declared war on Philadelphia Electric!

In a trenchant opening attack, Ballard informed the Commissions that Drexel's would make inordinate profits in the financing of Conowingo, that the project itself was not sound, and that it could not be completed on twice the capitalization submitted. He went further, announcing that unless it could be conclusively proved that Philadelphia Electric rates would be lowered by Conowingo, P.R.T. intended to build its own electric plants and discontinue buying power from the Company. Walter E. Long and Charles W. Kellogg of Stone & Webster testified in favor of Conowingo, but P.R.T. had stolen the headlines.

Business circles were astounded at Mitten's action. Many financial leaders believed that Mitten in his vendetta with Stotesbury was out to break Drexel's influence with Philadelphia Electric and grab that Company for himself. Few credited the reason Mitten gave for his intervention in the Company's affairs—that if Conowingo proved a fiasco, electric rates would go up and P.R.T., the Company's largest customer, would suffer unduly. Knowledgeable people noted that money from trolley operations was drying up, that Mitten was experimenting with buses and taxis, had gone into banking, and was looking for new ventures to manage.

The P.R.T. assault continued violently, Mitten raining blow after blow at Philadelphia Electric's management. Ballard filed a petition with the Public Service Commission, charging that the Company's rates were "unjust, excessive, unreasonable and discriminatory"; he asked that its books be audited.

174

With Philadelphia Electric's annual meeting only a month away, Mitten made an outright effort to obtain control of its management by soliciting proxies for himself and his associates. The bait he offered to the stockholders was a promise to increase the dividend rate from eight per cent to ten per cent. If, on the other hand, he should fail to obtain control, not only would the stockholders not receive a higher dividend, their present rate would be in jeopardy because P.R.T. would take its business away from the Company.

Mitten maintained that the day must come when P.R.T. and Philadelphia Electric would operate as one company. "Since it is far better for both P.R.T. and P.E., and for P.R.T. car-riders and P.E. customers that this great forward step be now taken, P.R.T. management plans to offer P.E. stockholders $1,200,000 a year through increased dividends to justify P.E. stockholders assenting to the transfer of P.E. management from its present destructive banker control to that of P.R.T.'s already proven dependable management. . . . P.R.T. must build its own powerhouses—operate P.E. powerhouses—or must buy elsewhere and itself distribute electricity."

Mitten's audacious attack came at a time when his own standing in the community was not high. Recently picturing P.R.T. as on the verge of bankruptcy, he had succeeded in winning a fare increase to eight cents. Having secured this additional income, Mitten had then paid a higher dividend, a step which had aroused general disgust and had brought on political action. Down to Philadelphia came Milo R. Maltbie, sent by Governor Gifford Pinchot to investigate P.R.T. Mayor W. Freeland Kendrick and many businessmen's organizations also entered the fight to repeal the eight-cent fare.

Returning from Palm Beach, where his winter vacation had been ruined by a fire that had destroyed much of the resort, Stotesbury went straight to City Hall to combat Mitten's charges. Before the Public Service Commission, he denied that Drexel's would receive $5,000,000 for the now famous option. Stotesbury was not the only one put in a bad light by inaccurate accusations. Vice-President Eglin had to be defended from the totally unwarranted allegation that Drexel's had bribed him with a payment of $430,000 to gain his support for their schemes.

Philadelphia Electric issued a statement comparing its rate reductions since 1920 with P.R.T.'s fare raises during those years, raises which had increased the price of trolley rides from five to eight cents. "If Mr. Mitten were an electric man there might be some sense in his 'offer.' But even at that, it is difficult to see how he can lay claim to being so successful in operating the P.R.T. when he is continually asking for more money to pay the fixed charges and operating expenses. . . . The actual intent is to strengthen the P.R.T. at the expense of the Philadelphia Electric Company."

While P.R.T. employees went the rounds soliciting Philadelphia Electric proxies, Mitten continued his attack. Drexel & Company was accused of "downright dishonesty"; a great point was made of McCall's illness and the lack of leadership that had resulted. But all this led nowhere; the stockholders preferred an ill McCall to a healthy Mitten. On April 5, Mitten wrote to McCall and Johnson, acknowledging defeat and taking a swing at Drexel's: "This management hopes most sincerely that the result of the contest will make you dominant in the affairs of your company and enable you to adequately protect the interests of those stockholders who have so signally expressed their confidence in you."

In retiring from one fight, Mitten announced that he must continue in another—his battle against the Conowingo project. Whether he did this to save face, to obtain

Conowingo for himself, to keep the door open for another attempt at winning control of Philadelphia Electric, or because of an honest conviction that Conowingo, a financial monstrosity, would raise his rates, cannot be determined.

At the Company's annual meeting on April 8, 1925, ninety-five per cent of the stock was voted, all of it for management. About four hundred stockholders actually attended the meeting, where they were addressed by William Clarke Mason who reviewed the entire history of Conowingo and its financing, refuting the recent "unwarranted attack" and defending the project.

Counsel for Mitten, however, continued to present Conowingo in the most unpromising light in their futile attempts to block its acceptance by the Commissions. Ballard characterized the project as "a scheme calculated to reap a profit for bankers and company stockholders with all the risk involved shouldered solely by the public —the rate payers." He introduced expert witnesses who maintained that the cost of Conowingo had been set too low. Henry M. Brinckerhoff, an engineer and power man, testified that Conowingo would cost the Company an annual net operating loss of $1,113,360, and that it would tie up $50,000,000 of capital to no purpose. When they realized that they could not kill the project, Mitten's lawyers sought to modify its financial arrangements. The objections they raised on interest rates and allied matters were largely sustained by the Commissions. Having accomplished this after many months of hearings, Mitten withdrew from the struggle, boasting that he had saved Philadelphia Electric $1,000,000 a year. He forgot about his threat to build his own powerhouses. With good relations restored, "Mitten Men and Management" solicited an account from the Company for their bank.

In March, 1926, Drexel's formed a syndicate with Brown Brothers and Harris, Forbes & Company to market $36,000,000 worth of 5½% Philadelphia Electric Power Company bonds: "We recommend these bonds for investment." Additional funds came from $12,000,000 in 8% preferred stock in the same company, which was allotted by Philadelphia Electric to its shareholders. The undertaking for which this money was raised was a giant one, for Philadelphia Electric proposed to create a hydroelectric development second in size only to Niagara. The Conowingo project, however, was basically different from that of Niagara, where the source of power, the endless rush of water from the greatest reservoir in the world, was constant. The flow of the Susquehanna was erratic, now heavy, now light. It could be used for hydroelectric purposes only in conjunction with a highly developed center for electricity which also had steam plants capable of taking care of the area demands. With Baltimore already receiving hydroelectric power from Holtwood, Philadelphia was the only center within practical transmission range of Conowingo that had these requisites. When the Susquehanna was running strongly, the energy it generated would carry Philadelphia Electric's base load, the steam plants furnishing the top demands. At other times, when the river was low, the steam plants would care for the base load, and Conowingo would be sparingly used to handle the upper levels.

Nestled against the hills on the east side of the Susquehanna, the village of Conowingo contained a garage, a railroad station, church, school, inn, several canneries, a number of homes, and about two hundred residents. It was there that the Baltimore Pike crossed the mile-wide river on an old-fashioned bridge. Baltimore lay forty miles away in one direction, and Philadelphia sixty-five miles away in the other. Through the town ran the tracks of the Columbia & Port Deposit Railroad, an important low-grade freight route, part of the Pennsylvania Rail-

EDISON BUILDING, 900 SANSOM STREET,
ON COMPLETION IN 1928

RAILROAD OVERBUILD
An engineering technique developed by Philadelphia Electric to
overcome right-of-way problems

road system, which connected Perryville, Maryland, with Columbia, Pennsylvania, forty-four miles upstream. This picture of a typical country village was soon to be abruptly changed. Since the site selected for the dam was two miles below Conowingo, its reservoir would flood the town, bridge, and railroad, all of which would have to be removed.

The plans for the powerhouse and dam were designed by Stone & Webster, who supervised the construction and themselves built the powerhouse and a section of the dam, the powerhouse being on the west side of the river near the main channel. The Arundel Corporation of Baltimore constructed the main part of the solid concrete dam, which, in its entirety, is 4,648 feet in length and rests on solid rock approximately ninety-six feet below the surface of the lake it forms.

On either side of the river, camps to house 3,800 workers were erected. A nine-mile standard gauge railroad connecting with the Pennsylvania Railroad at Havre de Grace was built along the tow path of the old Tidewater Canal on the west side of the river. Electricity was brought in by high-tension lines from Holtwood, and in March, 1926, the great hydroelectric project was at last under way.

Among the major engineering accomplishments connected with it was the speedy relocation of the Columbia & Port Deposit Railroad, which involved the construction of nearly sixteen miles of double-track roadbed over rugged terrain. Because the Conowingo Bridge was to be demolished and the Baltimore Pike carried over the river on the top of the dam, it was necessary to relocate eight miles of state highway. This stretch was completed in December, 1926, shortening the route between Philadelphia and Baltimore by several miles.

Work on the project was carried on without a single interruption from labor disputes, the magnitude of the enterprise attracting constant inspection parties. In June, 1927, a grand official inspection was sponsored by Philadelphia Electric. Special trains from Philadelphia, Baltimore, and Washington brought in one hundred and fifty prominent men. Among those present were Stotesbury, Lloyd, and Newhall of Drexel's, Rodman E. Griscom, and Mitten's lawyer Ellis Ames Ballard. Since the top men in Drexel's were mortally offended by the recent attacks on their character, by their representation as financial vultures, it is possible that the atmosphere of the party may have been a little constrained. To mark the interstate character of the occasion, representatives of Maryland and Pennsylvania clasped hands for the photographers across a symbolic Mason-Dixon Line. While Walter H. Johnson, the senior Philadelphia Electric man present, was permitted in the picture, Governor Albert C. Ritchie of Maryland is shown firmly gripping the hand of Edward T. Stotesbury, whose personal association with the project was of the slightest. Stotesbury invariably received top billing simply because he was Stotesbury; it was unthinkable to put him in a secondary position.

On November 16, 1927, the new highway across the dam was opened to the public, and preparations were made to dynamite the old highway bridge with a special explosive prepared by duPont. From far and near assembled an army of cameramen to photograph the scene. With the attention of the cameramen concentrated on an official who was describing what was about to happen, a workman named Kelly prematurely detonated the charges. Fortunately, the bridge was to be blown in two sections; all cameras were on target when the second section went up in the air.

While Stone & Webster and the Arundel Corporation were working at Conowingo, Day & Zimmermann were constructing the transmission lines—two lines of steel towers, each of which supported three steel-core aluminum power cables about one inch in diameter and designed to operate at 220,000 volts. According to the original plan, this power was to be brought into Schuylkill Station by 132,000-volt lines.

Liversidge took serious exception to this plan. He believed it would be too expensive, since the transmission would have to come into Philadelphia across densely built-up areas. Moreover, the extraordinary expense would not end when the lines arrived at Schuylkill Station, for the congestion of underground cables at that point was such that it would be impossible to distribute the power from there without additional heavy outlays in money.

Now, it so happened that the Company was working on a plan of interconnection with Pennsylvania Power & Light Company and the Public Service Electric and Gas Company of New Jersey, which proposed bringing 220,000-volt transmission into a substation upstream from Flat Rock Dam on the Schuylkill. At that point the power would be stepped down to 66,000 volts, fed by underground cables into the new Hunting Park Substation, and from there distributed by 66,000-volt lines to Richmond and Schuylkill Stations.

Liversidge felt that advantage should be taken of the cost saving that could be made by combining the interconnection and Conowingo transmission in one substation. His advice prevailed, and the site of the important substation was located at Plymouth Meeting near Norristown. The next problem to be solved was how to get the power from Plymouth Meeting into Philadelphia. To be sure, it would be transmitted part way by 66,000-volt aerial lines, but how to bring it in the rest of the way with the miles of expensive underground cable which would be required remained unresolved.

Plan after plan to convey the power to Philadelphia failed to win acceptance until George P. Roux made a workable suggestion. Down the Schuylkill Valley, near Plymouth Meeting, ran the tracks of the Reading Railroad on their way to the city. Why not erect the transmission towers along the Reading's right of way? With Conowingo nearing completion, time was running out and Liversidge was becoming desperate. He called on Agnew T. Dice, president of the Reading. To Dice, the attractiveness of Liversidge's request hinged on the railroad's contemplated electrification program. If he permitted Liversidge to build his transmission towers along the tracks—actually overbuilding the tracks on certain stretches—Dice could use this construction for his own electric lines and much money would be saved. Accordingly, he agreed to the proposal, subject to the approval of his chief engineer, Clark Dillenbeck. Then followed a long struggle with the engineer, which was eventually won for Philadelphia Electric by its assistant chief engineer, N. E. Funk. By happy coincidence, both Dillenbeck and Funk were of Pennsylvania Dutch extraction, a harmonious element which smoothed the path of Funk's negotiations. In an agreement reached in July, 1927, the Company obtained the use of the Reading's right of way from Shawmont to Westmoreland. Work was rushed to completion so that the three 100,000-kilowatt 66,000-volt lines could be extended from Plymouth Meeting to Westmoreland and the system's Hunting Park Substation before Conowingo went into operation. From Hunting Park, the energy was carried underground by 66,000-volt cables to the main steam generating plants.

While Liversidge wrestled with transmission problems, the directors gave consideration to the best way to supply some Conowingo power in Maryland. If this were not done, the charter obligations of The Susquehanna Power

Company could be questioned. Moreover, the reaction of Herbert A. Wagner, president of Consolidated Gas Electric Light and Power Company of Baltimore, to Philadelphia Electric's extension of its interests to Maryland was not altogether friendly. The directors suspected that if they did not take on Maryland customers, Consolidated would demand the right to purchase a substantial block of Conowingo power. To prevent this, Philadelphia Electric acquired a number of local electric companies.

For unified corporate control of its new properties, Philadelphia Electric formed the Susquehanna Utilities Company in 1927. Incorporated in Delaware, this holding company owned the stocks of six operating companies which distributed electricity in northeastern Maryland and southeastern Pennsylvania. Their territory lay in and about Conowingo on both sides of the river, and included Havre de Grace.

The decision of Consolidated Gas Electric Light and Power Company of Baltimore to compete with the Havre de Grace company owned by Susquehanna Utilities brought on the "Battle of Havre de Grace" when Consolidated extended its lines into the town. Albert R. Granger, general manager of Susquehanna Utilities, has written that in 1927 Consolidated "came out with display ads, citing lower rates, appealing on the basis of home pride for the support of the Maryland utility. Consolidated's men proceeded to take down our meters, depositing them on porches, building their own pole lines, installing duplicate street lights. Havre de Grace was thus furnished with the most striking street illumination it had ever enjoyed." The war carried on for a time, with many amusing incidents and a striking display of ingenuity by both Granger and his rival. Philadelphia Electric did not want trouble in Havre de Grace and was willing to sell out, but not to be kicked out. Eventually, Wagner called off the battle and accepted the Company's sales offer, informing the president of Philadelphia Electric, "if Granger hadn't gotten into the scrap we would have run you out of Havre de Grace in jig time."

Meanwhile, the monumental Conowingo project had been completed. Backed up behind its mighty dam was a lake fourteen square miles in area and fourteen miles long, in which were impounded 150,000,000,000 gallons of water. In place and ready to operate were seven huge water wheels, each rated at 36,000 kilowatts. Standing by, in reserve, were foundation provisions for four additional units, should their installation ever be required. The requisite machinery to generate a capacity of 252,000 kilowatts was in place. On March 1, 1928, power from Conowingo was transmitted to Plymouth Meeting!

Three weeks before this exciting event, Vice-President W. C. L. Eglin had died. More than any other man, he had been responsible for the creation of the great hydroelectric development. In the initial stages, he had controlled its destinies, and throughout the building phase of the project he continued as its chief engineer, co-ordinating the work of the contractors and keeping everything running smoothly.

Eglin had served the Philadelphia Electric system for nearly forty years, although he was only fifty-seven when he died. Starting as a dynamo tender at The Edison Electric Light Company of Philadelphia, he was soon its chief engineer. Ultimately, he rose to the position of vice-president and director of Philadelphia Electric, and attained national recognition as a foremost engineering authority in the electric industry. A tireless worker, it was he who designed and supervised the erection of Schuylkill, Chester, Delaware, and Richmond Stations. The recipient of three honorary degrees, president of the world-famous Franklin Institute for five terms, Eglin's career had culminated in his climactic achievement—Conowingo.

Conowingo has proved to be all that its engineers had hoped, all that Mitten and his cohorts had said was impossible. It has notably strengthened the Philadelphia Electric system and has brought about important economies. Ever since Conowingo went into operation, it has generated an average of 1,300,000,000 kilowatt-hours of electricity a year.

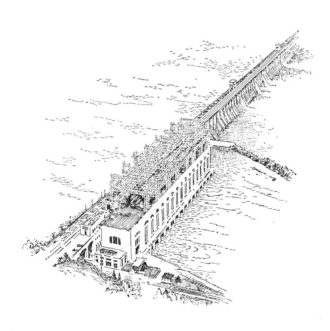

CHAPTER 13

The Prosperous Twenties

Accomplishment and optimism marked the mid-1920's. As memories of the great European conflict dimmed, and the hard times of the recent period of deflation gave way to an era of remarkable prosperity, a conviction seized the country that it was standing at the portal of extraordinary change. Man became excitedly aware that there was nothing his ingenuity could not conquer, nothing he could not achieve.

In April, 1927, science, having already provided the radio, once again annihilated distance, this time through television. Sitting in front of a screen in New York, a group of men watched Secretary of Commerce Herbert Hoover in Washington as he talked to Walter S. Gifford, president of the American Telephone and Telegraph Company. "It is a matter of great pride to me to have a part in this historic occasion," Hoover told Gifford. "I am glad to welcome television as the latest subject of scientific discovery." Ever since the invention of the telephone, television had been the dream of scientists; now it was a reality. Of course, it was far from perfected—at times one could see only Hoover's ear, and at other times the picture faded or rippled as if water were running over it. Years would pass before the machine could be sold to the public.

A little more than a month after television's debut, Lindbergh piloted the "Spirit of St. Louis" across the Atlantic to France, and became the hero of the world. Meanwhile, Henry Ford was busy in Detroit. Since 1908, he had sold 15,000,000 "Model T" cars, and now in secrecy and at enormous expense he was working on a new model. In December, 1927, after artfully creating an almost unbearable suspense in the public mind, he at last unveiled his famous "Model A"—"our most important contribution thus far to the prosperity of the country, and to the daily welfare of millions of people."

During the twenties, Philadelphians built as they had never built before, and the "downtown" area, traditionally the hub of business activity, lost out to center city, the area around Broad Street and City Hall to which many of the banks moved. Unfortunately, material progress was marred by a crime wave, which stemmed in large measure from prohibition. Despite the law, Philadelphia remained ostentatiously wet. The police had records of 8,000 places where liquor was sold, and speculated that there were probably twice that many. It did little good to close these bars, for they immediately reopened. "Sure, I got beer," a bartender told a reporter shortly after the seventh raid on his establishment.

To break political control of the police, Mayor W. Freeland Kendrick appointed a director of public safety who would not be subject to political pressures, General Smedley D. Butler of the Marines. One of the few men to hold two Medals of Honor, Butler was a veteran of fourteen campaigns and expeditions. "Old Gimlet Eye," as he was often called, and not without reason, was totally honest, a strict disciplinarian, blunt and hasty in speech. Entering upon his duties in January, 1924, Butler closed 2,566 speakeasies that year and sharply curbed crimes of violence. Unhappily, he was soon at odds with the politicians, and within two years even the mayor had to give him up. That he was an honest man had been known all along, but no one had counted on his being one hundred per cent honest. Butler created an impossible situation. With the Sesqui-Centennial International Exposition on the horizon, the general was trying to padlock the Ritz-Carlton Hotel for allowing liquor on the premises, and he was about to revoke the dance license of the Bellevue-Stratford. These were the final straws. Butler returned to the Marines where his colorful career could continue in a more congenial atmosphere.*

The Sesqui-Centennial, commemorating one hundred and fifty years of independence, was the great Philadelphia event of 1926, the year the Delaware River Bridge, since rechristened in honor of Benjamin Franklin, had its opening. Those who originally planned the exposition were mindful of the superb world's fair held in Philadelphia in 1876 to mark the nation's centennial, but there were many who hesitated to try anything so ambitious again. Edward T. Stotesbury and Samuel Vauclain, president of Baldwin Locomotive Works, argued for a purely local celebration on an "Old Home Week" theme. At a meeting called by the mayor in December, 1923, this modest plan was supported by 403 civic leaders— only forty-six voted in favor of a fair that would be international in scope. The site recommended was Fairmount Park, where the Centennial Exposition had been staged.

Then all plans were suddenly changed under the guidance of a professional fair director. The Sesqui-Centennial would take place at League Island; it was to be an international event; a municipal stadium was to be built; the fair would cost millions. Before long, the professional

*The description of General Butler rests on an article by Fred D. Baldwin in *The Pennsylvania Magazine of History and Biography* (July, 1960).

director resigned, but not before the course of the fair and its uncontrollable costs had been irretrievably set. Mayor Kendrick spurred on the plans, contriving all he could to make them successful. In January, 1926, he quashed a final effort of apprehensive citizens to postpone the celebration. And so it was that a strange new world, something out of "Arabian Nights," took form on League Island as the exposition was belatedly rushed to completion of sorts.

Coolidge visited the "Sesqui" in July, and, despite his reputation for taciturnity, spoke for nearly an hour in a plea for the restoration of the ideals of 1776. Drab skies and drizzling rain marked the occasion. Indeed, in the first eighty-four days of the fair, rain fell on fifty-three. The concessionaires began to complain that the fair had been misrepresented to them; they were losing money. Business was not improved by the Philadelphia Sabbath Association and allied groups, which held a mass meeting at the Academy of Music to protest the exposition's being open on Sundays. The boycott they declared probably had little effect; the fair's deficit mounted by the million for lack of patronage caused by factors other than religious. At length, on November 30, a final ceremony was held on the grounds. The mayor said a few words, rather forlornly admitting he was glad it was all over. The day was in harmony with people's spirits—dreary and cold.

To many, the outstanding event associated with the exposition was the Dempsey-Tunney prize fight held at Municipal Stadium in September. All records for receipts and attendance were shattered on this occasion when Tunney wrested the world's heavyweight title away from the champion. As soon as the boxers entered the ring, rain began to fall, increasing gradually to a relentless downpour. More clothes were ruined that night in Philadelphia than ever before in its history.

One of the features of the Sesqui-Centennial was its extraordinary use of lighting effects. The visitor entered the grounds under an eighty-foot-high replica of the Liberty Bell, which rested on two massive columns. The bell was illuminated with thousands of lights whose glow was said to be visible as far away as New York. Batteries of floodlights made possible nighttime pageants in the great stadium. Eight hundred and sixty floodlights of varied hues played on the building and shaft that supported the statue of William Penn. The "Tower of Light," two hundred feet high, lived up to its name; in addition, the beams of twenty-four immense searchlights crisscrossed the evening sky. To provide current for this display, officials of the exposition contracted with Philadelphia Electric for 12,500 kilowatts, the equivalent of Germantown's lighting load. The Company played another part at the fair by helping to sponsor the "National Home Electric." Walter H. Johnson turned the first spadeful of earth on the site of this building, and, before long, a Spanish-style residence was erected in which were demonstrated the wonders of electricity in domestic use.

The Company had no difficulty in taking on the fair's electrical demand, or in supplying Philadelphia's steadily growing requirements, because the fine new Richmond Station, which housed two 50,000-kilowatt generators, the largest made, had gone into operation in November, 1925. The rating of the generators was increased several years later to 60,000 kilowatts each. Designed by Eglin and Windrim, Richmond Station was as handsome as the other plants they had created. Moreover, it was one of the most efficient in the world, being able to produce a kilowatt-hour of electricity with the lowest fuel consumption attained up to that time. Eglin planned to add two more sections to Richmond sometime in the future, which would increase its total capacity to 720,000 kilowatts, but the additional sections were never built.

In fact, after Richmond Station's two large generators were installed, the capacity of the Company's steam generating plants was not increased for years. To a degree, the Company had caught up with the sharply rising need for electrical energy which had begun to level off. Then, too, Conowingo's giant hydroelectric power was soon to become available. Still another deterrent to increasing Philadelphia Electric's capacity lay in studies it was making of the advantages of an interchange of energy in bulk with other companies through an arrangement planned with Pennsylvania Power & Light and Public Service of New Jersey.

During the mid-twenties, the system's steam generating capacity had been enlarged from 339,000 kilowatts in June, 1924, to 529,000 kilowatts in June, 1926, the additions being at Chester and Delaware Stations in 1924 and at Richmond Station in 1925. In 1926, the stations were rated as follows:

Schuylkill A-1	64,000 KW
Schuylkill A-2	65,000 KW
Richmond	100,000 KW
Chester	120,000 KW
Delaware	180,000 KW

Tacony Station with its capacity of 15,000 kilowatts was held in reserve. At this time, 80,000 kilowatts were generated at 25 cycles and the rest at 60 cycles, the two systems being tied together by frequency changers. The distributing centers for this energy—the third largest power rating in the country—were Philadelphia Electric's thirty-five substations, which were grouped into five districts: Edison, Central, Southern, Northern, and Delaware County.

The Pennsylvania Railroad was one of the Company's largest customers. Its 102 miles of electric lines (Paoli, Chestnut Hill, and Atlantic City) were supplied entirely by Philadelphia Electric. Consequently, the railroad's announcement in March, 1926, that it intended to electrify its roads from Philadelphia to Wilmington and to West Chester via Media was good news. This electrification was an integral part of the railroad's major project which involved the building of an enormous passenger station on the west bank of the Schuylkill and the subway extension of its lines into a suburban station to be located in the very heart of the city. The Baltimore & Ohio publicized similar plans for a new station, and the Reading in 1926 was actively engaged in a survey to determine the feasibility of electrifying its suburban roads. Everyone agreed that the steam locomotive was doomed.

Imagine Philadelphia Electric's consternation, therefore, when, in February, 1927, the Pennsylvania Railroad let it be known that it might build a $10,000,000 power station on the Delaware near Trenton to supply 25-cycle power for the extensive electrification plans then in progress. Speculators sold Philadelphia Electric short at this news. Although at first alarmed by the railroad's proposed plant, Philadelphia Electric engineers soon concluded that it would neither be adequate for the purpose, nor economic in operation.

Other engineers must have viewed the scheme in the same light, for the Pennsylvania Railroad did not build the station. Instead, in July, 1927, the railroad signed a contract whereby it agreed to buy all its power for the next twenty years from Philadelphia Electric. The energy was to be generated at 60 cycles and converted to 25 cycles, 13,000 volts, single phase. This was the most important contract a railroad had ever executed with a utility company up to that time.

While taking on new business in the twenties, the Company proceeded steadily toward the completion of its two major changeover programs. The lesser of these was the replacing of arc lamps with high candlepower series incandescent lamps. At the end of 1923, Philadelphia Electric operated 19,034 municipal arc lamps and 110 commercial ones. In 1924, about 8,000 arc lights were changed to incandescent lamps, and in 1925 another 8,000 were converted. Well-lighted streets helped General Butler combat crime, and criminals no doubt glared with disfavor at the new ornamental light standards that Philadelphia Electric was erecting on the city's streets and boulevards. On the major arteries, 1,000-candlepower lamps were installed on twin standards; single standards on Roosevelt Boulevard and the southern part of Broad Street were supplied with 600-candlepower bulbs; parks and squares were lit with 250-candlepower lamps; while outlying country roads and suburban sections were illuminated with smaller lights of 100-candlepower.

With the disappearance of the light that had been so intimately connected with his career, A. H. Manwaring, engineer of transmission and distribution, retired on December 31, 1927, after more than forty-five years of service. In 1879, he had joined the Brush Electric Company of Cleveland and had been sent to Philadelphia to superintend the installation of equipment. It was Manwaring who set up the isolated Brush plants in the Continental Hotel and in Thomas Dolan's mills. In 1882, Dolan brought him into The Brush Electric Light Company of Philadelphia as assistant superintendent, and he had remained with the system ever since. Among his contributions were the broad carbon arc lamp, the electrically operated tower wagon for trimming arc lamps, the electrically operated pole truck, and the plow for the rapid installation of underground cable.

The changeover from direct to alternating current was a far larger project than the elimination of arc lamps. It took a great deal longer to accomplish, not being finally completed until 1935, by which time the changing of customers' installations had cost the Company nearly $8,000,000. This was a lot of money, but it was insignificant when compared to the advantages of a single system for Philadelphia—better continuity of service, reduced capital investment, and smaller operating expense. Although several cities had completed changeover programs before Philadelphia Electric, none of them was of the same magnitude.

Electric motors rather than lights created the most perplexing and multifarious problems for the changeover engineers. Most motors ran on direct current and had to be replaced or converted. Philadelphia Electric did not believe that its customers should pay for this changeover, and offered two plans for supplying alternating current machinery in place of direct current equipment. By one agreement, the Company leased alternating current apparatus to a customer, who would have free use of it as long as he remained a customer at the address recorded in the lease. By a direct exchange agreement, alternating current motors were traded to the customer for his direct current motors. There were at least two hundred and fifty kinds of apparatus in one hundred classes to be exchanged, including seventeen carloads of electric fans. In the "shirtwaist district," there were thousands of sewing machines of every type and age to be reckoned with. It took considerable ingenuity on the part of the changeover branch to solve the countless problems involved.

During the first four years of the program, the load on the direct current system increased rather than decreased. No one had thought it possible that the load in the Edison district would grow so fast, and it was obvious

PLYMOUTH MEETING SUBSTATION

Northern terminus of power lines from Conowingo and point of interconnection between the Company, Pennsylvania Power & Light, and Public Service of New Jersey.

W. C. L. Eglin

Walter E. Long

N. E. Funk

H. N. Ramsey

that the Company had started to make the changeover none too soon. By refusing to become discouraged, and by keeping relentlessly at the task, the changeover crews slowly began to win out, until, at last, direct current was eliminated from the system.

In 1935, Liversidge sat in his office, relaxed in the thought that one of the most fantastic efforts ever made by an electric company had been brought to a successful conclusion. Suddenly he was aware that the lights were dimming—they went out! Dashing down to the load dispatcher's office, he found nothing but pandemonium and darkness. A total shutdown at Schuylkill Station had interrupted the electric supply to a portion of the central city district, including a section of the new A-C network. "We can't get it back," cried the load dispatcher. "Every time we close in a feeder switch, it opens; it is impossible to hold it in."

The horrible thought crossed Liversidge's mind that perhaps Philip H. Chase's system would not work after all. Perhaps Insull was right. Maybe the changeover was nothing but a multimillion-dollar blunder. But Liversidge knew Chase's original calculation, and he knew that if he closed in on everything and blocked relays, from a theoretical standpoint the system would hold. He issued a series of orders: clear one bus at Schuylkill; after blocking the relays, throw all feeders in the area affected onto the cleared bus; place a generator on this bus at low voltage and then slowly raise the voltage. Liversidge waited, his eyes glued to a lamp. In a matter of seconds the lights were back, the telephone rang and the word came through—"everything's holding!"

Exhausted by strain, his nerves on edge, Liversidge did something he always regretted. Turning to the chief dispatcher, he barked, "Why in the hell did I have to come down here to tell you what to do? Why didn't you do it yourself?" Then, on legs that could hardly support him, he made his way back to his office.

The changeover simplified the marketing of electric motors in Philadelphia. Only alternating current motors were sold, and they could operate anywhere in the city. Philadelphia Electric promoted the sale of electric appliances of all sorts. In a five-year period ending in 1927, the Company sold $9,000,000 worth, which represented about forty per cent of the sales in the Philadelphia area. Next to Commonwealth Edison of Chicago, Philadelphia Electric was the largest retail distributor of electric household devices in the country. Among the major types of equipment it sold in these years were the following:

95,761 irons	2,377 sewing machines
54,047 cleaners	2,057 ironers
23,409 lamps	566 refrigerators
21,289 washing machines	340 oil burners

Despite hard campaigning, refrigerators were not yet popular. "Domestic refrigeration is here to stay," stoutly advertised Philadelphia Electric in offering easy payment terms on refrigerators or refrigeration units for iceboxes. Oil burners were also slow in winning public acceptance. In 1924, the Company vigorously advertised the advantages of automatic oil heating for the home. It took its first step in radio broadcasting that fall by sponsoring a series of nontechnical talks about electric service. More than 1,000 electrically driven, oil-heated furnaces were on its lines, it proudly announced. Three years later, there were twelve times that number, but this was merely the beginning.

Another form of heating—steam heating—was provided from the Edison Station to Philadelphia Electric's own buildings, to Gimbel's, the Jefferson Hospital, and to a few other places. Steam heating had not proved profitable, and, with the boilers at Edison due to be condemned at any time, there was a temptation to discontinue it. The Company, however, recognized a moral obligation to its steam customers. Moreover, by supplying steam heat to large users, it minimized the likelihood of their generating their own electricity. In 1927, the directors decided to build up the steam business and make it pay. A plant was erected at Ninth and Willow Streets, enabling the Company to shut down the inadequate steam plant at the Edison Station. To develop a market for steam heat, Day & Zimmermann were hired to survey business prospects.

Progress brought its special problems, not the least of which was the growing popularity of radios. More and more people were fastening earphones on their heads and listening intently to these novel machines. Scores of radio clubs were formed, and at their meetings it was often agreed that static and other interference were the fault of the electric company. In January, 1924, the Lansdowne Radio Club accused the Company of drowning out broadcast reception in Delaware County. A petition signed by owners of radios from the smallest crystal set to the most elaborate model was delivered to 1000 Chestnut Street.

This petition and other similar incidents led Philadelphia Electric to undertake the task of locating and minimizing sources of radio disturbance. During 1924, the technical section of the transmission and distribution department handled 800 complaints of this nature. Philadelphia Electric was one of the first large utilities to recognize its seeming responsibility to the public in this regard, and to realize that radio reception was a powerful agent for creating either good will or antagonism toward electric companies.

The enormous development of radio during the twenties was one of the phenomena of the times, and Philadelphia was a center of the industry. In 1922, A. Atwater Kent started making radios in a factory built on less than two acres. Five years later, his Philadelphia plant covered fifteen and a half acres. Demand for Kent's radios in 1926 was such that he stepped up production to 5,300 sets a day. At peak production, his output was eleven sets a minute. From having been a curiosity, radio was fast becoming as much a part of the American way of life as the telephone, the automobile, the motion picture—as electricity itself.

Liberal-minded statesmen dedicated themselves to the ideal of introducing electricity into every home in the country. They were particularly concerned over the lag in rural electrification. When Gifford Pinchot became governor of Pennsylvania in 1923, he called in Morris Llewellyn Cooke. He was looking for an expert on electricity and had heard that Cooke knew all there was to know about it. "Governor, I'm a mechanical engineer," said Cooke. "I know nothing about electricity." But this was no drawback. As Cooke pointed out, you do not have to know French to use plaster of Paris. Pinchot appointed Cooke director of the Giant Power Survey Board which had the responsibility of recommending a policy that would best secure "an abundant and cheap supply of electrical current."

"Giant power" was a term used for great pools of power at the major sources of supply—the coal mines and the waterways. Another term that came into popularity was "superpower"—the interchange of power between public utility systems. Under Cooke, the old study of building power plants at coal mines went futilely on. Because of the publicity given to this concept, Philadelphia Electric in 1925 warned its customers that the idea was not practical. "Electricity must be generated where there is plenty of water. An electric light and power plant requires 600 tons of water for every ton of coal in order to condense the steam and cool the turbine bearings. Most coal mines are not near water." But Pinchot was rapturously enthusiastic about Cooke's studies: "Giant power proposes to bring electricity in a cheaper and more reliable form than ever before to every home, every farm, every factory, every mine, every consumer of power in the state. . . . The power stations will be located at the very mouths of the mines and the current there produced will be transmitted to every hamlet and every home throughout the state. The savings on the transportation of coal will be enormous. Our minds are almost staggered by the possibilities of the new plan."

Promoters of visions like this were also receptive to the idea of public ownership of electric utilities, although on the municipal level, public ownership, once a fad, was now in a sharp decline in America. By May, 1926, 1,129 municipal plants had been abandoned in favor of private companies. Many politicians, however, were eager to stimulate the concept of broad public ownership. Far-reaching roles for the Federal government in utility ownership were suggested. Herbert Hoover rejected such ideas by declaring that the electric industry of the nation would break down if the burden of government ownership was placed upon it: "We find many people enthralled with the notions of 'superpower' or 'giant power,' who conceive it a superimposed financial and industrial structure over all existing structures. No superstructure of this sort is possible. Superpower means interconnection of systems and larger central stations scattered over the whole Union."

In line with Hoover's viewpoint and with his recommendation that power pools be created, Philadelphia

Electric joined with two other utilities to establish the first great American interconnection of electric systems. The project had its inception in a conversation between Norman J. Reinicker, operating superintendent of the Pennsylvania Power & Light Company, and N. E. Funk, operating engineer of Philadelphia Electric. These two engineers discussed the idea with their counterpart at Public Service Electric and Gas Company of New Jersey. Funk then brought the matter to Liversidge's attention, who, in turn, interested Eglin in the possibility. After months of the most exhaustive studies and committee work, Philadelphia Electric enthusiastically endorsed the project.

In September, 1927, a tri-party contract was signed by Walter H. Johnson, Thomas N. McCarter, president of Public Service, and Sidney Z. Mitchell, chairman of the board of Pennsylvania Power & Light. The contract provided for the interconnection of the three systems with 220,000-volt transmission lines ringing an area of many thousands of square miles, and creating the largest pool of electric power in the world—3,000,000 horsepower. No interconnection had ever before been attempted for the transmission of such large blocks of energy by independently operated companies.

From Siegfried, Pennsylvania, eight miles north of Allentown, a transmission line was to run eighty-two miles to a switching station at Roseland near Newark, New Jersey. Also from Siegfried, a forty-nine-mile line was to go to Plymouth Meeting, Philadelphia Electric's switching station where the Conowingo lines came in. The station at Roseland was to be connected with Philadelphia Electric by a seventy-seven-mile line, thus completing a ring into which all the generating stations of the three companies could feed. This was a giant project, and would cost many millions of dollars to build.

The advantages of the Interconnection were numerous. The peak loads of Philadelphia Electric and Public Service came in the evening, and their seasonal peak in December. Since the load of the Pennsylvania Power & Light Company was largely a coal mining and steel load, its peak demand was in the daytime, and its seasonal peak in the autumn. By connecting the systems with their diversified load characteristics, it was possible to make a favorable exchange of power in large blocks, with consequent economy of operation and savings in investment. By pooling the generating capacities of the group, a fewer number of generating units would be needed to carry the load, and fewer needed to protect the service. The production of low-cost current by Conowingo could be absorbed, high efficiency stations could be used to the maximum, and less economical generating facilities could be spared. The availability of all stations in the three systems to care for service in extensive and unexpected emergencies, such as a breakdown of generating capacity, shortage of fuel, and unforeseen increases in load, was another important advantage.

The interconnection between Philadelphia Electric and Pennsylvania Power & Light was completed in 1928, and in 1931 the tie-in with Public Service was made. In practical operation, the Interconnection soon proved its worth. It was one of the outstanding co-operative ventures in which Philadelphia Electric has joined.

These years, during which the Company was so actively increasing its business and broadening its interests, inevitably brought major changes in personnel. McCall's health had not materially improved after his serious illness, and in June, 1924, he was relieved of the details of running the Company by being appointed chairman of the board. His faithful friend and long-time associate Walter H. Johnson then stepped into the presidency;

Arthur B. Huey was elected senior vice-president, and Horace P. Liversidge was promoted to the vacant vice-presidency. When informed by McCall that this was to happen, Liversidge refused the position out of deference to his chief, Eglin. He feared that Eglin might be upset at his assistant's being given equal rank. "You'll do what you're ordered to do, won't you?" demanded McCall, who was never a man to be trifled with. Liversidge hastily assented. McCall then ended the matter: "I'm ordering you to be vice-president."

McCall continued to preside at board meetings, attending the last one of 1925 on December 22. It was his final appearance. On January 29, 1926, he died at the age of fifty-six, having devoted his life to Philadelphia Electric.

At the annual meeting in April, Johnson announced that the board of directors had adopted a resolution in recording McCall's death. The stockholders rose to their feet while Johnson, in a voice that faltered from time to time, read:

Joseph B. McCall, from whose monument—The Philadelphia Electric Company—invisible links stretch to almost every main industry and by far the greater number of hearthstones in the city he loved, was a businessman of genius and rare discernment. He was a pioneer in the great electrical industry that is revolutionizing the world, and one of the four or five outstanding executives of light and power companies serving American centers of population. As an employer, his interest in an army of employees was not bounded by the walls of the counting room and the powerhouse, but led him in a spirit neither perfunctory nor patronizing but that of a brother man, to further their welfare in all ways that he could. He was a friend who drew others affectionately to him, an optimist, a wit, a worker, a fair fighter, a real man.

Unfortunately, McCall's death left a void that could not immediately be filled by anyone in his organization. McCall had believed that Johnson could carry on for him, and certainly Johnson had been the recipient of major recognition in the electric industry—he had served as president of both the Association of Edison Illuminating Companies and the National Electric Light Association. Moreover, the directors had always liked Johnson. Several months after McCall's death, they expressed their confidence in him by raising his salary $15,000, making it twice as much as that of the vice-presidents.

Before long, however, the directors found it necessary to strengthen Johnson's hand. Liversidge was elected general manager, reporting directly to the president and helping him in the practical business of running the Company. Walter E. Long, who had distinguished himself in the Conowingo hearings, was added to the list of vice-presidents. Then, in April, 1927, an executive committee of directors was appointed, which, in effect, assumed control of the major executive functions. This committee met with the president in his office every Monday, and took over the responsibility of authorizing all capital expenditures. New faces appeared at the board. Morris R. Bockius, counsel for the Company, took McCall's place, and in May, 1927, two more directors were elected—Thomas Newhall of Drexel & Company, and Vice-President Eglin.

Through the years of the mid-twenties, the Company had prospered under McCall and Johnson. It had made repeated reductions in its rates. "Every time we made a dollar," said McCall in 1924, "we gave the public part of it. It has been one of our best assets." Philadelphia Electric continued to pay wage dividends to its employees, and benefited its stockholders with an extra dividend in 1926 and with stock allotments at par, although on one of these occasions the stock was selling at double par. Increased need for capital resulted in raising the authorized capital stock from 4,000,000 to 6,000,000 shares in 1927. Everything had the appearance of going well. By the end of 1927, the number of customers on the lines had swollen to 495,250, and the future of the Company looked more than promising.

One final triumph for Philadelphia Electric in 1927 was the completion of its new office building—the Edison Building—at the corner of Ninth and Sansom Streets. The number of the Company's employees totaled more than 7,000 that year, and more space simply had to be provided. Designed by Windrim and towering twenty-three stories high, the Edison Building is, in a way, a monument to Johnson, the man who ordered it built. While the executive offices and the commercial department remained at 1000 Chestnut Street, the other departments began their move to this new building in the last days of 1927.

"I consider it an honor," Thomas A. Edison wrote Johnson, "that your company—one of my pioneer companies—should have its building named for me, and I appreciate and accept the compliment with much pleasure." At his home in West Orange, New Jersey, the inventor tapped a telegraph key at 6 o'clock on the evening of December 31, 1927. This tap conveyed an impulse over ninety miles of Western Union lines to the Edison Building, where it put into operation a sensational floodlighting system that painted the nine upper floors with moving lights in all the colors of the rainbow. Lest its customers fail to recognize what this color opera was, the Company informed them: "Like a resplendent jewel, there suddenly flames into being a kaleidoscopic prism of colors as if by the touch of some prodigal Aladdin's fingertips. It is the towering top of the new Edison Building, bathed in a soft radiance of ever-changing lighting effect, that you see wreathed in colors."

And so 1927 came to its close with Johnson completing the fortieth year of his service with Philadelphia Electric and its predecessor companies. His career with the Company was now all but done, ending in a blaze of color that shone forth from the Company's newest structure. Normally, Johnson would have had to obtain only the approval of his board to light up the Edison Building, but times had changed. Johnson had been required to ask the president of U.G.I. if it would be all right. Control of Philadelphia Electric had, in fact, passed to U.G.I. Within a few weeks, a U.G.I. man would arrive to relieve Johnson of his duties.

CHAPTER 14

Absorbed by U.G.I.

For many years, Philadelphia's financial community had taken for granted the eventual consolidation of U.G.I. and Philadelphia Electric. It was said that the only reason why U.G.I. had failed in its 1913 effort to obtain the electric company was that a suitable position had not been guaranteed McCall.

Hardly a year went by without its rumors that the consolidation was actually to take place. The stocks of the two companies moved together, U.G.I. always selling at a little more than twice that of Philadelphia Electric, a ratio which was kept in balance by the conviction of brokers that Philadelphia Electric's stock would be acquired by U.G.I. on a two-for-one basis when the consolidation occurred.

U.G.I. was a holding company, owning a controlling interest in many electric utilities, as well as in gas companies and street railways. It managed the city gasworks, owned its own construction company, and was showing every sign of vigorous growth. In 1925, U.G.I. purchased the American Gas Company, of which Morris W. Stroud was president. Philadelphia Suburban Gas & Electric Company was a subsidiary of American Gas and came into U.G.I. at that time. In 1927, U.G.I. bought control of Day & Zimmermann, construction engineers and operators of public utilities in fifteen states. This acquisition considerably enlarged U.G.I.'s management organization, an organization which operated from Maine to Florida, and west to Iowa.

There was little question that U.G.I. was expansion-minded. Its selection of Arthur W. Thompson to succeed Samuel T. Bodine as president in 1926 gave proof of that. Thompson, a hard-driving, aggressive man, had been president of the confusingly named Philadelphia Company which controlled the Pittsburgh utilities, including the Duquesne Light Company. On coming to Philadelphia, he gave an interview to the press in which he pointed out the general tendency toward unification of public utility properties, especially by Electric Bond & Share, Samuel Insull, and the H. M. Byllesby organization. Economies, he stressed, resulted from such mergers.

There was no way of controlling merger rumors. Any action of Philadelphia Electric or of U.G.I. could set them off. When U.G.I. took over the American Gas Company, the news brought on a tremendous demand for Philadelphia Electric stock. In August, 1925, rumors were so rife and the Company's stock was bouncing about in such a dizzy way that Johnson issued a public denial of merger possibilities. But in November, rumors were out again and spectacular advances were scored by the securities of both U.G.I. and Philadelphia Electric. With the Company's stock selling at an all-time high of 64¾ in January, 1926, Johnson again denied that a merger was in the wind. The public, however, would not believe him until March, when the merger balloon was punctured and Philadelphia Electric's shares plummeted fifteen points.

Four months later, U.G.I. made an offer to Philadelphia Electric. A special meeting of the directors was called and Johnson hurried back from a vacation in Maine to be present when his board declined the proposition. In the meantime, unfounded stories circulated that Electric Bond & Share was interested in Philadelphia Electric; fear was expressed that Associated Gas and Electric was buying the Company's stock.

In December, 1926, the public learned that Philadelphia Electric was about to evaluate its properties. Again, Johnson denied merger rumors, declaring, "It is simply good housekeeping." The appraisal took six and a half months to complete and at one time had as many as eighty-five men working on it. The figure they established as the "depreciated value" of the Company as of June 30, 1927, was $234,154,753. While this figure could be useful in working out a merger, it could also be used for rate making, for guidance in issuing securities, and for accounting and tax purposes.

More merger talk broke out in May, 1927, when it was learned that Philadelphia Electric had created an executive committee of which Horatio G. Lloyd of Drexel's was chairman. These rumors were fortified by the announcement that Thomas Newhall, another Drexel partner, had just been elected to the Company's board.

Drexel's name was so coupled with the two utility companies that many believed the investment firm controlled the potential merger. The house of Drexel had been established in 1838 as a Philadelphia brokerage office by Francis Martin Drexel, an artist. His son Anthony J. Drexel became the dominant influence in the firm, which, in 1871, joined with J. Pierpont Morgan as Drexel, Morgan & Company. The names of the two interests later separated, but the partners in Drexel's continued as partners in the house of Morgan.

Edward T. Stotesbury, who had entered the employment of Drexel & Company in 1866, became the resident senior partner in 1904. By the mid-1920's, he had about reached the fulfillment of his often expressed ambition—

the acquisition of a $100,000,000 fortune. Not interested in public utility financing, he permitted Horatio G. Lloyd and Thomas S. Gates to become the active heads of the firm. They were the men responsible for its position in the utility field. Through them, Drexel's became the bankers for U.G.I., Philadelphia Electric, and Public Service Corporation of New Jersey. Stotesbury sat on the U.G.I. board; Thomas S. Gates was a Public Service director, and in 1927 also joined the U.G.I. directorate; Horatio G. Lloyd and Thomas Newhall were with Philadelphia Electric. To strengthen its hold on the utility business, Drexel's took in Edward Hopkinson, Jr., as a partner in 1926. Hopkinson had served as counsel for Drexel's during the Conowingo hearings and was one of the best-known banking and public utility lawyers in Philadelphia. In time, he became a director of both U.G.I. and Philadelphia Electric.

The position of Drexel & Company was thus unique in Philadelphia utility circles, and it is simplest, if not most accurate, to refer to all activities emanating from its handsome Florentine office building at Fifteenth and Walnut Streets as the work of Drexel's. Thus, it may be said that it was Drexel's which brought Arthur W. Thompson to U.G.I., while in actuality it was Thomas S. Gates who was responsible. And it may be said that it was Drexel's which was disturbed about certain conditions at Philadelphia Electric, when, in fact, it was primarily Lloyd and Newhall who were concerned. As far as the public was concerned, the absorption of Philadelphia Electric by U.G.I. was to be consummated through the agency of Drexel's, and to split hairs on that point was not very profitable.

Lloyd realized that top management at Philadelphia Electric was not as strong as it should be. Walter H. Johnson lacked the necessary leadership qualifications. A fine man for a smaller company, he had not developed as fast as Philadelphia Electric. Raised in the commercial and business side of the utility, he was unfamiliar with over-all operating problems and with expansion programs. So it was that after McCall's death, Liversidge and Walter E. Long actually ran the company. Lloyd attempted through an intermediary to persuade Johnson to become chairman of the board and let Liversidge take over. When this effort failed, only one course remained open. Liversidge never criticized Lloyd's decision to turn to U.G.I. for help.

Aside from strengthening management, a union with U.G.I. offered other advantages that were carefully studied by Long. With Conowingo about to pour its power into Philadelphia, it was well to have additional outlets for that energy, and U.G.I. had some to offer. Long reported favorably on this basis, and the move toward consolidation began.

The merger could have been avoided had Joseph B. McCall been interested in acquiring new territory, but McCall had always been reluctant to extend his interests beyond Philadelphia. Samuel Insull never could understand why McCall sat idly by while U.G.I. bought up the suburban companies ringing Philadelphia—economy of electric operations so plainly favored a uniting of the Philadelphia and suburban territories. By 1927, they could be united only at the cost of Philadelphia Electric's independence. The tail was to wag the dog; the big electric company had to go to the owners of the smaller properties.

To the north of Philadelphia lay an extensive area served by the Philadelphia Suburban Gas & Electric Company, owned since 1925 by U.G.I. For many years, Philadelphia Electric had been furnishing current to various companies in this district before their consolida-

WALTER H. JOHNSON

JOHN E. ZIMMERMANN

WILLIAM H. TAYLOR

HENRY B. BRYANS

WILLOW STEAM PLANT, PHILADELPHIA
CAPACITY, 756,000 POUNDS OF STEAM PER HOUR

tion into Philadelphia Suburban. Service was handled by 13,000-volt lines from Tacony Station to Jenkintown and Bristol. When Philadelphia Suburban came into being, it requested additional energy; at the same time, Public Service of New Jersey called for a supply of power at Trenton. In 1926 and 1927, Philadelphia Electric built a high-voltage line to supply both needs.

In addition to Philadelphia Suburban, U.G.I. owned the Counties Gas and Electric Company, which operated principally in Montgomery County, and which had a modern generating station on Barbadoes Island at Norristown. These two companies were merged by U.G.I. in 1927 to form the $75,000,000 Philadelphia Suburban-Counties Gas and Electric Company, which supplied substantially all the southeastern part of Pennsylvania adjacent to Philadelphia, including the residential Main Line area, the industrial Schuylkill Valley, and the territory extending from Coatesville to Trenton.

The main economic advantage to be gained by U.G.I. in an absorption of Philadelphia Electric was, of course, the combination of the Philadelphia and suburban electric systems. U.G.I.'s ability to accomplish this made the consolidation highly desirable, and beneficial to all concerned.

There were those, however, whose loyalty to Philadelphia Electric prompted them to try to prevent the move. Liversidge did what he could to block the consolidation. When he realized that it was inevitable, he considered an offer to join another company. By now, he was a national figure in the electric industry; in fact, in September, 1927, he had been elected president of the Association of Edison Illuminating Companies. Alarmed at the possibility of losing Liversidge, Horatio G. Lloyd sounded him out. "I have refused an offer only two weeks ago," the vice-president told Lloyd. "I will say to you that I have no other offer now. I intend to stick if you want me to, and, if I do, no matter how much I hate to think of what is going to be done—I'm not at all favorable—but, if I stick, I want you to know that I'll be just as loyal to the new combination as I was to the old."

In September, 1927, committees from the boards of U.G.I. and Philadelphia Electric reached an agreement on the consolidation of the two companies, the largest consolidation of public utility enterprises yet attempted in the United States. Philadelphia Electric was to retain its own corporate identity and separate organization, but its stock was to be exchanged for U.G.I. stock on the long-predicted two-for-one basis. Any fears that the two thirds of the stock necessary to put this plan in operation would not be turned in were soon put to rest. The stockholders were overwhelmingly in favor of the plan, promptly delivering 95½ per cent of Philadelphia Electric's common stock in exchange for shares of U.G.I.

Public opinion on the absorption of Philadelphia Electric was entirely favorable. According to the *Evening Bulletin:* "So far as public service goes, the Philadelphia community has been exceedingly fortunate in being served by two concerns like The United Gas Improvement Company and The Philadelphia Electric Company. Both have been progressive, enterprising, accommodating, and counting the good favor of their patrons as their chief asset." The *Philadelphia Record* found the consolidation interesting for several reasons, "not the least of which is that both concerns have been managed with so much enterprise, tact, and success that the Philadelphia public looks upon the merger with distinct approval."

On February 14, 1928, control of Philadelphia Electric passed to U.G.I. Walter H. Johnson retired as president and director, receiving the honorary title of assistant to the chairman of the board.* He was succeeded by William H. Taylor. Taylor, forty-seven years old, had been connected with U.G.I. since 1903. An engineer by profession, he was a thoroughly capable utility operator. Other changes on February 14 saw Samuel T. Bodine and Arthur W. Thompson, U.G.I.'s two senior officers, elected directors of Philadelphia Electric, with Thompson designated chairman of the board.

The way was now clear to consolidate Philadelphia Electric and Philadelphia Suburban-Counties Gas and Electric, but this could not be done overnight. On June 1, 1928, the first step was taken when their engineering operations and other functions were combined, and their joint territory divided into five major divisions: Philadelphia; Delaware, headquarters at Chester; Main Line, headquarters at Ardmore; Schuylkill, headquarters at Norristown; Eastern, headquarters at Jenkintown. Not until October 31, 1929, were the two companies actually merged into the newly incorporated Philadelphia Electric Company, a title identical to the Company's previous name except for the article "The," which was dropped.

It was in this way that Philadelphia Suburban-Counties Gas and Electric became part of Philadelphia Electric. The area it brought to the system was about 1,380 square miles in Bucks, Montgomery, Chester, and Delaware Counties, where it had been serving some 112,000 gas and 88,000 electric customers. Added to the system's generating capacity was the 48,000-kilowatt station on Barbadoes Island and the 30,000-kilowatt Cromby Station near Phoenixville, as well as a small plant in West Chester.

The merger put Philadelphia Electric into the gas business in its suburban territory. At West Conshohocken,

* Johnson retired as assistant to the chairman of the board in February, 1929, and died March 30, 1944.

coke oven gas, purchased from the Rainey-Wood Coke Company, was metered, purified, and stored. There was also a carbureted water gas plant at West Conshohocken with a capacity of 5,000,000 cubic feet a day. This plant acted as a compressor station, with a daily maximum output of 12,000,000 cubic feet. At Chester there was a coke oven plant, capacity 3,000,000 cubic feet a day, and another carbureted water gas plant, capacity 4,500,000 cubic feet, and at Oreland a peak load water gas plant with a capacity of 2,000,000 cubic feet. All these plants manufactured 520 Btu gas and were interconnected with various pumping mains and compressor stations. Included in the system were 1,540 miles of mains; gas holders were located at Oreland, Bristol, Pottstown, West Chester, Coatesville, Chester, West Conshohocken, and Upper Darby.

To supply increasing demands, in 1930 a 10,000,000-cubic foot gas holder, one of the largest in the country, was ordered to be erected at West Conshohocken. Meanwhile, under the direction of E. G. Boyer, manager of gas production, work went ahead on the development of the reformed oil gas process which was soon to make available for domestic and industrial purposes gas produced from a crude oil by-product obtained from the Sinclair Refining Company at Chester. The cost of this crude oil by-product was considerably less than the cost of manufacturing carbureted water gas. Before long, Philadelphia Electric was furnishing it to Pottstown, Reading, and Wilmington, where local gas companies shut down their carbureted water gas plants.

The benefits of the unification of the Philadelphia and suburban electric companies were soon evidenced in rate reductions. In May, 1929, Philadelphia Electric authorized a $900,000 reduction, and in September, Philadelphia Suburban sliced its rates by $700,000. On September 1,

1930, a little less than a year after the merger, Philadelphia Electric cut its rates an additional $1,864,000. With the consolidation of the properties, antiquated stations became a thing of the past. In 1930, the historic Edison Station, which had been put into operation by Professor Marks in 1889, ended its career, and the old Tacony Station, built by The Suburban Electric Company in 1891, was abandoned. Philadelphia Electric had not made any enlargements to its steam generating plants since 1925, but in 1930 it purchased a half interest in Deepwater Station. This electric plant had been built by the American Gas and Electric Company and U.G.I. American Gas and Electric disposed of its share to the Atlantic City Electric Company, one of its subsidiaries, and U.G.I.'s interest was acquired by Philadelphia Electric through a newly formed subsidiary, Deepwater Light and Power Company. Deepwater had a capacity of 106,000 kilowatts and was located on the east bank of the Delaware River, four miles south of Pennsgrove, New Jersey. Submarine cables brought its power under the river to Pigeon Point, where it entered the lines of the Delaware Power & Light Company for transmittal to the Philadelphia Electric system. A substantial part of this energy never actually reached the Company's territory, being sold to Delaware Power.

While Philadelphia Electric was shaking down into its new pattern of operations, a number of personnel changes took place. Ninety-one-year-old Jeremiah J. Sullivan, who had come from County Cork as a boy and who had been a director since 1899, and J. R. McAllister, a director since 1905, both died in 1928, and Charles E. Ingersoll, a director since 1904, resigned in 1931. Onto the board came a U.G.I. director, Thomas N. McCarter, the picturesque president of Public Service Corporation of New Jersey. Czar of New Jersey utilities, McCarter was wont to emphasize his remarks by bellowing at the top of his lungs and pounding on the table. New directors took the place of old, with Edward Hopkinson, Jr., of Drexel's replacing Thomas Newhall, who had retired from the banking firm to become financial vice-president of the Penn Mutual Life Insurance Company.

Changes affecting the officers found Vice-President and Comptroller Walter E. Long resigning in September, 1928, to become vice-president in charge of accounting at U.G.I., where he was eventually to become president. Into Long's place stepped Edward Porter. Porter had been with U.G.I. since 1894, and had been serving as its general auditor. In June, 1929, N. E. Funk was promoted to vice-president in charge of engineering, and, a few months later, Henry B. Bryans, the Company's assistant general manager was also advanced to a vice-presidency. Bryans had come to U.G.I. in 1907, and had spent many years with the suburban electric companies before they were brought into the Philadelphia Electric system.

These changes were of a relatively routine nature and presented no extraordinary problem. The most important personnel change of all in this period, however, was not so routine. It is doubtful that the personality of Arthur W. Thompson was well suited to the position he filled. Embarrassing problems arose in management, and the house of Drexel, which had brought him to the job, scarcely knew what to do. The difficulties stemmed in large measure, no doubt, from the condition of Thompson's health, which was visibly failing. In December, 1928, John E. Zimmermann of Day & Zimmermann, a man long prominent in Philadelphia engineering circles, was persuaded to lend a hand. Zimmermann became a director of Philadelphia Electric and chairman of a hastily reconstituted executive committee. Thompson, meanwhile, went on a leave of absence which terminated the next month in his resignation, his death following in November, 1930. Zimmermann, who protested that he did not want the positions, and accepted them "without obligation to continue the same for an indefinite period," became president of U.G.I. and chairman of the board of Philadelphia Electric.

The years 1928 and 1929, when U.G.I. was absorbing Philadelphia Electric and unifying it with the suburban company, were the greatest years the electric industry had ever experienced. Prosperity was at its height, and business was confidently willing to invest in the future. In 1928, the Reading Railroad announced a $20,000,000 program for the electrification of its Lansdale, Chestnut Hill, Hatboro and Langhorne lines, and the Pennsylvania Railroad outlined a seven-year schedule for the largest railroad electrification program in the world. Some 325 miles of road were to be electrified at a cost of $100,000,000.

Progress and excitement marked these boom times. At one end of the city in March, 1928, the magnificent new Philadelphia Museum of Art opened to the public, while in May, at the other end of the city, Federal receivers sold $10,000,000 worth of Sesqui-Centennial equipment for $500,000. In 1929, everyone flocked to the theaters to see talking pictures, such as "The Wild Party," which featured the "It" girl, Clara Bow. "Noah's Ark," starring Dolores Costello, came to the Aldine in March, proclaimed by Warner Brothers as "Love's call through the centuries sounded by the life-like voice of Vitaphone . . . the most stupendous pageant that ever thrilled mankind." This film was the biggest spectacular since "The Ten Commandments" in 1923, but the sound was poor. A reviewer for the *Public Ledger* commented: "The picture deserves better sound effects than it has got, though it may stump the studio engineers to reproduce audibly the destruction of the population of the earth and all its works."

Some undesirable strangers occasionally came to Philadelphia to see the movies. Emerging from a Market Street theater on May 16, 1929, "Scarface Al" Capone and a henchman walked into the waiting arms of a cordon of police and were whisked away. The reputed king of Chicago gunmen and bootleggers and his friend were both carrying fully loaded .38 caliber revolvers, which gave the city's authorities the welcome opportunity to jail them for a year.

In 1929, Martin Maloney, a Papal Marquis and founder of Philadelphia Electric, died at the age of eighty, leaving an estate estimated at $8,000,000; the Tacony-Palmyra Bridge opened; the city commenced negotiations with the United States Shipping Board leading toward the acquisition of Hog Island as the site of a municipal airport; and the controversial Thomas E. Mitten continued to make headlines. In September, the city controller brought suit to eliminate him from the transit scene, charging that the Mitten regime was marked by exploitation of the finances and management of P.R.T.

Mitten did not seem to be worried; he went fishing. Alone and at an early hour on October 1, he rowed out onto the lake at his vast estate in the Poconos. He anchored his skiff and then fell overboard, his heavy boots and clothing dragging him to the bottom. Attention immediately centered on P.R.T. affairs. Among the strange discoveries uncovered by the indefatigable Milo R. Maltbie was the fact that $320,000 had been charged to P.R.T.'s capital account for money spent on lawyers, engineering experts, and publicity in connection with the Conowingo fight and the attempt to gain control of Philadelphia Electric. Maltbie summed up the results of this improper charge to capital: the proxy campaign had failed; the fight against Conowingo had been abandoned; the demand for a review of Philadelphia Electric rates before the Public Service Commission had never been pressed. Later disclosures resulted in Mitten's entire estate being turned over to P.R.T. The day after the traction magnate's death, a Philadelphian, encountering three glum-looking members of the law firm which had represented him, facetiously remarked, "You look like the three little kittens who lost their mittens."

In October, 1929, the month that Mitten died, the world honored Thomas A. Edison, who fifty years before had produced the first incandescent electric light. Philadelphia Electric outdid itself in designing impressive lighting effects for the local celebration of "Light's Golden Jubilee." Another event also occurred that month, one which heralded far-reaching consequences— 1929's famous bull market collapsed.

CHAPTER 15

Hard Times

Throughout the stock market boom of 1929, utility shares had led the way. When the market had an occasional sinking spell, utilities were the rallying point for another upward surge. Investors had become "utility minded" in the solid belief that electric light and power stocks were the soundest of investments. They bought eagerly of Electric Bond & Share, Associated Gas and Electric, and Insull Utility Investments in the overoptimistic expectation that through the magic of holding companies the earning power of utilities would be greatly enhanced, and would justify the high prices of holding company securities.

Early in 1929, the houses of Morgan, Drexel, and Bonbright created the United Corporation, which soon held important minority interests in U.G.I., Public Service Corporation of New Jersey, and the Niagara Hudson Power Corporation in New York State. The same firms also formed Commonwealth & Southern, which controlled Commonwealth Power, Penn-Ohio Edison, Southeastern Power and Light, and Allied Power & Light Corporation, and had interests in numerous other operating companies. Investors looked to United Corporation and Commonwealth & Southern to link up the principal utilities on the Atlantic seaboard in a co-operative interchange of power which would permit tremendous economies in their operations. It was through such holding companies that public utilities became conspicuous in the market place.

In June, 1929, Stone & Webster reported that during the previous six years the utility industry had sold $11,424,000,000 worth of securities, about one fourth of the total issues offered to the public. In earlier years, electric companies had not been considered a good investment, and the expansion of operating companies had consequently been restricted for want of capital. Financing his growing company had been McCall's most difficult problem. Except in the case of a few large metropolitan companies like Philadelphia Electric, the most feasible way to finance operating companies was by making them a part of a holding company, whose securities, having behind them a whole group of operating companies, could be readily marketed. Through holding companies it was also possible to consolidate operations in geographical areas, with attendant savings in expenses by means of interconnections and co-ordinated service. Liversidge maintained that the holding company was just as important to the early expansion of the electric industry as was the improvement of generating and transmission facilities.

Unfortunately, this expansion was accompanied by inflation of stock values, which often resulted in unreasonably high rates. Companies had to earn enough to justify the investment. Not enough thought was given to the public welfare, and little concern was had for public relations. "Inevitably," observed John E. Zimmermann, "in an industry which had expanded so rapidly and has had to solve so many new and difficult problems in finance, engineering, and management, mistakes have been made, unsound financial practices followed in some instances and unwise managerial policies put into effect in others."

U.G.I. and Philadelphia Electric were well aware of dangers to the electric industry. Their bankers had set up United Corporation and Commonwealth & Southern to purchase properties which might otherwise fall into the hands of holding company entrepreneurs whom Drexel's and others distrusted. Philadelphia utility leaders, having safeguarded their interests close to home, began to feel concern at Insull's operations. Without any regard to geographical unity, he was purchasing companies all over the country, and was paying too much for them. These inflated values went into his holding company structures. There were other complaints about Insull leadership, and in 1931 both U.G.I. and Philadelphia Electric resigned in protest from the National Electric Light Association.

Long before this, Insull had managed to injure the industry's reputation. In 1926, he contributed $125,000 to the senatorial campaign of Frank L. Smith of Illinois. Since Smith was chairman of the Illinois Utility Commission, Insull's gift evoked an outcry. The public could stand just so much, and the Senate naturally refused to seat Smith. This incident helped bring on an eight-year (1928–1935) utility investigation by the Federal Trade Commission with monumental results for the industry, including a public relations blight.

Liversidge had had a premonition that something like this might happen. In October, 1929, a few days before the market crash, he was in Quebec, where, as president of the Association of Edison Illuminating Companies, he was scheduled to address their convention. In his address, he planned to compliment the large holding companies on the accomplishments in which they could take pride, but to warn them on the matter of public acceptance, the need for good public relations. He intended to forecast serious dangers ahead, a widening gap between the holding companies and the public they served, and a gap between management and employee groups. The speech had to be approved in advance by a committee, one of whose members was, next to Insull, probably the best-known man in the industry, a man whose personal fortune was estimated at $300,000,000. This tycoon was infuriated by the speech and, had he not been overruled by the committee, would have forced Liversidge to prepare another address.

To Liversidge, the holding company president had lost sight of the industry's objective—service; he had lost contact with his customers. Liversidge did not hesitate to point this out, reminding the great man that he had started his spectacular career at the bottom, repairing customers' equipment and doing other service jobs. "You were down on the street level when you did that and today you are in the top offices of a forty-story building. If I have any advice to give you, I'd say you had better come down to the street floor and walk around with the average citizen." After a little cogitation, the holding company man replied, "I'm inclined to think you are right."

Throughout 1929, the price of U.G.I.'s stock had advanced, spurred on by a five-for-one split. It crept up to 300, and after the split sold as high as 59. But in October, when the crash came, it declined to 26, went lower in November, and then climbed back to 49 in 1930. In 1931, it broke again, reaching its low in the depths of the depression the next year. The following figures give an idea of what happened to security values.

	High for 1929	Low for 1932
U.G.I.	59	9¼
United Corporation	75½	3½
Commonwealth & Southern	32	1⅝

Philadelphia Electric's common stock was not quoted because it was not traded, nearly all of it being owned by U.G.I. However, the Company did have a preferred issue outstanding, its five-dollar dividend issue, par one hundred. This issue was little affected by the depression, selling usually above par and never declining below 87. When additional shares were offered in 1931, the entire issue was oversubscribed in a single day.

Hysteria selling, however, rather than confident buying characterized these lean times and brought on horrifying failures. The most notable collapse of all was that of Samuel Insull. By 1930, the utilities built and managed by him produced one tenth of the nation's electricity. Their service extended to 5,000 communities in thirty-two states, most of which had been without electricity in 1914. In April, 1932, Insull's holding companies—none of the operating companies failed—went into receivership, taking with them the savings of thousands of investors. This disaster became a political issue in an election year, and Insull was forced to stand trial on many charges, but was acquitted on all counts. Despite the legal verdict, Insull's career remained a source of acute embarrassment to the electric industry.

The market crash stimulated politicians to turn their guns on public utilities. Both Pennsylvania and New York were the scenes of gubernatorial contests in 1930, and the successful candidates, Gifford Pinchot and Franklin D. Roosevelt, made utility regulation and rates major issues in their campaigns.

Pinchot, a progressive-prohibitionist Republican, declared at the outset that the Public Service Commission of Pennsylvania was "the catspaw" of the utility corporations and was "useless or worse." He announced his intention "to break the stranglehold of the electric, gas, water, trolley, bus, and other monopolies on the cost of living and the government of the state." By a slim margin, he won the Republican primary in May, 1930, and then continued his vigorous campaign, inveighing constantly against the utilities. In October, he charged that industries were leaving Philadelphia because Philadelphia Electric's rates were so high. U.G.I. mailed a letter to each of its 95,000 shareholders denying this, and pointing out that rates in Philadelphia were five per cent lower than the average in the United States. Praising Philadelphia Electric for its six voluntary rate reductions during the previous six years, the letter stated, "To attempt to break down the confidence of the public in the utilities in order to serve selfish political ambition is neither fair nor decent."

Although he failed to carry a single ward in normally Republican Philadelphia, and even lost that stronghold of Republicanism, Montgomery County, Pinchot eked out a victory in November. Stirred by bitter memories of the utter failure of the giant power schemes of his first administration, Pinchot lashed out at the utilities in his inaugural address on January 20, 1931. "The task today is to defeat the attack of the public utilities . . . upon the rule of the people." With reference to the Public Service Commission, "We have no more compelling duty than to destroy the corruption upon which the power of the utilities depends." And finally, "Back of the public utilities in their attack on our American form of government is the whole fabric of political corruption, the underworld, the protected racketeer, and criminals of low and high degree." That Pinchot did not back up these inflammatory statements with a single instance of corruption cannot be credited to any sense of timidity on his part. Had he known of any, he would have used the example for all it was worth.

No matter what a utility did, it was wrong. When Philadelphia Electric made one of its customary rate reductions, Pinchot was not pleased. In a radio talk in February, 1931, he warned the public to beware of the Company's "trick," for "the boasted rate reduction occurred in a consumption range rarely reached by the average consumer." Since this reduction was in the first step of the rate and benefited every residential consumer in Philadelphia, President Taylor protested to Pinchot that such a statement "may seriously affect the cordial relations which have existed for so many years between the Philadelphia Electric Company and its customers." This, of course, was exactly what Pinchot wanted to do. Taylor urged him "in the spirit of fair play, to correct the erroneous impressions created by your public utterances." The appeal went in vain.

Pinchot launched a sweeping investigation of the Public Service Commission and championed bills to abolish that agency of the legislature, substituting for it an executive agency—the Fair Rate Board—accountable only to himself. In an appearance before the judiciary committee of the state senate, Zimmermann protested against this arbitrary power: "Do you think that a man who attacks the utilities in such a violent manner and often without regard for the facts is fit to be entrusted with the sole power of hiring and firing the members of the Commission?" Evidently, the committee did not believe that Pinchot was ideally suited for the responsibility, for it killed his fair rate bills. In any event, had the bills passed, it is probable they would have been declared unconstitutional.

Pinchot was furious. He likened the Public Service Commission to a "malignant cancerous growth" which was "sapping the life blood of the people." But he could do nothing about it. In 1932, he traveled the state, making a political issue of alleged excessive electric rates. During all this time, he had failed to uncover any corrup-

Chester Station, 1954. Present Capacity, 284,000 Kilowatts

Delaware Station, 1957. Present Capacity, 467,750 Kilowatts

tion, but in the summer of 1932 he was handed some ammunition. A disgruntled person seeking to strike at Mitten Management fabricated a tale that Mitten had given large bribes to W. D. B. Ainey, who for seventeen years had been a member of Pennsylvania's Public Service Commission and was currently its chairman. Pinchot instantly accepted the story, announcing that he had "conclusive evidence that Ainey had sold the public out." A full-scale investigation was held, but no evidence of wrongdoing was uncovered. Ainey denied that he had received bribes from Mitten, and it was soon quite clear that he was innocent.

Then, a damaging light was brought to bear on Ainey. It was disclosed that in 1926 Arthur W. Thompson of U.G.I. had paid a hospital bill for Ainey amounting to $3,000. Pinchot was delighted. He wrote a friend, "We are having a gay old time up here, and I think we have got Mr. Ainey cold."* Another inquiry was ordered, but Ainey resigned. Protesting that he had never done anything wrong, the commissioner wrote that the precarious condition of his health and his lack of financial means for litigation prevented him from defending his reputation.

Here at last was a triumph for Pinchot, who ridiculed Ainey's reasons for avoiding investigation. But Ainey, a distinguished-looking man of reputation as a utility expert, a former president of the national association of utility commissioners, president of the state Y.M.C.A., a man generally believed to be a good public servant, had not exaggerated the condition of his health. He survived his resignation by only a month.

Pinchot was but one of many political leaders engaged in a bitter attack on the electric industry. Senator George W. Norris of Nebraska, referring to the "power trust," called it "the most disgraceful and far-reaching and

* M. Nelson McGeary, *Gifford Pinchot, Forester-Politician* (Princeton, 1960), 367.

shameful combination that has ever been organized by man," and declared that its leaders had "never done anything except to feather their own nests and deceive the very people who by their pennies contribute to their wealth."

Orators who indulged in diatribes naturally did not stress the accomplishments of the American electric industry. They neglected to mention that the United States enjoyed the most extensive and the cheapest electric service in the world; that the creation of the American electric power industry represented an outstanding national achievement; that while the cost of living in 1931 was fifty per cent higher than in 1913, the average cost of electricity to the consumer had shrunk thirty-one per cent during that period. If electric rates were high, at least they had been going down steadily, while the cost of almost everything else was rising.

It was rather ironic that government representatives should have been so critical of declining electric bills at a time when the taxes they were creating were rising sharply. How many liberal politicians who maintained that rates were too high voted against taxes proposed for utilities? In 1932, Philadelphia Electric's tax bill had risen to $5,856,697, up more than half a million dollars for the year despite declining earnings. Taxes had become an important part, and an uncontrollable part, of the rate structure. They tended to postpone rate reductions and threatened, indeed, to cause a rise in rates!

That the industry needed regulation was true enough, and many utility leaders looked forward to reforms in commission regulations, in financial statements, and in holding company operations. However, they refuted the charge that there was a "power trust," and they fought against public ownership of utilities. Much of the criticism directed at the industry by men like Senator Norris was difficult to come to grips with. Criticism was seldom directed at the relations of individual companies with their customers, but at the relation of the electric industry as a whole to society as a whole. It was futile to point out that the average operating company enjoyed good relations with its consumers and that there was, in fact, no grass roots outcry against electric rates.

Still, utilities were becoming so large that there was a distinct danger of their losing contact with their customers, of their becoming so impersonal that the customer could not make his individual problems known. Ever responsive to the times, Liversidge was conscious of the importance of favorable public opinion, which could best be earned by good customer relations. So important did this matter seem to him that he determined to set up a department for the purpose of giving customers close personal attention.

The organization of this department followed by several years the merger with the Philadelphia Suburban-Counties Gas and Electric Company, when accounting work had been decentralized into the five suburban division offices and the seven district offices which comprised the Philadelphia division. Calls of all sorts—for service, inquiries, and complaints—now came to these offices in far greater volume, thereby increasing their importance as centers for customer traffic.

The calls were taken by the telephone operators, who attempted, not always successfully, for which they were not to blame, to screen them to the proper department, where they were handled by people whose function was only secondarily that of servicing contacts with customers. In 1931, when the customers service department was created, this method was changed. A special group of employees, carefully selected and trained in the technique of answering calls, was established at the various offices. It was to these customers service groups that incoming calls were channeled, and it was their direct and primary responsibility to see that the customer obtained satisfaction.

Philadelphia Electric was the first utility to have such a department. So successfully was it organized, and so effective were its procedures, that it has been copied in part or in full by many other companies. Much credit for the evolution of the department goes to E. B. Myers, Philadelphia division manager who was designated manager of the department. It was Myers and his assistant and eventual successor Henry R. Flanegan who set up the customers service groups in district and division offices. Liversidge considered this work so vital that he kept it directly under his own control and did not assign it to one of the vice-presidents. Eventually, after personnel and public relations were combined and their manager raised to the rank of vice-president, the new department was put under his supervision.

In time, customers service was handling about 12,000 contacts a month, approximately fifty-five per cent of which were by telephone, thirty-five per cent by personal office visits, and the rest by mail. Although the service handles complaints, it is not to be thought of as a "complaint department." About fifty per cent of its calls are orders for turning service on or off; ten per cent are trouble calls—reports on fallen wires, gas leaks, blown fuses; another ten per cent are merchandising inquiries relating to business with that department; five per cent are miscellaneous queries, such as "Can I use my electric iron in Rome?"; and the remaining ten per cent are inquiries about bills and payments. Roughly a quarter of this latter type complain about "high" bills, and provide a reason for making a personal call on the customer, a rare and welcome opportunity in electric utility operations. Investigations of high bills include an analysis of the hours of electric use and the operating cost of the appliances connected to the total metered service. When customers understand how their charges are made up they are generally better satisfied.

Complaints are thus turned to good advantage by customers service operations. In handling all customer dealings, the goal of the department is not only the prevention or removal of grounds for dissatisfaction, but the building of favorable customer attitude. Customers service keeps the pulse of public opinion, and through its experience passed on to management influences Company policy.

The customers service department went into operation in the early stages of the depression. Actually, hard times had hit Philadelphia in the fall of 1930, and conditions were to grow steadily worse through 1932 as unemployment mounted. By December, 1930, it was clear that unless an extraordinary effort was made hundreds of Philadelphia families would be without food on Christmas Day. To forestall hardship, a committee for unemployment relief was set up to raise $5,000,000, with Horatio G. Lloyd as chairman.

In July, 1931, Lloyd was appointed administrator of the bureau of unemployment relief to handle a $3,000,000 emergency loan authorized by City Council. Distress continued to mount, and in the fall of 1931 a United Campaign was formed to raise $9,000,000, taking the place of previous Welfare Federation, Federation of Jewish Charities, and unemployment relief drives. Again the city responded well—Stotesbury gave $250,000, Mrs. Cyrus H. K. Curtis, $300,000. By December, the united fund had swept past its goal to $10,258,000.

Even this was not enough, for Philadelphia was experiencing the worst period of unemployment in its history. When J. Hampton Moore became mayor for the second time in January, 1932, the city was having difficulty in meeting its payrolls, its museums were open only part time, salaries of schoolteachers, policemen, and firemen had to be slashed, and the list of delinquent taxpayers filled eleven newspaper pages, each of eight columns in fine print. In June, 1932, Lloyd's committee for unemployment relief disbanded for lack of funds. With 57,000 Philadelphia families facing dire need, it was realized that relief was beyond private aid. Governor Pinchot responded to Lloyd's appeal and called a special session of the legislature.

Business was in desperate plight by this time. A. Atwater Kent's factory, which in 1929 had reached its maximum extent, covering thirty-one acres, and which was twice as large as any other radio factory in the world, restricted its operations until it had to shut down, never to reopen. Manufactories of all sorts were closing their doors. The effect on Philadelphia Electric was harassing but not crippling. By strict economies, the Company's net income available for dividends even showed annual increases, but for once its growth was stopped. Whereas in 1929 Philadelphia Electric had added 39,062 customers to its lines, and continued to add more in 1930 and 1931, in 1932 it lost 26,360, and its operating income declined by more than $3,000,000.

Among its falling power requirements were those of the street railways. On October 1, 1929, Philadelphia Electric had contracted to supply P.R.T. with its entire energy needs and had taken over the operation of its Beach Street powerhouse. Lessening demands for railway current brought on the abandonment of Beach Street Station in 1932, when its load was shifted to Schuylkill Station. Neshaminy Substation had closed in 1931 because buses had been substituted for trolleys on Easton Road between Willow Grove and Doylestown. Long country trolley runs had had their day.

Although there was no large-scale layoff of Philadelphia Electric employees, vacancies were left open, salesmen quit, and, across the board, some members of the force had to be let out. Frequently, these people could not obtain new jobs; in such cases, the Company provided for their relief with donations of food and fuel, and with orders on local stores for bread and milk. Gone was the wage dividend, the Christmas bonus, hopes of a raise. To retain as many people as possible on the payroll, work was distributed, so that certain employees worked only part time. As demands for power decreased, operations of generating stations were limited. In 1932, Schuylkill Station was shut down during the early morning hours and all day Sundays; Chester Station was closed from May 12 to September 16.

To alleviate suffering in the community, Philadelphia Electric workers gave generously, and the Company adopted the policy promoted by General Electric and U.G.I. of matching dollar-for-dollar the employees' relief donations. "Five days' pay will keep hunger away" was the slogan of the Company's relief drive which started in November, 1931: "Never since the World War has a greater crisis arisen demanding relief funds than will exist this winter among the unemployed." In response to the plea, nearly 7,400 employees, ninety-six per cent of the total, pledged $170,000, more than fifty per cent pledging a full day's pay each month for five months. The Company matched this sum, and in 1932 gave $165,000 more, "due to the unprecedented amount of unemployment with its consequent distress."

At a time when wage earners were acutely apprehensive of their future, Philadelphia Electric took a step to broaden one of their security bases. Because of the rigid medical examinations required for membership in the Company's beneficial association, many employees were deprived of its benefits. To take the place of that coverage, a group insurance plan, paid for in part by Philadelphia Electric, was adopted. Enthusiastically accepted by the employees, this plan provided them life insurance and disability protection without regard to their physical condition, age, or length of service.

During the lean times in the early thirties, Philadelphia Electric workers all turned salesmen. Their first job was to sell coke. At Chester, the coke oven plant was manufacturing gas very economically. Through the distillation of coal, gas passed into the mains, and one of the residues of the process was coke, which was sold to a local blast furnace. On February 15, 1930, the depression forced the furnace to shut down, and the Company was faced with the alternative of selling thousands of tons of coke a year or closing its gas plant. It decided to market the coke in the domestic field, using its employees as a sales force. In four months' time, the improvised coke salesmen had sold $160,000 worth of the fuel. By 1938, when the Chester coke ovens were shut down and the coke campaign came to its end, 425,000 tons of coke had been sold, or given to people who were too poor to buy it.

Because of declining electric demands, the Company embarked on sales campaigns to add load building equipment to its lines. To head up activities of this sort, George E. Whitwell, an outstanding sales executive, was brought to Philadelphia in April, 1931, and made vice-president in charge of the commercial and new business departments. Albert R. Granger has recalled how Whitwell started, selling equipment to Philadelphia Electric's own people. "He would arrange different groups afternoons and evenings at the Edison Building, and with his personal magnetism did a wonderful job in selling the employees commodities for which we were all making current. I know that he sold me one night and I converted a coal-fired boiler and installed a gas water heating system which was truly marvelous." After a campaign of selling to the employees, such as the one in 1931 when they purchased 589 electric ranges, the employees themselves became salesmen and in three months sold 2,269 ranges to the public as part of the Company's endeavor to raise the average domestic consumption.

In the fall of 1931, Whitwell organized a drive to sell 500,000 electric light bulbs, which was about as many as any utility had ever sold in a similar campaign. After working hours in October, the employees went out to ring doorbells in their effort to fill every light socket in every house: "Don't be a bulb snatcher!" In the middle of the campaign, when everyone was all excited about it and comparing sales quotas, newsboys rushed into the Company's offices crying, "Extra! Extra! All about Philadelphia Electric's Lamp Campaign!" The whole front page of the *Public Ledger* was devoted to the story! Near riots took place in some departments. Employees, unaware that the paper was one of Whitwell's publicity stunts, rushed into the streets to buy additional copies. The campaign not only went over the top, it set a world's record with the sale of 1,039,000 bulbs!

The key position of Philadelphia Electric as an outlet for electrical equipment aroused much protest and antagonism among other dealers, and Liversidge stepped in to eliminate causes of complaint. Since about 1908, the Company had conducted a wholesale electrical equipment supply business under the name of The Philadelphia Electric Supply Department. Through this branch it purchased much of the equipment it needed, obtaining it at wholesale rates and saving the manufacturers' commissions. In December, 1928, after many meetings and strong protests from the wholesalers' division of the Electrical Association of Philadelphia, this department was discontinued. The Electrical Association also objected to the Company's policy of free lamp renewals, which had been much abused, and in 1933 the Company ceased giving out new bulbs for old.

As the depression deepened, appliance dealers became increasingly concerned about Philadelphia Electric's retail activities, although actually it was the Company which had pioneered nearly every appliance enjoying local acceptance. To avoid criticism, an appliance sales policy was established which would "best serve the interests of the Company as well as promote relations between Philadelphia Electric and dealers in electrical appliances in its territory." During 1932, successful efforts were made in developing the sale of load building electric appliances through co-operation with retail agencies. In this endeavor, the Company worked closely with the Electrical Association of Philadelphia, of which Liversidge was now president. In reply to the question of how he always happened to be in the right place at the right time, he replied, "If you want to get hit on the head by an apple, stand under an apple tree."

It was in 1932 that Philadelphia Electric adopted a merchandising policy which sought to standardize sales practices and conditions in order to promote profitable dealing in appliances by all logical outlets. Liversidge's role in this co-operative work was honored late in the year when he received the James H. McGraw Award, the highest honor in the electric industry. "He observed in his own city," read the citation, "the demoralizing effects of discord between the power company and the electrical trade. Four years ago, he set himself to expounding the principles and advantages of co-operation within his own company, to synchronize the policies of the utility with the essentials of intelligent trade practice, and to establish harmony within the electrical community. . . . He has become the outstanding exponent of a practical co-ordination in sales policies and trade relationships."

In the early thirties, everyone was urged to spend, not to hoard. To stimulate business recovery, and to alleviate unemployment, Hoover requested industry to continue construction programs. In 1930, Philadelphia Electric spent $24,300,000 on new construction, made its services available to more people, and reduced its rates. In October, 1931, it purchased the Philadelphia Steam Company whose territory lay west of Broad Street adjoining Philadelphia Electric's own steam area. President Taylor announced a plan to spend $4,000,000 in developing central heat. "Fewer smokestacks in the business districts, purer air and cleaner buildings will be accomplished by completion of the program. Building managements will find the care of structures considerably simplified. The development is in line with the best thought of engineers and public health authorities. The growth of central station steam heat service is most satisfactory. There already is an impressive list of buildings using the service. We are to see completed within a year a thirty-three-story building—the Philadelphia Saving Fund Society Building at Twelfth and Market Streets—without a single stack. Every service, including the heating, is to be supplied externally."

In December, 1931, Taylor made public a construction budget of $20,519,645 for 1932, and reported on studies of rate cuts. Wage levels and employment volume for 1931 had been maintained, as well as good service and a large building program; liberal contributions had been given to charities. By such means, Philadelphia Electric had aided the general welfare in a time of acute distress.

In July, 1932, one of the blackest months of panic and business despair, the Company announced the awarding of an $8,500,000 contract to Westinghouse Electric and

Manufacturing Company. Westinghouse was to build one of the largest generators in the world, 165,000-kilowatt capacity, for Richmond Station, and was to build it in Philadelphia where eventually 800 men would be employed on the project. The generator would be needed in two years to help handle the railroad electrification load.

One of the more novel uses of electricity, for air conditioning, was showing signs of its potential in these years. Actually, air conditioning had been in limited use in manufacturing establishments for some time. In 1922, the motion picture industry began to adopt it for its theaters, and by 1931 Philadelphia Electric had installed air conditioning in several of its offices. Its use was spreading to auditoriums, restaurants, trains, and stores. The most notable local example was the completely air-conditioned Philadelphia Saving Fund Society Building.

The early years of the depression had swept the community with fearful effect, but Philadelphia Electric, although experiencing a difficult time, had withstood the shock admirably. While the use of electricity in 1932 had declined throughout the nation to 85½ per cent of its 1929 output, Philadelphia Electric had retained ninety per cent of the boom year's load. Its earning power remained good. Of the $34,032,933 received in dividends by U.G.I. in 1932, $18,100,000 came from Philadelphia Electric.

Thus, when times were at their worst, President Taylor was being realistic when he said, "We look to the future with optimism, confident that business will return to normalcy within a reasonable time, and our policy of expansion gives expression to that confidence and belief." Vastly increased use of electricity by railroads, in air conditioning and refrigeration, and for highway illumination awaited the re-establishment of business. However, the expression that "prosperity was just around the corner" was wearing a little thin.

CHAPTER 16

The New Deal

CONFIDENCE IN THE leadership of the utility industry was shaken in 1931 when responsible corporations like U.G.I. and Philadelphia Electric resigned from the National Electric Light Association (N.E.L.A.). Their resignation represented a protest against holding company policies practiced by Samuel Insull and by Howard C. Hopson of Associated Gas and Electric, as well as a protest against the political activity in which N.E.L.A. had engaged. The Association attempted to right its course by electing to its presidency the distinguished George B. Cortelyou, head of New York City's electric and gas utilities. It was not long, however, before Cortelyou concluded that the politically tainted N.E.L.A. should be abandoned in favor of a new trade organization whose reputation would be free of stigma.

To bring this about, the Edison Electric Institute (E.E.I.) was formed on January 12, 1933, and in the following month N.E.L.A. was dissolved. Most of the electric industry, including Philadelphia Electric, promptly joined the new organization. George B. Cortelyou served as its first president; among its initial trustees were John E. Zimmermann and Thomas N. McCarter. Philadelphia Electric's Vice-President George E. Whitwell was chairman of sales, one of the nine technical committees, and it was under his forceful leadership that major national programs promoting electric refrigeration and electric cooking were carried on. In 1934, Cortelyou was succeeded as president by McCarter, and in 1936 McCarter was followed by Charles W. Kellogg, who, in his days with Stone & Webster, had supervised the building of several Philadelphia Electric power stations, including Conowingo.

While the electric industry was putting its affairs in better order, Franklin D. Roosevelt entered the White House. Business, particularly what was known as "big business," had been largely discredited in the public eye by the stock market crash of 1929 and the unprecedented and ever-deepening depression which followed. Millions were unemployed, other millions had suffered severe financial reverses; a mood of bitterness prevailed. Traditionally, American business had developed through rugged individualism. By and large, it had been permitted to operate without much government regulation and had succeeded in making America the greatest industrial nation in the world. The result seemed to justify the means, and most people had been convinced that government should keep out of business. But the agonizing depression altered this opinion, creating an attitude favorable to strict regulation through Federal agencies.

Roosevelt thus came to power at a time fertile for liberal policies. He promptly initiated his "New Deal," promising a more abundant life for the underprivileged, freedom from fear and want, and committing himself to mammoth public power projects which would provide cheaper electricity. The political atmosphere became charged with concepts of social and economic reform.

Before long, agencies to provide relief and to further New Deal policies came into being, their names usually shortened to initials—the "alphabet soup" agencies. In June, 1933, the National Recovery Administration

(N.R.A.) was set up, its administrator, General Hugh S. Johnson, exercising wide control over industry. Calling for shorter hours and higher wages, Johnson launched an intensive drive for jobs, hoping to put 5,000,000 unemployed back to work by Labor Day. Industries were required to accept N.R.A. codes which pledged co-operation with its program. On August 16, 1933, Philadelphia Electric signed the President's Re-employment Agreement and also subscribed to the N.R.A. electrical code, which guaranteed employees the right to organize and bargain collectively, limited the maximum hours of labor to forty a week, fixed minimum rates of pay at fifteen dollars a week, and restricted child labor.

In the fall of 1933, President William H. Taylor addressed 8,000 Philadelphia Electric employees at Convention Hall. "We have confidence in the New Deal," said Taylor, "and have decided to take a chance by increasing our expenses at the rate of hundreds of thousands of dollars a year, by adding as of November 1, 1933, ten per cent to the wages and salaries of those working on the new limited schedule of hours, in addition to the six per cent effective as of August 16 last." Thus, the Company entered into the spirit of N.R.A., realizing full well that the price it would have to pay for the national recovery effort would be one of ever-increasing costs for labor, materials, and services. N.R.A. was not destined for a long life—in May, 1935, the Supreme Court in a unanimous ruling declared it unconstitutional—but during the period of its activity it did much to further New Deal policies in controlling business, stimulating the labor movement, and bringing on inflation.

As "pump primers," methods to force money to flow again, President Roosevelt set in motion two gigantic relief and credit agencies. The Public Works Administration (P.W.A.) provided Federal funds for large construction programs, such as the electrification of the Pennsylvania Railroad. P.W.A. grants created jobs for thousands, and in Philadelphia financed low rent housing projects and a huge school building program.

The second agency, the Works Progress Administration (W.P.A.), supplied work and wages for the unemployed on Federal made-work projects. In Philadelphia, the largest W.P.A. project was the leveling and grading of the municipal airport on Hog Island, a task which dragged on drearily for years. Despite the millions poured into P.W.A. and W.P.A., the pump seemed always in need of more priming. In September, 1936, there were 66,800 men and women in Philadelphia receiving wages from the Federal government. Despite such employment, the economy was still unhealthy; millions of people remained out of work. It was true that in 1936 and 1937 business did show improvement, but in the fall of 1937 a severe recession set in.

By this time, the city of Philadelphia was virtually bankrupt, unable to meet its payroll. In January, 1938, the city adopted a two per cent sales tax, but its financial position continued to deteriorate. The following year, the sales tax was raised to three per cent, and an unsuccessful effort was made to institute a one and a half per cent wage tax. After five years of unprecedented government spending, the national picture in 1938 was darker than ever. In April, Roosevelt called for nearly $5,000,000,000 to underwrite a comprehensive recovery program through government spending, lending, and credit expansion, but month by month the situation worsened. By August, 1938, some 1,774,255 Pennsylvanians were on the public assistance rolls, the greatest number since the dark days of 1933.

The local and national economic plight took its toll on Philadelphia Electric. Locally, the Company lost municipal business through economy moves which darkened the

THE 165,000-KILOWATT UNIT AT RICHMOND STATION
FROM A PAINTING BY THORNTON OAKLEY

WISTER SUBSTATION

Designed to harmonize with its Germantown residential area

city's street lights. Worse yet, the city did not pay its electric bill. According to the *Philadelphia Record* of November 19, 1938, by the end of the year the city would owe Philadelphia Electric $3,300,000. Failure to pay this money was a serious matter because it depleted the Company's working capital to such an extent that it had to borrow from the banks. On the national front, the Company felt the pressure of the government's gigantic spending. Federal taxes, which were $3,500,000 in 1932, increased to $5,000,000 in 1938; state and local taxes nearly doubled.

While the results of depression, inflation, and recession during President Roosevelt's first six years in office were reflected in many ways in Philadelphia Electric's performance and on its balance sheet, an even stronger influence was brought to bear on the Company by New Deal policies regarding electric rates, regulation of the industry, and the advancement of public power projects. The President had been in office little more than a month when he urged on Congress the creation of the Tennessee Valley Authority (T.V.A.) to develop the Tennessee Valley basin and Muscle Shoals. The measure passed in May, 1933, and its administrator, David E. Lilienthal, soon announced that T.V.A. would serve as a "yardstick" for measuring the fairness of utility rates. T.V.A. had two major objectives: to protect the public more effectively against unreasonable utility rates and financial abuses, and to promote greater use of electricity all over the country.

Investor-owned utilities viewed the building of power plants and the sale of electricity by the government as an infringement on private enterprise. Alarm grew as political leaders encouraged public ownership with increasing gusto. In November, 1934, President Roosevelt flatly declared that community operation of electric power facilities would spread throughout the country "before we are through." The next month, Senator George W. Norris, the great advocate of T.V.A., urged four Tennessee Valley cities to build distribution plants for T.V.A. power, even if it meant "the almost complete destruction" of existing plant values. Small wonder that utility leaders feared that private investment would be destroyed! They brought action testing the right of the government to generate and sell electricity in the Tennessee Valley, but the Supreme Court ruled in favor of T.V.A. Utility stocks became a drug on the market, for how, people asked, could taxpaying, investor-owned utilities compete with the extension of nontaxpaying, government-subsidized operations?

Public ownership of electric systems was given another spur with the establishment in May, 1935, of the Rural Electrification Administration (R.E.A.), headed by Morris Llewellyn Cooke. Through Federal financing, Cooke strenuously promoted publicly owned co-operative ventures "to bring electricity to the farm."

Naturally enough, the enthusiasm for public ownership evidenced in Washington filtered down to state and municipal levels. In 1933, a move to set up a municipal plant in Camden gained support, and Public Service Corporation of New Jersey found itself embattled in an attempt to deny this P.W.A.-financed project entrance into its territory. In New York City, Mayor Fiorello H. LaGuardia applied for Federal assistance in 1934 to construct a municipal electric plant to supply the needs of the city government and provide competition for Consolidated Gas if that company did not lower its rates. How much P.W.A. money he would need, said LaGuardia, "depends on how far we go. If the utility people behave like decent, honest, law-abiding citizens—a very remote and almost impossible supposition—we consider one plan.

Otherwise. . . ." Consolidated Gas was soon threatened from another direction, for in January, 1935, the United States Treasury Department asked for a P.W.A. allotment of $3,780,000 to construct a Federal power plant in New York City.

Meanwhile, in 1934, Philadelphia Electric was having difficulty with City Controller S. Davis Wilson, who was also attacking P.R.T. and U.G.I. Wilson championed some dissatisfied customers and brought a case before the Public Service Commission, maintaining that he would show how Philadelphia Electric was being "milked by Morgan and Company," and charging that its rates were excessive. Commissioner Frederick P. Gruenberg, who conducted the hearings, was not impressed by Wilson's arguments in this case, which was ultimately dismissed. Irritated at the commissioner, Wilson accused him of collusion with Philadelphia Electric. This wild, unfounded charge, which shocked even Pinchot, did not advance Wilson's cause. The Commission barred him from appearing before it again, and branded his conduct "unwarranted, offensive, contemptuous, and insolent." Gruenberg threatened to sue Wilson for slander.

The next year, Wilson, a registered Democrat, obtained the Republican mayoralty nomination, and in November, 1935, defeated Democrat John B. Kelly. As mayor, Wilson did not continue his unprofitable attack on Philadelphia Electric, although he did declare, "I want to see this municipality operate every public utility." He expended a large part of his energy in a fruitless effort to bar U.G.I. from a new lease of the city gasworks. The public used to become excited over this issue, but by 1937 it evidently had more confidence in U.G.I. than in its mayor.

Philadelphia Electric's customer relations were so sound that it was not threatened by municipal agitation.

However, in common with other utilities, the Company did encounter major problems at the state level.

Caught up in the New Deal cyclone that swept the country in 1934, Democrat George H. Earle was elected governor of Pennsylvania. In his inaugural address, Earle called for lower utility rates, and pledged, "This administration will introduce a public utility law so stringent that no Public Service Commission can stultify it without full public knowledge."

Meanwhile—Earle's law was not passed until 1937—the Public Service Commission, its members nearly all Pinchot's reform appointees, were busily reducing rates. In 1934, the Commission limited the return allowable to utilities to six per cent (it had been seven per cent), and between January 1, 1933, and June 30, 1936, it obtained rate reductions totaling $15,000,000 from Pennsylvania operating companies. These reductions were nearly all achieved by informal conferences at which the commissioners set up a tentative rate base and endeavored to show the utility that it was earning more than a fair return. In general, the alternatives were either voluntary reduction of rates or formal proceedings if the Commission felt that such proceedings could be successfully maintained. Officials of Philadelphia Electric were in frequent conference with the commissioners, and the Company lowered its rates substantially in 1933, 1934, 1935, and 1936. Nonetheless, these reductions were not large enough to satisfy Governor Earle. In September, 1936, he charged that rate schedules were producing more than the maximum six per cent profit allowed, and declared that no real rural electrification plan had ever been worked out in Pennsylvania. He demanded that the Commission co-operate with the R.E.A. to electrify farm homes in all parts of the state. Richard J. Beamish, the vocal counsel for the Commission, took up the cry. In a radio address, he asserted that rates were too high, rural electrification had been a "fake," utility executives were in partnership with the Republican state organization, and that "through mergers, write-ups and dizzy bookkeeping methods, Pennsylvania operating companies were being milked of their profits for the benefit of big-wig New York heads of holding companies."

The end of the Republican-dominated Public Service Commission had been in sight since Earle's election. In 1937, it was dissolved and superseded by a five-man Public Utility Commission. Committed to a policy of sweeping rate reductions, the new Commission was granted extremely broad powers, including the right to declare temporary rate reductions. Its expenses were to be paid by the utilities themselves.

The Commission moved rapidly, declaring rate reductions for one company after another. In October, 1937, it ordered Philadelphia Electric to slash its rates by $3,146,000, the largest reduction yet imposed on a Pennsylvania utility. Beamish, now a member of the Public Utility Commission, glibly suggested that $3,000,000 more should be cut off. Fortunately, the other commissioners were more interested in making fair rates than headlines.

Although it was the aim of government to increase the prices of commodities, services, and labor, government officials were at the same time dedicated to the principle of reducing electric rates. They argued that if the rates were reduced more people would buy electricity and the utilities would not suffer. Unlike some of the other major systems, Philadelphia Electric had always made its rate reductions voluntarily until the enforced reduction of 1937. Of course, had it not done so, similar reductions would have been imposed upon it. The Company's record of rate reductions during the early Roosevelt years is as follows:

Year	Electric	Gas	Steam
1933	$2,170,000	$180,000	
1934	51,000	27,000	$58,000
1935	3,087,000	50,000	
1936	1,249,000	11,000	
1937	3,146,000		

While regulatory commissions lowered rates at a quicker pace than the industry deemed altogether convenient and while rising taxes hit utilities hard, the threat of competition by publicly owned systems did not prove as damaging as had been feared. The municipal plants to serve New York City and Camden were never built. In Pennsylvania, the trend toward municipal ownership was not consequential, and the R.E.A. systems were neither numerous nor large. No municipal plant or R.E.A. cooperative was built in Philadelphia Electric territory. Lansdale, to be sure, had a successful municipal plant, but it did not stem from this period; its operation was nearly as old as Philadelphia Electric itself.

The New Deal legislation that was to have the most pronounced effect on the Company's history had to do with holding companies. In February, 1935, the administration introduced bills in Congress to abolish holding companies, with the exception of a few whose operations were of economic necessity to a geographical area. Speaking in favor of the Wheeler-Rayburn bills, Senator Burton K. Wheeler of Montana explained that they were designed to stop "the concentration of economic power," a necessary move "to avoid Fascism or Communism." The so-called holding company "death sentence" in these bills evoked horrified outcries from utility leaders.

John E. Zimmermann pointed out how Philadelphia Electric's territory, a logical entity, had been brought together through U.G.I., a holding company: "What valid reason can be advanced for believing that a system which has planned, financed, and built an 'electric America' should now be ruthlessly broken up?" The nation's utility companies massed forces under the leadership of the E.E.I. to combat the passage of the holding company act. Philip H. Gadsden, chairman of the E.E.I.'s committee of public utility executives and a vice-president of U.G.I., led the industry's attack on this legislation. Zimmermann, too, played an active part, circularizing U.G.I.'s stockholders to protest the bills. Many people believed that the immediate investigation of Zimmermann's income tax returns by the United States Bureau of Internal Revenue was a vindictive reply to his activity.

After five months of the most intense and bitter debate, the Wheeler-Rayburn bills were enacted into law in August as the Public Utility Holding Company Act of 1935. The Act provided that the Securities and Exchange Commission (S.E.C.) be given jurisdiction over holding companies and their subsidiaries, with the Federal Power Commission being given jurisdiction over companies engaged in interstate transmission or wholesale sale of electricity. All holding companies were ordered to register by October 1, 1935, with the S.E.C., which was then to examine their organization, and to simplify their corporate structure or apply the "death sentence" as it saw fit. However, the great bulk of the industry believed the Act unconstitutional, refused to register, and filed suit to test its validity.

The S.E.C., under the leadership of its chairman, William O. Douglas, agreed not to enforce the law until the Supreme Court decided on its constitutionality. As a consequence, the matter remained open for nearly three years. U.G.I. refused to accept the terms of the Act. Philadelphia Electric, which had also refused to accede, was later absolved from doing so by an S.E.C. ruling that, since the Company was predominantly an operating rather than a holding company, it was not required to register.

While the holding companies were beset in their struggle with the 1935 Public Utility Holding Company Act, a labor movement, unleashed in part by New Deal policies, was making rapid progress. In 1935, John L. Lewis, impatient with the conservative leadership of the American Federation of Labor (A. F. of L.), established a Committee for Industrial Organization (C.I.O.). By means of a new technique—the "sit-down strike," developed for mass production industries—the C.I.O. organized a large part of the vast automobile industry. In 1937, the United States Steel Corporation capitulated by recognizing a C.I.O. union. From coast to coast, a kind of warfare was carried on between labor leaders and harried management as industry after industry was organized.

In June, 1937, attempts were made to organize the workers of the P.R.T. and of the Philadelphia Gas Works Company, operated by U.G.I. These efforts failed. The 2,300 gasworks employees were satisfied with their own union and rejected the C.I.O., while P.R.T.'s employee union also triumphed in a four-cornered fight.

It is noteworthy that during this period of general labor unrest Philadelphia Electric continued to enjoy satisfactory relations with its employees. It had long ago been firmly established that Philadelphia Electric Company was a good employer. That reputation had been so well maintained and strengthened that the employee body was content with its lot.

The major changes which came about during President Roosevelt's first term and a half were momentous ones for the electric industry. Nearly all of them took place during a fairly constant period of depression, characterized by rising taxes and costs of operation, strict regulation, and rate reductions. Moreover, through Federal subsidy, the concept of publicly owned utility systems was vigorously promoted. The government also lent encouragement to the labor movement. These trends have been discussed in general terms with only occasional references to Philadelphia Electric. How did the Company make out in these trying years of 1933 through 1938? What was it able to accomplish?

In common with other systems, Philadelphia Electric found itself faced by a challenging situation. In a time of depression, it had to increase its business materially; it had to take on additional load at an extremely rapid rate. Failure to do so would mean that the Company could not procure sufficient revenue to offset the rate reductions necessary to meet the competition of government-subsidized power. Additional revenues were also needed to meet the rise in expenses caused by heavy tax increases and mounting costs of nearly everything needed in the Company's day-by-day operations.

It was through the expansion of the domestic use of electricity that the Company conquered the depression and maintained its competitive position. The key to this success was the mushrooming popularity of electric refrigerators, the enormous growth of the refrigeration load. Of the 103,564 refrigerators sold in Pennsylvania in 1933, nearly half of them, 47,100, were connected to Philadelphia Electric lines. During the years 1933 through 1938, approximately one half of the Company's residential customers discarded their iceboxes and purchased their first electric refrigerators. National sales indicate the pace at which household electric refrigerators were gaining acceptance.

Refrigerator Sales

1932	769,666
1933	1,065,105
1934	1,372,526
1935	1,590,023
1936	2,079,535
1937	2,369,025

Other uses for electricity remained to be developed. In 1933, it was estimated that there were not more than 10,000 electric ranges in the Company's territory. Electricity for water heating had limited popularity. For years, the sales organization worked to build up the load from these two appliances. In 1936, more electric water heaters were sold than in the previous four years; results, if rather slow, were at least encouraging. In 1937 and 1938, the number of domestic electric ranges increased thirty per cent. The home use of deep freezers remained for future years, but as early as 1933 Philadelphia Electric's first one, a made-to-order freezer for Mrs. Isaac Starr of Chestnut Hill, was installed. Mrs. Starr's son, Floyd T. Starr, was an ardent gunner and wanted an appliance in which he could keep the ducks and deer he shot for year-round eating. The Starr freezer was so novel that, although installed in a residence, it was referred to as "the first commercial refrigeration installation of its kind."

Many increasing uses of electricity in the home—more lights, more radios, more appliances—combined to raise the average residential load. By 1936, Philadelphians were using more kilowatt-hours of electricity for radios alone than the entire use of residential electricity in 1920. Thus, while the industrial use of electricity fell off during the depression, its use in the home rose sharply. In 1929, the greatest year utilities had thus far experienced, Philadelphia Electric's average residential customer used 499 kilowatt-hours (KWH) of electricity. In the depression years, his average use far outdistanced that record.

1933	645 KWH
1934	675 KWH
1935	718 KWH
1936	793 KWH
1937	874 KWH
1938	959 KWH

The Company's load-building campaigns were remarkably successful because of the leadership of the vice-president in charge of sales, George E. Whitwell. It has been mentioned that he was the first chairman of the sales committee of the E.E.I., where he headed up national programs to increase the use of lighting and to combat the downward trend in the demand for electricity. In 1933, he launched a crusade to educate the public in the conservation of eyesight, and a bureau of the E.E.I. was established to organize the resources of the electric industry in its support. Through his "Better Light —Better Sight" campaign, a new business was created for the manufacture of scientifically designed reading lamps. As the originator of this movement, he shared the James H. McGraw Award in 1935 with Merrill E. Skinner of Niagara Hudson Power Corporation, who served as first chairman of the Better Light—Better Sight Bureau. It was also in 1935 that Whitwell was made chairman of the National Kitchen Modernizing Bureau, which put on a country-wide campaign—"Modernize—Electrify your Kitchen."

The promotional techniques sponsored nationally were, of course, intensively used in Philadelphia Electric territory, where, indeed, some of them had originated. The sales department devised methods for utilizing, from time to time, virtually the entire Philadelphia Electric force to promote the sale of load-building appliances. For example, early in 1934, the "All Employee Electric Range and Electric Water Heater Campaign" was put on to sell five hundred of these units. As usual, the goal was surpassed; 867 were sold, the employees alone enthusiastically buying 118 of them. Later in 1934, the retail sales department held its first air-conditioning campaign. The thirty-one installations sold were considered an encouraging result. There were several more campaigns in November, 1934, including the sale of 1,041,000 Mazda lamps. In 1935, the All-Employee Sales Campaigns were more ambitious than ever; the lamp campaign set a record of 1,357,000 sales. A new method was tried in 1936—Employee Prospect Activity, in which employees suggested possible purchasers of electric appliances. That first year, 7,139 appliances were sold through this effort, and in 1937 more than half the electric water heaters installed on the Company's lines were the result of Employee Prospect Activity. The work of the sales department was a vital factor in maintaining and increasing the Company's electric output during years filled with complicated problems. As rates went down, electric sales went up, and the measure of Whitwell's success, and the achievement of the Company generally, can be expressed in terms of kilowatt-hours sold. In 1933, the Company sold 2,574,566,593 kilowatt-hours; in 1938, it billed its customers for 3,430,377,231.

Income from the increase in the Company's output merely matched increased costs of operation and offset a decline in the gas business. Annual surpluses were small and, since market conditions were such that new stock could not be sold, Philadelphia Electric had little money to put into improvements. Nevertheless, the system continued to be well maintained and certain improvements and extensions were made to it.

Some modernization came purely for reasons of economy. In 1934, the substations at Chestnut Hill and Manayunk were converted from manual operation to remote control, anticipating the automation that was later to become so prevalent in small substations.

Lack of money brought to a halt the policy of replacing overhead distribution lines with underground cables along important traffic arteries and in certain merchandising centers outside the main business district. However, fourteen miles of streets were changed in 1933 and twelve and a half in 1934 before the program was temporarily ended.

In 1935, the Pennsylvania Railroad completed the electrification of its road from New York to Washington, thereby substantially increasing its requirements from Philadelphia Electric. The Company furnished current for nearly the entire stretch—from Newark, New Jersey, to Perryville, Maryland. To handle the increased load, the new 165,000-kilowatt turbogenerator at Richmond Station, an $8,000,000 addition to the system's generating capacity, was placed in commercial operation in September, 1935.

As new apparatus went on the lines, old equipment was removed. On October 4, 1935, Liversidge shut down a rotary converter at Cherry Substation, taking the last central city direct current equipment off the system. The Evening Bulletin Building, the largest conversion job of the entire changeover, had been completed in June, and City Hall on October 4, the day Liversidge opened the switch. The territory between Vine and Pine Streets, river to river—an area of 240 city squares where half a million people lived or worked—was thus successfully

255

changed from D-C to A-C at a cost of $7,637,345. During the entire complicated change, not a single serious controversy had arisen. Indeed, customer relations were strengthened by the move. What customer could complain about receiving a brand new desk fan for his 1892 model? Some of the relics gathered by the Company are now to be seen in the Philadelphia Electric Company's historical collection at 2301 Market Street, others at the Henry Ford Museum in Dearborn, Michigan. The completion of the Company's changeover, coming at a time when many other companies were just initiating similar changes in their systems, was an outstanding tribute to the foresight and pioneering spirit exemplified by Philadelphia Electric.

By the fall of 1936, it had become apparent that increasing load requirements would soon call for additional capacity in the southern area of the system. The board decided to order a 50,000-kilowatt unit, costing about $5,000,000, for Schuylkill Station, and to modernize much of the machinery there. Schuylkill, the Company's oldest plant, had gradually been surpassed in efficiency as new and more modern stations had been built. During the depression, it was several times shut down for extended periods, and by 1936 its use was merely that of a stand-by station.

The new Schuylkill unit utilized a principle called "topping." Where inefficient low-pressure units existed in a station, high-pressure boilers were installed to supply a "topping" turbine which exhausted steam into the old low-pressure header system, the steam then flowing to the old turbines. The resulting combination was very efficient and restored the old machines to useful service. When first built in 1903, this station used 5.6 pounds of coal for each kilowatt-hour generated. Its modernized part, completed in 1938, had a coal rate of 0.89 pounds per kilowatt-hour. A marked economy had been built into the system.

Another noteworthy economy was achieved in 1937. Philadelphia Electric had outstanding approximately $130,000,000 in relatively high-interest-bearing bonds. Market conditions being propitious, the Company refunded all its bonds, replacing them with a single issue of $3\frac{1}{2}\%$ bonds due in 1967. The issue, underwritten by Morgan, Stanley & Company and others, yielded the Company a price of $100\frac{1}{2}$. Its interest rate was near the record low, and its size the largest ever floated by an electric utility. Through this refunding operation, Philadelphia Electric effected a saving of more than $1,000,000 a year in interest payments.

In 1937, the Company obtained a $5,000,000 bank loan to help meet its construction program and its working capital needs. This was the first time in five years that it had been necessary to secure outside financing. In the past, some financing had been done through the sale of stock, but that was now impractical. During the recession of 1937 and 1938, utility stocks sold at even lower prices than in 1932. The political situation in Washington and in the state capitals with respect to utilities was such that few cared to buy their junior equities. Discussing this matter with Franklin D. Roosevelt at a White House meeting in December, 1937, William H. Taylor informed the President that future plant expansion was being retarded, that it was impossible to obtain "junior money," that investors were held back by fear. President Roosevelt blamed the situation on the utilities themselves for overstressing the New Deal-utility controversy.

Another need for money was rural electrification. In September, 1936, the Company decided to provide electricity for everyone in Philadelphia Electric territory who could possibly be reached. The Company did not want any R.E.A. co-operatives established in its bailiwick. Accordingly, an initial plan calling for 400 miles of poles and lines to be built along country roads was put in motion. Farmers were supplied current at the same rate as people living in densely populated areas. This program not only kept the R.E.A. out, but brought onto the Company's lines new customers whose business was soon a distinct asset to the system. The program also quieted political pressures. Not long after its inception, Governor Earle in January, 1937, warned the "big four" electric companies which served eighty-five per cent of the state's consumers—Philadelphia Electric, Duquesne Light, Pennsylvania Power & Light, and subsidiaries of Associated Gas and Electric—that they must provide real rural electrification on reasonable terms or step aside for someone who would.

During the years 1933 through 1938, operating revenues increased from $60,000,000 to $68,000,000, but net income failed to hold its own against rising costs and taxes. The decline in net income was very small, to be sure, only a little more than $300,000, but while this falling off was too minute to be cause for alarm, it was not reassuring. Facing a future which promised still higher taxes and more rate reductions, and unable to raise substantial sums of money to enlarge the system's capacity, the situation must have looked a little bleak to the directors. Still, they continued to vote the invariable forty-five-cent quarterly dividend on the common stock, 97.3 per cent of which was owned by U.G.I. The holding company's other investments did not stand up so well. Net income of U.G.I. had fallen from $36,532,876 in 1932 to $26,053,950 in 1938. One of its largest holdings, Public Service Corporation of New Jersey, had cut its dividend rate from $3.30 to $2.20 a share. Some of U.G.I.'s companies had ceased paying dividends altogether.

HORACE P. LIVERSIDGE TERMINATING DIRECT CURRENT SERVICE, OCTOBER 4, 1935

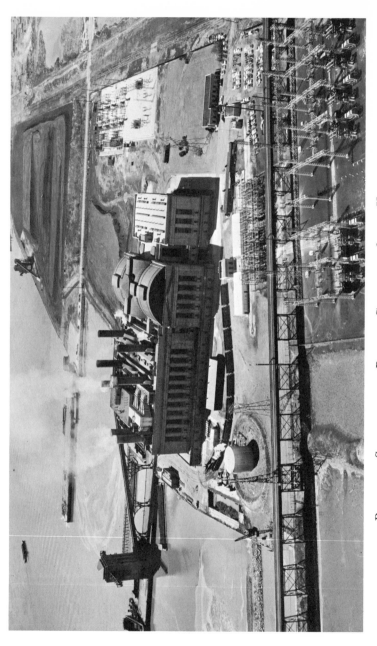

RICHMOND STATION, 1954. PRESENT CAPACITY, 483,000 KILOWATTS

In the thirties, a number of important personnel changes took place. Several directors died or retired, the most prominent of whom was Horatio G. Lloyd, whose death occurred on January 21, 1937. For fifteen years he had been a powerful factor on the board. A soft-spoken man of great personal modesty and old-fashioned courtliness, Lloyd was a leading figure in American financial life. He had, in particular, won the respect of Philadelphians for heading the War Chest Campaign in World War I, and for his leadership during the depression in disbursing more than $14,000,000 of relief funds. In 1938, the board lost another notable director when Thomas N. McCarter resigned. McCarter's place on the executive committee was taken by Director William W. Bodine, executive vice-president of U.G.I. Bodine was the son of Samuel T. Bodine and the grandson of William G. Warden, both of whom had served as president of U.G.I.

In 1936, the Company lost through death two of its oldest employees. On June 15, Joseph D. Israel died. Graduating from the University of Pennsylvania in 1887, he had gone to work for Professor Marks and had supervised the laying of the Edison Company's underground network. Together with W. C. L. Eglin, he had been one of Marks's key men. Israel had worked for the system forty-nine years, many of them as manager of the "Central District." On December 8, 1936, Vice-President Charles J. Russell died after forty-six years of service. Russell, the recipient in 1909 of the first Doherty Gold Medal for his paper "Load Factor, Diversity Factor, and Power Factor," was an expert on rates.

Retirements under a Company ruling which set an age limit of seventy years (unless waived by the president with the approval of the board of directors) sidelined two long-time officers in 1937, A. V. R. Coe, Philadelphia

Electric's secretary since 1899, and H. C. Lucas, its treasurer since 1911. A service annuity plan, worked out in 1938 but never put completely into effect and superseded by another plan in 1940, provided for retirements at an earlier age than seventy. Any male employee aged sixty-five, and any female employee aged sixty, who had worked twenty years was privileged to retire.

It was in September, 1938, that the most vital personnel changes of all took place. President William H. Taylor's health had broken; he had not attended a single board meeting that year. To make a position for him, John E. Zimmermann, while retaining the chairmanship of the executive committee, resigned as chairman of the board. Taylor was then elected chairman, but, unable to fill the office, he resigned it in 1940, and died on October 9, 1945.

On September 27, 1938, Horace P. Liversidge, who had been elected to the board two years earlier, was named president of Philadelphia Electric. The following month, Henry B. Bryans was elected executive vice-president, and Liversidge's former office of general manager was abolished. Liversidge's election to the presidency was a welcome one to Philadelphia Electric people, for they had implicit confidence in him. Although hard times might loom ahead, everyone knew that the Company's affairs were in the best of hands.

Some months before Liversidge became president, the nation's holding companies had capitulated to a Supreme Court ruling favorable to the Public Utility Holding Company Act of 1935. As of December 1, 1938, all holding companies were required to submit proposals for the integration and simplification of their properties. U.G.I., among the rest, bowed to the S.E.C. ruling.

No one now knew what Philadelphia Electric's future was to be. Would U.G.I. be permitted to retain ownership of the electric company, or would it be forced to dispose of its stock? With Liversidge at the helm, was Philadelphia Electric to regain an independent status? Independence, as Americans well know, has its all-compelling allure. With the future so very uncertain, small wonder that many employees fondly hoped that the Company was now headed toward a "new deal" of its own.

CHAPTER 17

Divested From U.G.I.

L IVERSIDGE DESCRIBED the years during which Philadelphia Electric was owned by U.G.I. as "a period of dissatisfaction and misunderstanding." His reaction was the not unusual one of an operating company executive who had experienced the embarrassing problems which can confront a utility controlled by a holding company. In such a combination, fundamentally different points of view not infrequently arise to vex the relationship between operating and holding company men.

Although orders handed down by U.G.I. often caused Liversidge to feel harassed and frustrated, the turmoil he underwent was shared by only a few of his fellow executives. To all intents and purposes, Philadelphia Electric ran itself, and most of its employees were unaware of the holding company. At the outset, President Taylor had made it clear to U.G.I. that all its orders must be channeled through him. Consequently, except for limited and amicable instances, there was no U.G.I. contact with the Company's personnel except at the top level.

The position of Philadelphia Electric as a satellite to a holding company was not basically sound. While it is true that holding companies performed valuable functions on behalf of operating companies, the situation in Philadelphia was such that U.G.I. could do little for the electric company after it had consolidated the suburban companies into it. The normal advantages of holding company management had to do with economies in the purchase of supplies through large-scale ordering, expert supervision by the holding company's corps of specialists, and financing through the holding company's credit.

Philadelphia Electric was simply too large to need this kind of help. To be sure, exceptions to this statement can be made. In its executive vice-president, William W. Bodine, U.G.I. had a man of extraordinary financial ability. Bodine exercised general oversight of Philadelphia Electric's finances, and it was he who arranged the refunding of its bonded indebtedness in 1937 and the sale of the $130,000,000 issue. But, on the whole, Philadelphia Electric could afford as good men as U.G.I., and Philadelphia Electric executives felt perfectly competent to run the business. They did not need U.G.I. guidance in operations, sales, or other forms of management. At times, indeed, such guidance as they received was directly to the Company's disadvantage. Thus, the holding company structure was unnecessary and uneconomical when applied to Philadelphia Electric. This was the price, and a low one at that, which the Company paid for the expansion of its territory.

The great benefit to Philadelphia Electric of coming into the U.G.I. system was the opportunity for growth. U.G.I. merged into the Company its extensive suburban territory with its large and promising Philadelphia Suburban-Counties Gas and Electric Company. Thus, it broadened the Company's activities by placing it in the gas business in the suburban area. Moreover, it gave Philadelphia Electric the top management that its directors had thought necessary.

It was U.G.I. that put in William H. Taylor as president, a position which he filled capably. Taylor was an effective leader, a good organizer and operator. It was he who was responsible for perfecting the merger of Philadelphia Electric with the suburban company, and it was he who had the difficult task of reducing their joint forces, which after the merger were far too large. In 1928, the combined personnel of the two companies totaled more than 9,000 men and women; within a few years, Taylor had pared this figure to an effective working staff of about 6,500.

During Taylor's regime, Philadelphia Electric was converted from a high-rate, low-use company into a low-rate, high-use utility, following the pattern of the times which saw increasing use of electric service accompanied by declining rates. Each year, Taylor asked Whitwell to estimate how much new business he could attract to compensate for rate reductions so that earnings would not decline. The amount of income lost in Taylor's frequent tariff cuts represented roughly the Company's anticipated growth factor as expressed in new income. Within ten years, the average residential rate was reduced forty per cent.

Men leaving a conference with Taylor could seldom remember a thing he had said. The truth was that he talked very little, but he was a great listener, and he reached his decisions slowly and with care. One possible drawback to his effectiveness was his reticence to meet the public; he made as few public appearances as possible. Instead of Taylor, it was Liversidge who was popularly considered "Mr. Philadelphia Electric." On the other hand, Taylor having been for so many years in U.G.I. had the confidence of that organization and was ideally equipped to deal with it.

Responsibility for the management of U.G.I.'s numerous gas, electric, and other properties was divided among its vice-presidents, each of whom was assigned the supervision of a number of companies. Philadelphia Electric, however, was too big to be handled in that way; it was kept directly under the eye of John E. Zimmermann, president of U.G.I.

Zimmermann, a seasoned, able engineer, was a big man of formidable appearance. He gave the impression of unbending determination. Very formal, rather impatient, exceedingly strong-willed, sometimes given to sudden rage when crossed, he was a leader of dominating personality. In addition, he was a fighter who was to spend years in an unsuccessful battle with Roosevelt and the Holding Company Act. It was on Zimmermann that the conflict of interests inherent in the U.G.I.-Philadelphia Electric situation focused.

This conflict was virtually unavoidable, for U.G.I. was primarily interested in gas, while Philadelphia Electric was primarily an electric utility. With Philadelphia Electric doing everything in its power to increase its business, it was inevitable that U.G.I. men should view it as a competitor to the city-owned, U.G.I.-managed gasworks. Trouble ensued. The electric officials found that they were constantly on the carpet denying intent to hamstring the gas business and justifying their efforts to obtain more electric business. Philadelphia Electric's advertising came under criticism. One of the Company's ripest areas for development was the suburban residential load. Suburbanites read the metropolitan papers, and Philadelphia Electric naturally advertised extensively in them. But city dwellers also read those papers, and U.G.I. officials complained that this advertising infringed on their Philadelphia gas field. They took their complaints to President Zimmermann.

Zimmermann had had years of experience in utility management and it was to be expected that he would exercise his right to dictate orders to the big local electric company. The background of many of his orders re-

265

flected his interest in the U.G.I. system as a whole and not necessarily in what was best for Philadelphia Electric. For example, at the height of one of the Company's campaigns to sell electric ranges, Zimmermann stepped in and ordered it stopped. His advisers had told him that the campaign was in direct competition with U.G.I.'s gas interests. Not only would this order have cost the Company its investment in hundreds of ranges and embarrassed it in the eyes of every electric dealer in its territory, it would have slowed the Company's growth. Liversidge managed to persuade Zimmermann to rescind the order by stressing that Philadelphia Electric had to take on as much new load as it could, and as fast as possible, if the high rate of return expected from it by U.G.I. was to be maintained. There was no question about the validity of that argument.

The top management team during most of the U.G.I. period—Taylor as president and Liversidge as general manager—was extremely effective in dealing with the holding company. Taylor always maintained good relations with Zimmermann, although in frequent disagreement with him. He had his methods, but when it came to a fight it was usually Liversidge who took over. This was as it should have been, for Taylor with his many responsibilities as president could not afford to be in conflict. On the other hand, Liversidge as the operating head of the Company was the one who had to execute the orders, and when he disagreed with one of them he went all out to get it changed. "Conditions got rather strained," he once said, "because it seemed to me that every time Zimmermann and I met around the same conference table I had the unhappy mental reaction to be ready to jump on anything he had to propose."

The following story illustrates the guile that Liversidge could command in a difficult situation. Not long after

HORACE P. LIVERSIDGE

President 1938–1947
Chairman of the Board 1947–1955

Zimmermann had become president of U.G.I., he ordered Philadelphia Electric's executives to move to U.G.I. headquarters, its office building at Broad and Arch Streets. Liversidge was appalled. The Company would lose its identity; the public would not know to whom to look; the employees would not know to whom they were responsible.

He went immediately to see Zimmermann, ostensibly to find out where President Taylor's office was to be, but actually to get the order rescinded. Taylor's office, he found, was to be in a splendid location right next to Zimmermann's. Sizing up the situation, Liversidge talked with Zimmermann about the routines which the new office arrangement would probably bring about. He mentioned that it was his practice to bring his operating plans into Taylor's office for approval. But now with Taylor's office next to Zimmermann's, Taylor would undoubtedly show the plans to the holding company head. "There's nothing wrong in that?" queried Liversidge.

"Oh no," replied Zimmermann. "That's the reason I want Mr. Taylor and you people here closer together so that we can understand just what is going on and have a better understanding all around." On this point Liversidge could do nothing but agree with him completely.

But he went on to remark, "Mr. Zimmermann, I'm quite sure that the plans laid down by Mr. Taylor, when you have a chance to look them over, will be changed. No two men think alike and it might be that you might change them for the better, but, nevertheless, you are going to suggest certain changes to be made."

"Yes," conceded Zimmermann. "I wouldn't be at all surprised but that will happen."

"Quite often?"

"Yes."

Liversidge subtly led Zimmermann into a trap. "So, Mr. Taylor will bring those same plans and specifications back and he will give them to me with the changes that are to be made and those changes will be made. Later, they will be taken back to you for your approval, your final approval."

"Yes," agreed Zimmermann.

"May I stop right there," said Liversidge. "The moment you put your signature on those new plans and specifications, which are yours, not ours, you are assuming the full responsibility for what has been done and what will be done. Up to the present time Mr. Taylor and I assume that responsibility and if you do not like the way we are doing things you can fire us, but you are not firing us, Mr. Zimmermann, after *you* change the plans of procedure. I could say a great deal more but I am telling you that now to warn you as to the dangers that you may find in the over-all development of trying to incorporate into one family the executives of an operating company with the executives of a holding company."

For a time, deep in thought, Zimmermann paced up and down his big office before he reached his decision. "Well, Mr. Liversidge, suppose we leave things as they are. We will make no change."

Taylor's methods of dealing with Zimmermann were nearly as effective as Liversidge's, if occasionally unorthodox. At one time during the depression years, U.G.I. had been making wage cuts. Zimmermann, who had reduced his own salary, called Taylor to his office. When he suggested that Philadelphia Electric institute a broad salary slash, Taylor simply rose to his feet and left the room without saying a word. Zimmermann spent several days trying to get him on the phone, but Taylor was not available. Finally, the holding company president went in person to Taylor's office to tell him that the wage cut would not be necessary.

Speaking of Taylor, Liversidge noted: "He would not argue with Mr. Zimmermann. If he knew the thing that Mr. Zimmermann was asking him to do was wrong, he would say, 'I don't agree with you Mr. Zimmermann,' turn around, put on his hat, and walk out, leaving Mr. Zimmermann talking to the walls of his office. Then, I would go up and have an hour-long, knock-down, drag-out argument."

Actually, considering the times, the years under U.G.I. were good ones for the Company, and, despite the several anecdotes just related, Zimmermann, Taylor, and Liversidge got along well together and respected each other. The last reference Liversidge ever made to Zimmermann was almost affectionate: "He was a warm-hearted, nice chap."

The strain of his battle against the Holding Company Act of 1935 took its toll on Zimmermann and by 1940 he was on the way down physically. In that year, he was advanced to chairman of the board and Bodine became president of U.G.I. Zimmermann remained as chairman of Philadelphia Electric, but relinquished the chairmanship of its executive committee to Bodine.

By this time, U.G.I., the oldest public utility holding company in the country, was deeply involved in efforts to prove that its system did not violate the terms of the Holding Company Act. It had attempted in a letter of November 17, 1938, to Chairman Douglas of the S.E.C. to show that its properties actually were integrated as required by the Act. U.G.I. had, in fact, two major integrated businesses, one operating in the region of Philadelphia and Delaware, and another in Connecticut. It also held large investments in Public Service Corporation of New Jersey and in Niagara Hudson Power Corporation. In addition, it owned upstate Pennsylvania gas and electric properties, and many other companies of diverse types scattered as far afield as Arizona.

U.G.I. concluded its presentation to Chairman Douglas with the following summary: "Thus it is seen that insofar as its principal investments go, U.G.I. today is an integrated holding company within the spirit of the public policy declared by Congress in the Holding Company Act of 1935, including its substantial minority interests in other regional holding companies and certain incidental nonutility investments." This point of view was wholly unsatisfactory to the S.E.C., which, in March, 1940, instituted integration proceedings.

In January, 1941, the S.E.C. issued its tentative conclusions for the guidance of U.G.I. It stipulated that U.G.I.'s control should be limited to a single integrated system composed of Philadelphia Electric, Delaware Power & Light Company, and their subsidiaries. U.G.I. could not retain its properties in Arizona, New Hampshire, Tennessee, Kansas, and Connecticut, and would probably have to rid itself of all its other properties and stock holdings.

Although U.G.I. sold its $27,500,000 interest in the Connecticut Light and Power Company in April, 1941, it petitioned for judicial review, but efforts to hold a major part of its empire together proved unavailing. In December, 1942, U.G.I. surrendered by reaching a final determination acceptable to the government. The purpose of its "plan for the divestment of certain securities" was to make an initial distribution to its stockholders of more than two thirds of its assets, and to distribute more from time to time. In short, the so-called "death sentence" implicit in the Act of 1935 was to be applied, and U.G.I. was to be limited in operation to a geographical area of its choice. Looking on the cheerful side of the situation as best he could, President Bodine pointed out that the plan was advantageous to U.G.I. stockholders, "as it will transfer to them the direct ownership of such of the Company's investments as are of a size to be readily distributed in kind, and should make possible a substantial reduction in expenses and taxes. It will afford a wide distribution of ownership of Philadelphia Electric, which company has been enlarged and developed over a period of years through extensions, mergers, and consolidations of many urban and suburban companies, serving a compact area from opposite Trenton on the Delaware River to Conowingo on the Susquehanna."

U.G.I. could have retained Philadelphia Electric, Delaware Power & Light, and its large holdings in Public Service of New Jersey had it so desired. The maintenance of this tri-state integrated system, however, would have been unwarrantably expensive. The plan adopted by U.G.I. of letting these major holdings go (Philadelphia Electric alone represented sixty-two per cent of U.G.I.'s assets, and in 1942 furnished more than two thirds of its income), and of falling back on its upstate Pennsylvania properties was calculated by the S.E.C. to save the stockholders $1,134,133 in taxes annually.

As part of the program of divesting itself of its equity in Philadelphia Electric, of liquidating this major asset by distributing its stock directly to U.G.I. shareholders, it was necessary to retire U.G.I.'s outstanding five-dollar dividend preferred stock. To accomplish this, Philadelphia Electric's authorized 15,000,000 common shares (10,529,230 outstanding) were reclassified in order to create from among them 2,369,076 shares of one-dollar dividend preference common stock. On the basis of this reclassification, U.G.I., as owner of 97.3 per cent of Philadelphia Electric common, received 2,304,958 and a fraction shares of the one-dollar preference and 7,939,303 and a fraction shares of the new common in exchange for the 10,244,262 shares of Philadelphia Electric in its portfolio. In June, 1943, U.G.I. declared a partial distribution of capital and turned over virtually all of its Philadelphia Electric stock to its shareholders, thereby increasing the number of direct owners of Philadelphia Electric securities by approximately 100,000 individuals. Through this wide distribution and through listing its stock on the exchanges, Philadelphia Electric found itself in a much better position to do its own junior financing than it had been in under the holding company.

John E. Zimmermann did not live to see Philadelphia Electric divested from U.G.I., for he died on May 30, 1943, several weeks before the act was consummated. His death heralded many changes on the boards of both companies. Since the S.E.C. had ordered that there were to be no interlocking directorates, William W. Bodine and Walter E. Long resigned as Philadelphia Electric directors, while Liversidge (who had taken Taylor's place on the U.G.I. board in 1940) and two other directors resigned from U.G.I. so that they could remain directors of Philadelphia Electric.

Adjusting itself to the loss of the U.G.I. directors, the board of Philadelphia Electric elected to its membership John A. Diemand, president of the Insurance Company of North America; Walter D. Fuller, president of the Curtis Publishing Company; and Edward Porter, Philadelphia Electric's vice-president in charge of finance and accounting. Director Harold S. Schutt was appointed chairman of the executive committee in Bodine's place.

So it was that Philadelphia Electric found itself once again independent, having been absorbed by U.G.I. in 1928 and divested from it fifteen years later. In taking leave of the holding company, a few comments about its future course are in order. Bodine resigned as its president in September, 1943, to become financial vice-president of the Penn Mutual Life Insurance Company and ultimately, 1949–1957, chairman of its board. He was succeeded at U.G.I. by Walter E. Long, under whom the task of further divesting U.G.I. of assets and of simplifying its corporate structure was carried on until 1953, when all the transactions required by the S.E.C. were completed. U.G.I. ceased to be a holding company and became an operating company doing business solely in Pennsylvania. It had no subsidiaries, since its former upstate gas and electric properties, which it had elected to retain, were all merged into divisions of U.G.I. itself.

The day of the vast utility holding company with its diverse and widely scattered properties had been legislated to its close. For the most part, the management of the investor-owned utility industry had reverted to operating companies. But these companies were little like their counterparts before the holding company era. Many of them were large systems representing the merging of scores of early companies into geographically integrated and closely knit organizations. Philadelphia Electric was one of the largest of these systems, a position it owed in part to holding company ownership. Emancipated by the Act of 1935, Philadelphia Electric emerged from U.G.I. a far stronger company than it would have been had the absorption never taken place.

CHAPTER 18

World War II

In 1939, the nation entered a new and dangerous period of growth. Financial uncertainties and disasters of the long depression, re-emphasized by the recent recession, gave way to prosperous times. To a degree, the business upswing was nurtured by normal demands, but, in large measure, it was encouraged by government spending for defense purposes. Ominous forces of aggression were on the move in the late 1930's, and those who had tried to confine the ambitions of dictators had found appeasement the most temporary of expedients. In Asia, Japan had become an awesome military power whose might was displayed in a bloody struggle with China. In Europe, Hitler had gathered Austria and Czechoslovakia under the swastika and was now threatening Poland. Mussolini had waged war in Ethiopia as a prelude to his 1939 invasion of Albania. Over the horizon loomed the brooding and enigmatic figure of Stalin.

At the outset of 1939, Philadelphia Electric was guided by a group of directors whose membership was soon to be radically changed by death and resignation. Martin V. Bergen was the senior member, having been elected in 1915 when the Company operated under a New Jersey charter and required a man of Bergen's legal influence in Camden. Although his roots were in New Jersey, Bergen made his home at the Racquet Club in Philadelphia,

West Conshohocken Gas Plant, 1957

ELECTRIC LOAD DISPATCHING HEADQUARTERS, 1000 CHESTNUT STREET

where he entertained his friends with stories of how he had coached the Princeton football team before the turn of the century.

Jeremiah J. Sullivan, Jr., had come on the board in 1929 to fill the vacancy caused by his father's death. Close to Liversidge and deeply interested in the financial aspect of the Company's operations, he had become one of the most influential of the directors. Samuel Lloyd Irving of Chester, president of James Irving & Son, had been elected in 1936, the first director deliberately selected to represent a part of the Company's service area other than Philadelphia. Charles E. Brinley, president of Baldwin Locomotive Works, a brother-in-law of John E. Zimmermann and a director of U.G.I., had joined the Philadelphia Electric board in 1938. Zimmermann and Bodine, of course, represented the main U.G.I. control over the electric company's directorate. Other directors in 1939 included the Company's chairman, William H. Taylor—a director in name only, since the condition of his health prevented his attending meetings after 1937— President Liversidge, and Edward Hopkinson, Jr., of Drexel's. Hopkinson did not stand for re-election in April, 1939, and Walter E. Long of U.G.I. took his place.

In the following year, Taylor resigned and Executive Vice-President Henry B. Bryans became a director. Bergen died in 1941, his vacancy being filled by Harold S. Schutt. Schutt was president of the Philadelphia Suburban Water Company, which was owned by the Estate of Clarence H. Geist, who had been the largest individual stockholder of U.G.I. As representative for the Geist family, Schutt was a member of the U.G.I. board. The 1943 changes—Zimmermann's death and the resignations of the U.G.I. officers Bodine and Long, together with the election of their successors, John A. Diemand,

Walter D. Fuller, and Edward Porter—have already been mentioned.

The wartime board of directors was a strong one, as was the top management team of utility men who operated the Company. The organization over which Liversidge presided was well seasoned. In addition to Executive Vice-President Bryans, there were five other vice-presidents: Arthur B. Huey, legal department; N. E. Funk, engineering; George E. Whitwell, sales; Edward Porter, finance and accounting; and L. B. Eichengreen, gas.

Other key men at Philadelphia Electric included I. L. Craig, rates and standard practice; A. M. Boyd, personnel; R. Z. Zimmermann, service operations; Alex Wilson, electric operations; R. G. Rincliffe, purchasing; and E. B. Myers, customers service. Myers was also manager of the Philadelphia division. The suburban chiefs were Regional Vice-President Albert R. Granger, Delaware division; Regional Vice-President H. H. Ganser, Schuylkill division; W. T. Ryan, Main Line division; and W. G. Sterrett, Eastern division. Vincent A. Sommar was secretary of the corporation and Clifford Winner, treasurer.

Several important changes in the upper levels of management took place during the war years. Vice-President Huey died in 1939 and Bernard P. Carey, who had joined the Company as a clerk in 1913 and who was now president of the Pennsylvania Electric Association, was appointed general counsel in charge of the legal department. Four years later, he was advanced to vice-president.

Death removed Vice-President Eichengreen in 1940. President of the Pennsylvania Gas Association, Eichengreen had joined U.G.I. in 1909, and in 1928 had become manager of Philadelphia Electric's gas department. He was succeeded in that department by E. G. Boyer, a national authority on gas who was to win many awards and distinctions in that field.

In 1941, H. N. Ramsey, who had been with the U.G.I. system for many years before coming to Philadelphia Electric, was appointed purchasing agent. Rincliffe, the former agent, was transferred to the station operating department. A graduate of Yale and the Massachusetts Institute of Technology, Rincliffe had been employed by the Company or its predecessor companies since 1923 and, marked for promotion, was on the road to the vice-presidency he achieved in 1945.

An effective new executive was introduced into personnel and public relations during these years. George R. Conover had long ago attracted Liversidge's attention. Liversidge had been instrumental in making him managing director of the Electrical Association of Philadelphia in 1928, and in 1939 brought Conover into Philadelphia Electric as manager of public relations. Somewhat to Conover's dismay, the president soon turned over to him the additional responsibility of personnel. That these combined jobs did not prove too much for the genial Conover was evidenced in 1944, when he was made a vice-president.

The men who managed Philadelphia Electric, whether they had been brought up in the old company, had joined it through U.G.I., or, like Whitwell and Conover, had come in from other backgrounds, realized in 1939 the urgent necessity of increasing the system's output. An impressive future awaited the development of its central city steam heat facilities. Quickening industrial and commercial life and the amazing growth of the residential load indicated the compelling necessity for more electric generating capacity. The gas end of the enterprise needed rejuvenation.

The gas business in Philadelphia Electric's service area stemmed from the incorporation of two companies in

1852—The Norristown Gas Company and The West Chester Gas Company. In 1856, the Pottstown Gas Company, The Bristol Gas Light Company, and the Chester Gas Company were also founded. Between 1868 and 1899, fourteen more companies came into being in the suburban counties, providing coal gas or carbureted water gas for lighting purposes. By 1900, coke oven gas plants were being installed and the merger movement which was to bring all but one of these gas companies into U.G.I. and thence into Philadelphia Electric was well under way.

The use of gas for lighting in the suburbs had nearly disappeared by 1920, but gas continued to flow through the mains for cooking and for industrial processes. Gas house heating began to be promoted in a small way. In 1929, the year when the system's gas supply was augmented by the reforming of refinery oil gas, there were 868 gas house heating customers. This number increased to 2,149 in 1935 and to 3,085 in 1940. The slow rate of gain in this important usage is a measure of the doldrums experienced by the gas department during the decade of the 1930's.

There were several reasons why Philadelphia Electric's gas business had not prospered. For one, management was not sure that it wanted to continue handling gas. Uncertainty on this point was intensified in the early 1940's by the attitude of the S.E.C. when it was dismembering U.G.I. For a time, the S.E.C. was of the opinion that Philadelphia Electric should not be allowed to sell both electricity and gas. Another reason for want of energy in gas promotion was the fact that Philadelphia Electric's income was so largely produced by electric sales; no one wanted to interfere with the rapid rise of the electric load. In addressing U.G.I.'s 1942 annual meeting, William W. Bodine referred to the relative progress of electricity and gas: "The gas end of the business has not grown in the last ten years to any degree comparable to the electric load. In that period, gas sales of our subsidiaries have increased but six per cent, whereas electric sales have increased more than eighty-five per cent."

Electric sales did not encounter the severe competition that gas experienced, particularly in space heating. Gas was in competition with coke for house heating and was undersold by "bootleg" coal. During the depression, many anthracite mines closed down, and unemployed miners trespassed on coal lands to engage in surface mining. These operations were not legal, but everybody sympathized with the miners who were trying to eke out a living by selling their coal to anyone who could hire a truck and come and get it. From Pottsville, Scranton, Wilkes-Barre, and the Poconos, hundreds of these trucks rolled into the Philadelphia area and went from house to house peddling "bootleg" coal at lower prices than the Company sold its coke. These illicit activities continued until the advent of World War II, when jobs once more became plentiful. Consequently, Philadelphia Electric had ample gas production facilities in the 1930's but lacked an adequate market.

With the gas business pretty much at a standstill, President Taylor authorized its promotion after Boyer had worked out an agreement with the Rainey-Wood Coke Company. Although Philadelphia Electric owned gas manufacturing plants, it depended for a large part of its supply on the purchase of Rainey-Wood's coke oven gas. The contract price was relatively high and did not stimulate new business. Under the revised arrangement, Rainey-Wood agreed to sell gas over and above contractual limits at lower rates. This enabled the Company to utilize inducement rates and encouraged it to seek industrial and residential customers. Determined efforts were made to increase the residential load by converting coal furnaces to gas and by pressing sales of gas refrigerators, ranges, and water heaters. For years, gas sales had been on a decline. Then, in 1938, a modest turning point was achieved. "For the first time since 1930," commented Liversidge in Philadelphia Electric's annual report for 1940, "residential gas sales, excluding house heating, exceeded those of the previous year." By the beginning of the war, the gas department was moving rapidly ahead with extensive improvements under way, notably at Chester, where in 1942 a battery of twenty-five coke ovens was being installed to help raise the Company's daily production by 10,000,000 cubic feet.

Meanwhile, the Company continued to increase its electric output. In 1939, a topping installation somewhat similar to that completed the year before at Schuylkill Station was begun at Chester. The $7,000,000 Chester program provided for a 50,000-kilowatt generator and two high-pressure steam boilers, each of 600,000 pounds capacity an hour. The country was moving toward a wartime control of industrial activity when Liversidge in October, 1939, announced the addition to Chester Station. "The new unit as designed," he said, "satisfies the preferred standard ratings suggested by the National Defense Power Committee. It will reinforce the already existing capacity of the system [total effective capacity in 1939 was 1,092,415 kilowatts; peak load, 907,000 kilowatts], provide adequate reserves under the established policy of the Company, and be available in the event that conditions abroad increase production demands on local industry."

While Liversidge was making this statement about the Chester addition, far more ambitious steps were being taken to enlarge the system's capacity. Late in October, 1939, Philadelphians learned that the Company intended to build a $45,000,000 station in South Philadelphia. A sixty-two-acre Delaware River tract at Delaware and Oregon Avenues was acquired for this purpose from the Pennsylvania Salt Manufacturing Company in the largest single purchase of city real estate in ten years. "Although the demand at present for this increased capacity is not urgent," reporters were told, "we must be ready to meet the expected demands of increased industrial activity when they come." A year later, with Southwark Station still on the designing boards, Philadelphia Electric awarded Westinghouse a contract for a 90,000-kilowatt low-pressure generator for Chester Station, where the new 50,000-kilowatt unit was then being installed. In 1942, a 20,000-kilowatt generator was added to Deepwater Station. Every effort was made to increase generating capacity so that the Company would have substantial reserves for emergency demands.

A wartime tempo accelerated industrial Philadelphia months before Hitler's troops invaded Poland on September 1, 1939. Once again, the Delaware River shipyards teemed with activity such as they had not known since World War I. In July, 1939, thirty-two vessels for the Navy were on their ways or on designing boards. Strenuous efforts were being made to reopen the great Kensington yards where the Cramps had launched 524 hulls before shutting down in 1927 after nearly a century of activity. In September, the month that World War II broke out, Pennsylvania payrolls gained 65,000 workers.

As the war progressed with the fall of France in June, 1940, American defense spending reached new heights. President Roosevelt called for military conscription of the country's youth, and heavy new taxes were proposed, including the excess profits tax. Baldwin Locomotive Works at Eddystone began to manufacture tanks. In August, 1940, the Frankford Arsenal, where 4,700 people were employed, converted its operations to a twenty-four-hour, three-shift schedule, and advertised for 3,800 skilled mechanics. While England withstood the fury of German aerial attack, the United States mobilized its National Guard. C. Jared Ingersoll, son of a former Philadelphia Electric director, was appointed chief ordnance officer for the area, "virtual czar" of national defense industries in Philadelphia. In October, Bendix Aviation Corporation took over the huge Atwater Kent radio plant, idle since 1932, and reopened it for the manufacture of airplane parts. Edward G. Budd Manufacturing Company and Midvale Steel began to produce artillery and ammunition. Budd was soon turning out 5,600 twenty-pound fragmentation bombs a day. In Ardmore, the Autocar Company started to make "half-track" vehicles for the Army. Unemployment melted as a business boom swept over the United States.

Initially, the war preparedness program was superimposed upon civilian production, and there were many—in particular Leland Olds, chairman of the Federal Power Commission—who believed that war production in itself would require corresponding increases in power facilities. Time and again, the imminence of a disastrous power shortage was predicted. Liversidge was not worried. In September, 1941, he said: "So far as we can now tell, skilled manpower and available factory space will be completely drained throughout this area before the power resources of Philadelphia are exhausted." Force was lent to his point of view because work on the foundations of Southwark Station, initially planned to be of 300,000-kilowatt capacity, had started in April, 1941.

By the end of the year, following the December 7 attack on Pearl Harbor, the United States was at war with Japan, Germany, and Italy. The country was soon on a full-scale war economy. The manufacture of civilian commodities, such as electric appliances, automobiles, and other durable goods, was shut down. Shortages and priorities became the order of the day. When Japan's conquests cut off ninety per cent of the world's rubber supply, tire rationing regulations were adopted. Public utility operations marked as nonessential, and for whose vehicles no new tires or recaps were to be available, included meter reading, collections, claims, legal department and similar activities. In common with other systems, Philadelphia Electric ceased reading residential and small retail customer meters on a monthly basis and changed to quarterly readings with estimated billings for the intervening months.

Although not countenanced by investor-owned utilities, fear of a power shortage haunted Federal officials. Steps were taken to conserve power. In February, 1942, Congress enacted wartime daylight saving. The change had an appreciable effect on Philadelphia Electric's peak load, reducing the evening peak about 180,000 kilowatts during the first week the new time was in operation, and creating a net saving in peak load of about 84,000 kilowatts, or eight per cent. Early closing of gas stations, voluntary restrictions on the use of power—a Philadelphia Electric conservation slogan read "Use all the gas and electricity you need, but be sure you need all you use"—blackouts, brownouts, dimouts, all served to lessen the load.

In 1943, when the War Production Board requested public utilities to conserve manpower, transportation, fuel, and critical materials, the Company organized a conservation committee to formulate ways of reducing civilian use of gas and electricity. A program was developed of newspaper advertisements, radio broadcasts, window displays, and outdoor advertising, all of which carried the idea: "Don't waste electricity or gas because it isn't rationed." Restrictions on electricity reached their height just before Christmas, 1943, when the director of War Utilities requested that Christmas street decorations, exterior home decorations, community Christmas trees, and holiday lighting for commercial establishments be dispensed with.

Early in the war period, intensive studies were made to determine what the national war power requirements would be. In July, 1941, the Federal Power Commission presented an estimate that was horrifyingly large. Unconvinced by this finding, the War Production Board drafted Constantine Bary, Philadelphia Electric rate engineer, to assist in making another estimate. After completing his study in October, 1941, Bary predicted a 1943 peak load for the United States of 37,500,000 kilowatts. As it turned out, the actual peak load was 37,300,000 kilowatts; Bary's figure came within one half of one per cent of the true demand, whereas the Federal Power Commission's estimate was fifteen per cent too high. Bary's associated studies were responsible in no small way for shaping the policy of the War Production Board on electric power expansion. They contributed considerably toward expediting the war effort through the elimination of unnecessary power projects, which, had they continued, would have interfered with the supply of wartime necessities.

Bary realized that the war load would not be an additional load, but would supplant that needed for the production of peacetime goods. There were other factors influencing his estimate. From 1939 through 1944, total electricity sales grew eighty-seven per cent. If load factor had remained the same, it would have been necessary to increase generating capacity about eighty-seven per cent, or from 40,300,000 to 75,500,000 kilowatts. Actually, capacity was increased to only 50,300,000 kilowatts.

Higher load factor resulting from longer hours of operation and the use of spare capacity through interconnections provided the difference. Leland Olds's prediction of February, 1942, that by 1943 between thirty and forty per cent of curtailable energy would have to be shut off did not come to pass. There was no power shortage during World War II.

Government curtailment of construction projects, however, did interfere with the normal growth of individual systems. In November, 1941, the Office of Production Management (O.P.M.) held up delivery of Chester's 90,000-kilowatt unit, which had been ordered to help meet the 1942 peak load. Manufacturers simply could not satisfy all turbine orders at this time. The naval carrier program alone required four turbines on each of eight ships. They were also in heavy demand for cruisers, destroyers, and for vital industrial needs. Not only was Philadelphia Electric counting on its new unit, but within the Pennsylvania-New Jersey Interconnection both Pennsylvania Power & Light and Public Service of New Jersey had ordered turbines. The O.P.M. ruled that only the New Jersey unit could be allowed, selecting it because it was the largest on order in the Interconnection. Subsequently, it developed that Westinghouse much preferred to build the less complicated machine for Chester, so that Philadelphia Electric obtained its new generator after all.

The Chester turbine, a $3,400,000 installation, went into operation on schedule. It was the first time a machine of its size had been shipped without being assembled and turned over under steam at the factory. Normal procedure was impossible, so rushed was the manufacturer. When the Chester unit went on the lines, the total effective generating capacity of the system was raised to 1,242,165 kilowatts. The 1942 peak of 1,118,000 kilowatts was readily met, and the 1943 peak of 1,172,000 kilowatts would not be too large to handle. For future peaks, Philadelphia Electric would need help.

This help would not have been necessary had the big Southwark Station been ready when expected. Unfortunately, that project was indefinitely postponed when the War Production Board canceled its preference rating in August, 1942. Some 2,200,000 kilowatts of electric generating capacity in various stages of completion by many utility companies was brought to a halt at this time. Because of the deferment of Southwark Station, the Company was unable to provide for all its needs during the peaks of 1944 and 1945, when new high demands of 1,254,000 and 1,292,000 kilowatts were recorded. At such times, Philadelphia Electric bought power from the Interconnection.

At other times, however, it sold power to companies in need. On December 30, 1942, and again on January 21, 1943, severe sleet storms broke down the transmission line from Niagara Hudson Power Corporation to the New York State Gas and Electric Company at Binghamton, creating a deficiency of electric supply in central New York. On both occasions, it was a matter of only a few minutes before bulk power up to 35,000 kilowatts from Philadelphia Electric was flowing into the Scranton Electric Company for delivery to the tie line to Binghamton.

As the Binghamton example shows, the Company, through the Pennsylvania-New Jersey Interconnection, was tied in with New York State, which, in turn, was connected with the New England utilities. Through the New York tie, in 1945, Philadelphia Electric received excess hydro energy generated by the Hydro Electric Power Commission of Ontario. Not only was the system connected to the northeastern utilities, but it was also tied in with Delaware, Maryland, and Washington, D. C.

Invaluable as the interconnections proved, they did not solve all problems. Philadelphia Electric's steadily increasing power deficiency reached its most critical point in the spring of 1945, shortly before Germany surrendered. In these waning months of the war, peak loads in the Pennsylvania-New Jersey area were running 80,000 to 100,000 kilowatts higher than the previous year. This added load, coupled with the necessity of adhering to equipment maintenance schedules, left generating capacity short of the amount usually considered adequate for reserve purposes. Despite full use of the tie lines with the Baltimore-Washington and the New York-New Jersey areas, it was impossible to provide the necessary reserve capacity on exceptionally dark Mondays and Tuesdays—days of the week when housewives did their washing and ironing. To assure protection for the interconnected area when dangerous peaks arose, Philadelphia Electric and the other major utilities agreed to drop the voltage at their generating stations two per cent or more as required. A two per cent voltage drop reduced the area load by about 65,000 kilowatts; a drop of five per cent added 140,000 kilowatts to reserve power. The effect of lowering the voltage was not startling—lights became a trifle less bright, machinery operated at slightly reduced speed.

Inability of the companies included in the Pennsylvania-New Jersey Interconnection to maintain suitable reserves was not their fault, for their construction programs had been stopped by the government. The War Production Board had clarified this point in 1942: "Necessity for diverting critical materials and equipment to the direct war program makes it impossible to carry out a utility expansion program that would preserve the standards of reliability of service observed in peace-times. Civilian inconvenience and sacrifice must be expected, particularly during periods of drought or other adverse weather conditions, or in case of unexpected large increases in power requirements for war production."

The added load taken on by Philadelphia Electric during the war was impressive, raising operating revenues from $71,442,625 in 1939 to $100,629,586 in 1945. Kilowatt-hour sales spurted from 3,818,877,626 to 6,609,769,287 in 1944 (they declined slightly in 1945). The gas department did well, with sales mounting from 8,678,000,000 cubic feet in 1939 to 13,481,000,000 in 1945. As for the steam heat business, demands on it were such that by mid-1942 the Company had to decline taking on new customers.

From these figures, it might be supposed that Philadelphia Electric was enjoying prosperous years. Such was not the case. Uncontrollable expenses rose more sharply than revenues. Prices of everything, despite government controls, went up steadily, although not as steeply as they were later to rise. Taxes climbed from $9,806,465 in 1939 to $22,652,393 in 1945; net income shrank from $22,595,521 in 1939 to a low of $15,751,521 in 1943, after which it steadied and showed a little improvement.

Contributing to the declining profit margin were two more rate decreases imposed on the Company by the Public Utility Commission. On March 1, 1939, Philadelphia Electric was required to make a $1,650,000 rate cut, and on September 1, 1941, an additional decrease of $4,000,000 became effective. These reductions torpedoed the Company's dividend. Since 1931, the dividend had held steadily at forty-five cents a quarter, $1.80 a year, but this level could not be maintained after the rate cuts. In 1941, the dividend dropped to $1.40, and then continued dismally down to $1.20, where it remained for years, with one exception—in 1943 an extra twenty-cent

dividend was declared in connection with the reclassification of the stock when Philadelphia Electric was being
"spun off" from U.G.I.

Although stockholders are not usually pleased to learn
that rate cuts have been imposed, it might be assumed
that customers would be delighted. However, with respect
to the $4,000,000 cut, largest in the Company's history,
Liversidge informed his directors, "There has been no
pronounced public reaction either favorable or unfavor-
able to the electric rate reduction."

The abnormal problems confronting utilities during
the war aroused the concern of the Public Utility Commission. In June, 1943, it issued a statement of policy on
earnings. Noting that it was imperative for public utilities
to maintain a strong financial position so that high-level
service would continue and so that the companies could
enter the postwar period prepared to deal promptly with
deferred maintenance and property rehabilitation, the
Commission stated that it would not inquire into existing
rates that might be producing increased earnings as a
result of war conditions. It urged utilities to conserve
earnings for such maintenance needs as were being incurred but which could not be taken care of because of
wartime priorities.

When the Commission published its new policy, Philadelphia Electric, in common with other systems, was
contending with shortages of all kinds, including manpower. All work it could forgo without seriously affecting
service had been discontinued. So restricted was the
Company's construction program that it required no new
capital after 1941, when it sold $20,000,000 of 2¾%
bonds to pay off bank loans. During the war, money
seeking investment was dammed up and interest rates
declined, creating a favorable market for refunding operations. Philadelphia Electric replaced its five-dollar divi-

dend preferred stock with a 4.4% issue in 1942, and in 1944 refunded its entire $130,000,000 issue of 3½% bonds with two new $65,000,000 series paying 2¾%. In completing this transaction, the Company drew the largest check it ever made out. On November 1, 1944, Treasurer Clifford Winner signed a check in favor of the Fidelity-Philadelphia Trust Company for $138,950,500, the amount necessary to redeem the principal of the old issue, to provide a six per cent premium of $7,800,000, and to pay $1,150,500 interest from September 1 to December 2, 1944, the day the bonds were called.

Fiscal policies, construction programs, earning power, the procurement of supplies, and virtually every other area of the Company's operations reflected wartime conditions. In personnel matters, the pinch was particularly acute. When the war started, Philadelphia Electric employed about 7,400 people. By early 1945, this number had dwindled to 5,800. The largest loss was to the armed services, which took 1,201 employees, twenty-two of whom lost their lives. Other reductions in the working force came from the curtailment of construction and sales activities. When the War Production Board issued orders early in 1942 which virtually terminated the supply of electric and gas appliances, the sales department was reorganized. Appliance sales were eliminated at seventeen locations and the force was cut by about 275 people, most of whom had been engaged in promoting residential sales. The change in meter reading to a quarterly basis released another 225 positions, the employees involved filling vacancies elsewhere, or entering the service.

Philadelphia Electric's manpower shortage was solved in part by longer working hours in a number of departments which went on a forty-eight-hour week. Some employees eligible for retirement voluntarily stayed on the job. Many transfers were made—chauffeurs became pipe-

Turbine Hall, Southwark Station. Present Capacity, 378,000 Kilowatts

GIRDLER CATALYTIC REFORMING UNITS AT WEST CONSHOHOCKEN GAS PLANT

fitters, a janitor became a machinist, appliance salesmen became station equipment servicemen. The severity of the manpower problem can be measured by the Company's employment applications. In April, 1940, it received 1,675 applications for work; in April, 1942, only 748 job seekers applied; and in April, 1943, the number dropped to 296, most of whom were unskilled laborers.

During the war, there was much labor unrest and many strikes, including a notable one in the utility field. The Los Angeles municipal power system was the largest city-owned public utility in the United States. On February 14, 1944, it was shut down when nearly 2,600 employees, members of the International Brotherhood of Electrical Workers, A. F. of L., walked out protesting that a wage increase was too small. The strike lasted until the Army took over the system ten days later at the mayor's request.

Philadelphia Electric had its own labor problems. In the early 1940's, criticism of the Company's personnel policies began to be expressed by some workers. At this time, there was no policy of general or periodic salary increases, and wages ranged widely for the same type of job. Not only were wages not standardized, they were low. The Company's sick benefit and vacation allowance plan had become outdated. There was no absent time allowance for men paid on an hourly basis. Lack of adequate fringe benefits and a want of progressive personnel management stirred employees to action in February, 1942, when a group of them decided to set up an independent union, primarily for the Company's outside workers. While those concerned in this movement had confidence in Liversidge, the gap between them and the president was too great; there was no adequate bridge. George R. Conover, who had just been placed in charge of personnel, talked to the employees involved, urging patience and asking for the opportunity to correct matters with their guidance. As a consequence, no union was formed. Instead, the Independent Group Association, to which nearly half of those employed by the Company now belong, was set up. The Association's dues are nominal, one dollar a year. Through it, the gap between management and employees has been bridged. Association representatives meet periodically with the vice-president in charge of personnel, and bring in whatever grievances, demands, or suggestions they have. Philadelphia Electric is the only major utility company in the country which enjoys this sort of labor organization. It has worked well, has helped avoid trouble and controversy, and has been of inestimable value in the maintenance of a healthy tone in labor-management relations.

Although the formation of the Independent Group Association cleared the air, there remained a special situation at Chester Station which was resolved in another way. A well-meaning but unfortunate Company policy had given the Chester workers a grievance. During the depression, Chester had been on shorter hours than most of the Company's other stations because it was one of the older and less economical generating plants. Rather than discharge workers, the Company decided to provide work for all, but on a part-time basis. This policy, however, caused dissatisfaction because it did not protect seniority, affecting everyone in the same degree. Memories of the depression were still vivid during the war when the workers at Chester were approached by the International Brotherhood of Electrical Workers, whose organizers emphasized the power of union affiliation in securing working contracts. With such contracts, it was stressed, workers would be in a better position to protect their interests in the event of a postwar business collapse.

On October 18, 1943, the Pennsylvania State Labor Board conducted an election of the Chester Station employees to determine if they wanted the union. Of the 141 men eligible to vote, 137 cast ballots. The decision was close: 69 voted for the union, 67 against it. An I.B.E.W. local was formed and has since represented Chester Station in collective bargaining.

Although the organization of the Independent Group Association and the forming of a union at Chester were important personnel matters, they were overshadowed by the wartime problem of manpower conservation. But manpower was not the only necessity that was in short supply. Copper, steel, and rubber became scarce commodities, and certain standards long considered basic ceased to exist as the Company fell back on substitute materials. Iron wire was substituted for copper wire where feasible. Copper wire and lead cable were salvaged and reused where possible. The mileage of the Company's vehicles was cut forty per cent to save tires, gasoline, oil, and maintenance. Tons of paper were saved by eliminating bill stuffers, advertising booklets, and various items of stationery. As a contribution to the nation's scrap drive in 1942, the old Edison generating station was razed so that its million or more pounds of steel and iron could go to war. Cromby Station near Phoenixville and Swede Street Station in Norristown met a similar fate.

While the supply of coal never ran out, the coal bureau had to keep continually on the job to see that enough was available. Whenever economical to do so, power was purchased from anthracite-burning Pennsylvania Power & Light and from Public Service of New Jersey, which was equipped to burn oil. Full use was made of Conowingo's hydroelectric supply. Even so, the Company's coal rate— the amount of coal required to generate a kilowatt-hour of electricity—suffered.

During the war, preference in coal purchasing was given to by-product plants making coke for steel mills. Better-grade coal generally has by-product qualities, and although those qualities were not important to Philadelphia Electric, they were important to the coking companies. As a result, much of the best coal the Company had previously used went elsewhere, and the generating stations had to get along with an inferior grade. This adversely affected the coal rate, which also suffered from the prolonged operation of the less efficient generating stations. But even though the coal rate rose under these pressures from 0.993 pounds per kilowatt-hour in 1940 to 1.063 pounds in 1944, it remained lower than the national average.

The problem of procuring coal was far less serious to the community than the threat to its oil supply. The war was still in its early stages when an oil shortage hit the eastern seaboard. To relieve this situation, the government built the "Big Inch" (24-inch diameter) pipeline from Longview, Texas, to a point near Phoenixville, Pennsylvania, where the line branched into two 20-inch lines, one running to a New Jersey terminus at Bayonne, the other going southeast to the refineries at Marcus Hook and South Philadelphia. About ninety-one miles of pipeline lay in Philadelphia Electric territory. On July 19, 1943, the line went into operation, disgorging 385,000 barrels a day into the oil-hungry East and releasing an estimated seventy tankers for military use. While the pipeline was to have little immediate effect on Philadelphia Electric, its conversion after the war from oil to natural gas transmission was to be of prime consequence in the development of the Company's gas business.

Throughout the war years, Philadelphia Electric did everything it could to ensure an adequate supply of power to its service area and to protect its system against interruption from sabotage or direct enemy action. Eight days after Pearl Harbor, John S. Wood, director of industrial sales, was appointed emergency defense co-ordinator of the Company in charge of its volunteer defense corps, which reached a peak enrollment of 5,000 people and participated in sixty-five alerts. Training courses were given in first aid, fire fighting, war emergency police protection, and the procedure to be followed in shutting off gas services. The effectiveness of this program won for the Company the National Security Award "for extraordinary achievement in establishing superior security and protection measures against enemy air raids, fire, sabotage, and avoidable accidents. . . . the award indicates a fine spirit of co-operation of management and employees beyond the call of routine duty."

Early in the war, Liversidge was troubled by the lack of liaison between the government and the utility industry. He felt the urgent need of placing the operating utilities in a position where they could be of service to the government. With the help of others, he evolved a plan to this end and presented it to President Roosevelt. With Roosevelt's blessing, the Council of Electric Operating Companies, supported by more than one hundred utilities, opened its headquarters in Washington on April 1, 1942. During its first year, the Council co-operated with the Selective Service System and the War Manpower Commission in the classification of critical jobs for the guidance of draft boards. It assisted the Signal Corps and the Navy in procuring specialists and administrative executives for war services; and it formed committees of operating men to co-ordinate the power industry with the War Production Board and other war agencies in determining power-pooling policies and the distribution of surplus materials.

While Liversidge believed that the Council filled a useful role in the promotion of the war effort and created a friendly bond with Federal agencies, he was ever intensely aware of the problem of maintaining friendly ties at home in the field of customer relations. He kept hammering away at the concept of high-grade service that would guarantee total acceptance of the Company by its customers. At a time when the public was frustrated and harassed by shortages and inconveniences, Liversidge stressed the ideal of service. On March 25, 1941, he informed his directors: "No more significant emphasis has been placed on the many phases of our operation than that which concerns our relations with customers and the public, and I feel that our efforts have been more than ordinarily effective. However, with present conditions undergoing rapid changes, we are undertaking a Company-wide survey of the supervisory personnel in order not only to re-emphasize the importance of good customer relations, but also through this medium to concentrate on future ways and means to improve our service still further."

And again, in December, 1943, he reported: "There has been no curtailment in our policy of catering to customer needs and requirements to the maximum extent possible under present wartime conditions. . . . It is particularly pleasing to note that there have been numerous instances in which customers have made a point of complimenting us for prompt and courteous service and have contrasted our handling of their problem with the arbitrary and even brusque treatment frequently accorded them elsewhere and blamed on the war. It is being stressed among all service group employees that the unusual and unexpected courtesy shown to customers has a 'long pull' value now greater than ever before."

Liversidge's zeal in promoting the ideal of service was recognized just two months later when he received an honorary degree of Doctor of Science from his alma mater, the Drexel Institute of Technology. The citation accompanying the degree stressed the human qualities which underlay his personnel and public relations policies: "His technical achievements as an engineer, including many notable improvements in the equipment of generating and substations, have been supplemented by outstanding contributions to the promotion of cordial relations with the consuming public and with his co-workers, whose respect for him and loyalty to him constitute an impressive tribute to his genius for leadership."

Liversidge was not the only Philadelphia Electric man honored for his work on the home front. Vice-President Whitwell in 1942 was elected president of the Chamber of Commerce and Board of Trade of Philadelphia. In 1944, he added the presidency of the Pennsylvania Electric Association to his many responsibilities. Vice-President Funk was singled out in 1943 for the presidency of the American Institute of Electrical Engineers. Throughout the war period, Philadelphia Electric men were active in bond rallies, blood drives, and every sort of civilian enterprise calculated to advance the war effort. In addition, the Company lent the services of some of its most highly qualified specialists to government agencies, including the Army and Navy. K. M. Irwin, C. C. Farrell, Lewis B. Beatty, and J. A. TenBrook were among those engaged in such assignments.

Of course, the big job for the average employee was to see that customers received all the electricity and gas they required. In this they were successful, even though the electric peak load in 1944 was nine times the peak of World War I, and the gas peak was more than six and a half times greater.

With the war raging into its final phases, Philadelphia Electric found itself embattled with a problem that had nothing to do with the war—the old question of the value of its properties. Their valuation was important because rates were based on an allowable percentage of return on that value. Some years earlier, the Company had been required to classify its plant on the basis of "original cost" in accordance with the accounting requirements of the Federal Power Commission, and had come up with the figure of $54,886,626 for Conowingo (as of March 1, 1934), and $314,883,995 for the rest of the system (as of January 1, 1938). This latter figure was prepared by Day & Zimmermann.

In 1944, the Federal Power Commission issued orders requiring the Company to show cause why it should not reduce the value of its Conowingo account by $6,133,037, and the value of its other account by $37,105,567, plus additional adjustments of about $7,000,000, pending further studies. Large as these figures were, they were relatively small compared to similar demands made on other systems.

After extended conferences, Philadelphia Electric in 1945 agreed to write off $28,652,670 from its principal account. This adjustment represented the difference between plant cost, as reflected on the Company's books, and "original cost," as recognized by accounting requirements. "Original cost" was defined as the cost to the person first devoting a property to public service, and not the cost to the present holder of the property. A large part, $18,577,258, of the adjustment was the expenditure incurred many years before in amalgamating the large number of predecessor companies into the present consolidated system. To a major extent, the remaining adjustments, $10,075,412, represented the difference between property values appraised under newer methods and values which had once been recognized for ratemaking purposes but which were no longer allowable.

It took until 1947 to settle the "original cost" of Conowingo at $50,895,903, or $3,970,722 less than the Company had claimed. Thrown out were the cost of Drexel's option and the profits realized by other banking interests in putting together and promoting the real estate holdings and hydroelectric rights which Philadelphia Electric took over to create Conowingo.

The Company came through the war years with less wear and tear than it had in World War I. It was aided by a better-directed national war effort and by a more decentralized industry. Relatively, the demands on Philadelphia Electric had not been as great. By 1944, the rapid rise in industrial power needs had begun to level off and the worst was over, even though Germany did not surrender until May, 1945, and Japan not until the following August.

When demands by the Army and Navy on manufacturers of electrical equipment eased, the Company filed an application with the War Production Board for authority to resume construction of Southwark Station. In September, 1944, permission was granted, Southwark becoming the first large utility project so released during the war. Another indication that the war effort was over the hump had occurred the month before when restrictions on gas house heating had been lifted. Before this action, Philadelphia Electric had been able to take on only those hardship cases approved by the War Production Board. During the last four months of 1944, a large number of gas heating installations were made, and in 1945 the Company was swamped with orders which it attempted to supply to the best of its production and transmission capabilities. A renewed construction program at the Chester gas plants was undertaken to increase manufacturing capacity twelve per cent. New transmission mains were also laid.

There were many evidences that the end of the war would bring increased demands on the Company. In its last appliance sales campaign of 1941—all records for domestic appliance sales were smashed that year—proof of greatly increased purchasing power in such Philadelphia districts as Kensington, Frankford, and South Philadelphia had been noticed. Despite the curtailment of appliance sales in 1942, the kilowatt-hour consumption per residential customer had risen from 1,025 in 1939 (the year it had first averaged more than 1,000) to 1,324 in 1945. The increased spending power of thousands of workers made this possible. In 1944, the rate of increase in kilowatt-hours for residential customers was actually more than seventy per cent higher than the best rate of increase during the period when electric ranges and water heaters were most aggressively promoted. Moreover, the base of the Company's business had been broadened with the influx of war workers and the building of vast housing projects. Philadelphia Electric took on 59,000 residential customers during the war—a ten per cent growth.

Throughout the war, the sales department had maintained an active interest in all new developments relating to the utilization of electricity and gas. A variety of surveys was completed, and plans were developed to promote potential markets. The most promising fields appeared to be in gas house heating, better industrial lighting, air conditioning, television, and a more widespread use of electric and gas appliances. An enormous building boom was anticipated.

With the end of the war, these plans went into operation. In co-operation with the Electrical Association of Philadelphia, the sales department had helped organize the retail appliance dealers division of the Association, set up to exploit to the full the huge market that came into existence with the lifting of restrictions on the manufacture of durable goods. In addition, and again in cooperation with the Electrical Association, the department pressed a continuous advertising program for the modernization of home wiring. Through the industrial expansion committee of the Philadelphia Chamber of Commerce and Board of Trade, of which J. F. Gaskill, manager of the Company's industrial sales department, was chairman, plans were developed to attract new industries to Philadelphia Electric's service area.

Thus, as ninety per cent of the Company's permanent employees who had entered the service began to return to their old jobs, Philadelphia Electric was alive to every possibility for extending its facilities. Its major problem was its deficiency in generating capacity. Far greater gas output was also needed. Indeed, a construction program of staggering magnitude lay ahead.

Liversidge had the future very much in mind on November 28, 1945, when he arose to address the Newcomen Society at the Bellevue-Stratford Hotel. The history of Philadelphia Electric Company was the subject of his talk, but he projected his thoughts into the days to come, when new ways of doing things would require inestimably greater output from his Company. The future, he felt certain, would not find Philadelphia Electric wanting. "We look forward with confidence to brighter days ahead," he concluded, "eager to meet the challenge of a public demand for electric service as nearly perfect as it is humanly possible to provide."

CHAPTER 19

Postwar Years

ALTHOUGH Liversidge and Americans in general were hopeful of prosperous times with the re-establishment of peace, business prospects bore a forbidding aspect. The end of the war in August, 1945, brought a sharp reduction in industrial activity, and serious concern arose over the possibilities of a severe recession, if not a return to the depressed conditions of the previous decade.

At this time, Philadelphia Electric was building its delayed Southwark Station, an addition that was badly needed because peak electric demands were greater than the Company's output. Southwark would bring 169,000 kilowatts onto the lines in 1947, and another 169,000 in 1948, increasing total capacity to 1,590,250. With that much power soon to be available, management felt relieved that it had not committed the system to further increases in the face of a possible depression that would retard the economic growth of the country and lower demands for electricity.

Abruptly, the economic situation made an about-face, projecting so startling a rate of business growth that the entire utility industry was to be kept scrambling for years in its efforts to meet the nation's needs. Impressive new peak demands were registered in 1946, and Philadelphia Electric completed its first full postwar year with no appreciable loss in sales. From then on, the growth of the Company's business followed the phenomenal pattern of the times. It was in 1945 that the system first earned more than $100,000,000; in 1955, revenues soared well above the $200,000,000 mark. Steam heat and gas revenues had trebled. Electric revenues were far more broadly based and could not show so steep a climb. Even so, they had doubled. To supply the enormous new demands of its customers, Philadelphia Electric had acquired additional sources of gas and had doubled its electric generating capacity. In these unprecedented years of growth, the value of the Company's plant had risen from $425,335,000 to $868,350,000.

Many factors in the nation's economic life were responsible for the rapid growth rate the country was experiencing. By the end of the war, the American people had accumulated enormous savings and were clamoring for the commodities they had been denied since 1941. Manufacturers quickly reconverted their factories and began to pour out civilian goods. So great was the demand that it was several years before the initial postwar appetite of the buyers' market could be satisfied. Sales were then sustained by a widespread purchasing power that stemmed from higher wages. Moreover, the end of the war released dammed-up inventive potential, and many new products appeared to entice the buyer.

Domestic food freezers, which were not being manufactured in 1941, went into 87,000 American homes in 1946. The next year, 300,000 of them were sold. Their sales continued to increase until 1954, when the combination refrigerator-freezer made its first substantial impact on the market.

Meanwhile, television, after a retarded start, had become a star performer. In 1941, there were about three hundred sets in the Philadelphia area, and plans for the city's first commercial television broadcasts were announced, only to be halted by the war. As late as 1947, there were but a few thousand sets owned locally.

Dealers had difficulty in selling television because there were no regularly scheduled daytime programs and it was thus difficult to demonstrate models to customers. Clara Zillessen, Philadelphia Electric's advertising manager, evolved a plan to promote sales through a Company-sponsored afternoon show, "Television Matinee," which began in February, 1947.

At this time, studio conditions were crude. Lights were so strong that metal objects became too hot to handle. Substitute materials, such as mashed potatoes masquerading as ice cream, were used. Gelatin was made seven times normal strength to prevent it from melting. In October, 1949, having served its original purpose, the name of the show was changed to "Television Kitchen," a program advertising the uses of electricity in cooking. Under the charge of Mrs. Florence P. Hanford, home economist for Philadelphia Electric, this show is the oldest singly sponsored telecast in the world. In another pioneer effort by the Company to encourage new ideas, "Television Kitchen" has been televised in color since November, 1956.

Before television was available, Philadelphia Electric's home economists gave public demonstrations of electric cooking and of the use of various electric appliances. These demonstrations, held in the Edison Building's auditorium, and in public halls, theaters, and department stores, could be watched by only a few hundred spectators at a time. It has been estimated that Mrs. Hanford is sometimes seen in a single television demonstration by as many as 100,000 people.

Television was a significant postwar load builder, its growth for some years being limited only by the ability of manufacturers to produce receivers. In 1952, Philadelphia Electric estimated that eighty-five per cent of its residential customers owned sets. That percentage has continued upward to the near-saturation point of ninety-five per cent. Today, at least 1,000,000 homes served by the Company contain one or more television sets.

Television was only one of many new or improved electric devices eagerly purchased for the modern home. Automatic laundry equipment, clocks, incinerators, automatic toasters, razors, and air conditioning were all priced within the means of the average American. While not solely responsible, air conditioning played the major role in eliminating deep summer valleys in electric demand. In contrast with Philadelphia Electric's June, 1940, peak, which dipped to seventy-five per cent of the previous December peak, comparable figures in 1953 showed a dip to only ninety-five per cent, and air conditioning was becoming more popular every year. In 1953, for example, 26,000 unit air conditioners, mostly for home use, were installed in the system's service area. The next year, 31,000 more were added; in 1955, the figure was up to 40,000.

By this time, air conditioning had become an accepted requirement in all new office buildings, stores, and hotels. Older buildings were being renovated to include it. Cost became secondary to comfort; the management of one office building that had cost $10,000,000 twenty-five years earlier spent $5,000,000 on an air-conditioning system.

The purchase of heavy-duty appliances increased residential consumer use of electricity to the point that wiring, particularly in older houses, was no longer safe. Consumer use is measured in kilowatt-hours. In 1945, the average residential customer was using 1,324 kilowatt-hours a year; in 1955, the average use was 2,619 kilowatt-hours. Obviously, something had to be done to strengthen wiring. In 1953, Philadelphia Electric and the Electrical Association of Philadelphia inaugurated an intensive home wiring modernization program, bringing together all segments of the electric industry into one activity. The Company promoted this program by extensive advertising, and extended loans to customers to help finance wiring jobs.

The residential load increased not only because the individual homeowner was using more electricity, but because of an enormous suburban building boom which brought thousands of customers onto the Company's lines. The trend in new home construction was to include a larger number of major electric and gas appliances, such as automatic washers and dryers, incinerators, and air conditioners, in the purchase price of the property, thus providing for greater use of electricity and gas at the time of occupancy. From 1945 to 1955, Philadelphia Electric connected an average of nearly 29,000 new electric customers a year. It was, of course, also making impressive gains in gas customers, but that is another story. However, both gas and electricity shared in the business created by the large communities which were replacing farm areas around the city. In the 1950's, the most spectacular of these developments were Levittown, with its more than 17,000 homes, and Fairless Hills, both built to house United States Steel Corporation workers brought in to man the new $400,000,000 Fairless Works on the Delaware River at Morrisville.

The Fairless Works became the focal point of a Delaware Valley renaissance, spurring on industrial and residential growth. Giant new structures were erected at record-breaking speed, and industry made a definite shift toward the suburbs. In prewar days, suburban industrial sales amounted to only thirty-six per cent of the total; by 1955 they accounted for forty-six per cent. The

PLYMOUTH SERVICE BUILDING, OPENED NEAR NORRISTOWN IN 1956

"Operation Snowdrop"
Surveying damage caused by the great March, 1958, storm

demand on the system for more and more power mounted steadily.

While Vice-President Funk and his engineers worked tirelessly to increase generating capacity, Vice-President Whitwell and his cohorts in sales were indefatigable in their pursuit of new business. During the war, the sales department had made surveys of homes in the Company's service area to determine what appliances they lacked. Later, Philadelphia Electric's salesmen arrived, and, if they did not succeed in making the sales themselves, they often aroused enough interest so that the customer eventually bought the appliance from a dealer.

The Company's promotion of industrial development was carried on under the leadership of J. F. Gaskill, who by personal contacts persuaded many industries to move to the Philadelphia area. Through such work, Philadelphia Electric made a very real contribution to the area's growth. Local banks and railroads were also active in this endeavor. Great credit, for example, goes to the Pennsylvania Railroad for its help in influencing United States Steel to locate its Fairless Works at Morrisville.

In that connection, Martin W. Clement, president of the Pennsylvania Railroad, told Liversidge that Philadelphia Electric should do more to promote the Delaware Valley. Liversidge discussed this criticism with Vice-President Conover, who had several times suggested public relations programs to stimulate area development. One such program was worked out to promote initially the Port of Philadelphia and, later, the entire service area. On June 30, 1951, this national advertising campaign was launched in an issue of the *Saturday Evening Post*. The Company had no hesitation in publishing the advantages of Greater Philadelphia as a good place in which to work and live, for the Company's growth and prosperity were linked to that of its service area, which was then on the threshold of its greatest industrial expansion.

The port was one of the city's spectacular features: it was the nation's fastest growing seaport, soon to become the largest port of entry in terms of tonnage in the United States. Philadelphia Electric's port advertisements were colorful and imaginative, and went all over the country, indeed, all over the world. The Company's program was the only one designed solely to put Philadelphia "on the map." Whether the program has actually stimulated area development is an intangible, but from a public relations point of view it has done a great deal to bring Philadelphia Electric's name before its far-flung army of stockholders, to interest its customers favorably, and to promote the city in a manner that has won warm recognition from civic authorities and trade bodies.

By the time this program was instituted, Philadelphia had many new improvements to boast about, and others were on the way. A massive modernization program was in progress which was changing the city's appearance, eradicating obsolete methods and archaic roadblocks to its development. For two hundred and sixty-four years, Philadelphians had used ferries to cross the Delaware to Camden. The peak of this service was reached in 1925, when ten vessels provided trips every three minutes. But the Delaware River Bridge (now Benjamin Franklin Bridge) was opened the next year, and on March 31, 1952, ferryboat service ended, its prospects ruined not only by the Delaware River Bridge but by the Walt Whitman Bridge in South Philadelphia, whose construction was soon to provide another highway link to New Jersey.

It was in 1952 also that the Philadelphia Orchestra gathered at Broad Street Station to play "Auld Lang Syne" as the last train pulled away from the famous depot. The station and its celebrated "Chinese Wall," the fort-like structure on which trains had rolled in from west of the Schuylkill, was demolished, opening up a blighted center city area on which a modern, planned complex of office buildings, a hotel, and other structures—"Penn Center"—was to rise. Urban redevelopment changed other blighted sections at an impressive rate; the long-planned superhighways that were to penetrate the city and make it more accessible were at last abuilding. Large new apartment houses crowned the heights of the Schuylkill along the approaches to the city. At Hog Island in 1953, a fine new building replaced the utterly inadequate terminal of Philadelphia's International Airport.

Something was even being done about the city's street lighting. During the depression, curtailments in street lights lost Philadelphia Electric about half its street lighting load. This business remained stagnant until 1941, when the Company initiated an improvement program, which the city adopted. Unfortunately, the program was no sooner started than wartime restrictions ended it.

Street lighting, based on a set price per lamp per year, was not a particularly profitable part of the Company's work. Not only did the Company supply the electricity through its distribution system (the city also furnished some distribution lines), but it provided nearly all the utilization equipment—the standard, the bulb, and the globe. An enormous stock of these units in many varieties and sizes had to be kept on hand. Maintenance of the equipment necessitated painting the standards, washing the globes, and replacing worn-out bulbs. Many controversial problems having to do with cost and maintenance arose with municipal officers. Rates, meanwhile, did not keep pace with the rising expenses incident to the service.

In 1951, Whitwell proposed a fifteen-year, multimillion-dollar plan for the rehabilitation of the city's lighting, which, despite improvements since 1946, was still considerably below recognized standards. As the first part of this program, the Company installed 103 mercury-vapor lights on Chestnut Street in November, 1951. These lights gave nine times the average intensity of the incandescent lights they replaced, but they were not the first of their type in Philadelphia, for the city itself had already erected some on Vine Street. In the adoption of new types of lighting, Philadelphia Electric had been conservative. It had viewed the fluorescent lighting of the mid-1930's with initial disfavor, and later had been slow to accept mercury-vapor lights.

Plans to modernize street lighting had not proceeded far before an arrangement with the city took the matter out of Philadelphia Electric's hands. On January 1, 1955, ownership of all city-owned distribution facilities—conduits, cables, wire, transformers and related equipment—was vested in the Company, and ownership of all utilization equipment—lamp posts, foundation brackets, and lights—went to the city, thereby eliminating certain areas of controversy resulting from joint responsibility. With this change, the Company's role was limited to supplying electricity to lamp posts as it would to a home; the rate for the service was based not on the number of lamps, but on the kilowatt-hours of electricity used. In the suburbs, the old rate method still prevails, the Company charging a flat annual price per lamp.

"Excess cost" had been the chief point of controversy between Philadelphia Electric and the city. In making installations for the city, the Company had not been willing to shoulder all the costs if it appeared that they were uneconomically large, if the cost of the job ran in excess of what the Company could expend for the revenue expected. That part which the Company did not feel it should pay, the "excess cost," became a bone of contention. This problem has been avoided in the suburbs, however, because developers have generally been held responsible for assuming "excess cost" in the installation of street lighting for new developments.

The rapid growth of suburban communities can be illustrated in the number of their street lights as contrasted with those in the city.

Year	Suburban Lights	City Lights
1940	24,500	32,300
1945	26,800	33,800
1946	27,700	34,150
1950	32,300	37,100
1955	45,300	47,400

While by 1955 the number of lights in the city and suburbs was roughly comparable, the average Philadelphia street light was much stronger than those in the adjoining counties. In terms of lumens (there are about ten lumens per candlepower—a hundred-watt bulb generates 1,640 lumens), the total generated light for city and suburban street lamps presents a more divergent series of figures.

Year	Suburban Lumens	City Lumens
1940	23,350,000	80,500,000
1945	40,960,000	84,111,000
1946	42,270,000	91,064,000
1950	53,650,000	216,838,000
1955	98,676,000	287,211,000

The power demand required by new and improved street lighting, by industry, and by the vast residential and commercial growth of the service area presented the Company with a serious problem. As has been noted, before the second unit at the $46,000,000 Southwark

Station was available, Philadelphia Electric was unable to meet peak demands without purchasing current from the Interconnection.

In common with most of the electric industry, the Company operated on a five-year plan in calculating future capacity requirements. Generally speaking, it takes between three and five years from the time a major turbine is ordered until it is installed and in operation. By September, 1946, Liversidge knew that the capacity of the system in 1948, even with Southwark in full swing, would not be sufficient. Two generators were ordered to reinforce the 48,000-kilowatt Barbadoes Station, which was no longer able to supply the demands of its area. The cost of this addition was to come to $23,000,000.

Immediately following the war, steam turbine manufacturers were booked to capacity for three years ahead. To expedite matters, an organization of engineering committees met with the manufacturers to determine on standardized equipment which would satisfactorily meet the requirements of a majority of utility companies. Acceptance of standardized equipment in lieu of "tailor-made" units permitted the manufacturer to speed up delivery dates. Although Philadelphia Electric played an important role in establishing the standard turbogenerators, the only ones it ever purchased were the two 66,000-kilowatt units for Barbadoes. The machines it was subsequently to order were all much larger than the standard sizes.

Long before the two Barbadoes units went into operation in 1949, a 182,000-kilowatt generator had been ordered for Richmond Station, at an estimated cost of $20,000,000. Meanwhile, the big Southwark Station, its handsome exterior the work of architect Paul Cret, put its first generator into commercial service on August 1, 1947. When its second unit went on the lines early in

1948, Southwark's 338,000-kilowatt capacity supplied approximately one third of the total steam-generated output of the system. Ernest Hopping, the Company's chief mechanical engineer, had been in charge of much of the design of Southwark Station. On his retirement in 1950, James Harlow took his place.

In October, 1950, steam was turned into the new Richmond unit, increasing Richmond Station's rating to 467,000 kilowatts and making it the Company's largest generating plant. But this addition simply enabled Philadelphia Electric to keep up with current demand; two more generators were on order for Delaware Station. Enlarging Delaware was to cost $41,000,000. Its two new generators, each having an effective capacity of 136,000 kilowatts, were somewhat smaller than the Company might have wished, but were as large as the space available at Delaware Station could accommodate. With demands continuing upward, orders were placed for two more units, one of 165,000 kilowatts and the other of 220,000 kilowatts, to be installed in a new $59,000,000 Cromby Station on the Schuylkill near Phoenixville, where an earlier generating station of the same name had been taken out of service in 1928. Ground was broken for Cromby on May 31, 1951.

In 1953, the two 136,000-kilowatt units at Delaware Station went into operation. Significant of advances in the art of electric generation was the fact that while it required 146 men to operate the 195,750 kilowatts of capacity in the old part of Delaware Station, the new part with its 272,000 kilowatts called for only twenty-four more workers.

When the generators at Cromby came into service in 1954 and 1955, the system's capacity was raised 385,000 kilowatts, but, even so, forecasts pointed to the need of much greater capacity. A 185,000-kilowatt machine was ordered for Schuylkill Station, where in 1955 some 44,000 kilowatts of capacity were lost with the dismantling of the last of the vertical turbines, three small units which had been installed in 1911 and 1913. Orders were also placed for two more enormous generators, more powerful than any owned by the Company. Another new plant would have to be built to house them.

In the years 1946 through 1955, the Company brought its capacity up from 1,246,250 to 2,477,250 kilowatts, an impressive ten-year increase. But all through this building period, increased capacity had done little better than hold its own when measured against the system's peak demands. The following table shows how closely rising peaks pursued mounting capacity:

Year	Peak KW Demand	KW Capacity
1946	1,316,000	1,246,250
1947	1,369,000	1,421,250
1948	1,477,000	1,590,250
1949	1,488,000	1,758,250
1950	1,678,000	1,879,250
1951	1,747,000	1,886,250
1952	1,818,000	1,886,250
1953	1,873,000	2,136,250
1954	2,000,000	2,286,250
1955	2,230,000	2,477,250

Although the Company's capacity was enlarged in 1950 because of the new Richmond unit, the net gain to the system was decreased by the sale of Deepwater Station, which had been contributing 54,000 kilowatts to Philadelphia Electric. Since 1930, the Company had jointly owned and operated this plant in New Jersey. The other owner, American Gas and Electric Company (now American Electric Power), had used its share of Deepwater to supply its subsidiary, Atlantic City Electric

Company. Because of "integration" proceedings, American Gas and Electric was forced to divest itself of Atlantic City, and in 1946 Philadelphia Electric seriously considered purchasing the New Jersey property. For a variety of reasons, it declined the opportunity, but continued as joint owner of Deepwater until 1950, when it sold its interest to Atlantic City Electric for $6,200,000. Philadelphia Electric thereby received money to support its expansion program, and Atlantic City Electric obtained sufficient generating capacity to meet the needs of its rapidly growing southern New Jersey area for some years to come.

Building new plants and increasing the size of old ones called for corresponding additions to the transmission and distribution facilities. Southwark Station, for example, was interconnected with the rest of the system by three 66,000-volt underground lines, two from Southwark to Schuylkill, and one from Southwark through Delaware Station to Westmoreland Substation. A fourth line from Schuylkill to Westmoreland completed the loop. The amount of bulk power to be transmitted from Schuylkill Station to West Philadelphia after the building of Southwark created a problem, because if overhead lines were to be used, the vulnerability to multiple losses resulting from the congestion of the lines made this solution impractical from the point of view of system reliability. In 1946 and 1947, a $650,000 tunnel was dug under the Schuylkill to accommodate the necessary river-crossing circuits.

Next, consideration had to be given to the development of communities and industries in lower Bucks County following the construction of the Fairless Works, which brought on a rapidly increasing load concentration in the Company's northeastern territory. This section had been an outlying rural area of light load density, and had been supplied by means of transmission lines from Richmond Station. By 1951, it had become necessary either to build a generating station there, or to reinforce the transmission system.

Across the Delaware River in New Jersey, the Public Service Electric and Gas Company found itself in quite a different position. Because of the development of South Jersey, Public Service had expanded facilities at its Burlington station. With ample power there, it was now experiencing heavy load growth in the vicinity of Camden, south of Burlington. Planning engineers of Philadelphia Electric and Public Service tackled their problems jointly, effecting solutions on the basis of mutual use of facilities as if the two systems were parts of one over-all company. Their objective was to draw on New Jersey's Burlington plant to supply Philadelphia Electric's northern area, and to draw on Richmond Station to supply Camden. An existing double-circuit 66,000-volt tower line between the Company's Emilie Substation in Levittown and Public Service at Trenton was converted to a single-circuit 132,000-volt line in 1951, and a new 132,000-volt cross-river tie was established between Burlington station of Public Service and Philadelphia Electric's Emilie Substation in 1952. These lines reinforced the transmission system supplying the Bucks County area. Additional power for South Jersey was provided by extending a new 132,000-volt tie between Richmond Station of Philadelphia Electric and Camden substation of Public Service in 1951. Through this co-ordination, needed capacity was found for both systems with a minimum of capital expenditure. The new transmission lines permitted use of the stations of both systems to solve local supply problems and at the same time to increase materially the ability of the Interconnection to exchange capacity economically.

While economies in the transmission of power were important, the Company's largest expense was for coal, and the greatest economy it could achieve was to lower the coal rate by taking advantage of every advance in the art of electric generation. Each new generator it purchased improved the coal rate, for generators were becoming available in ever-larger sizes and were operated under much greater pressures and temperatures. The increasing efficiency of these units had a spectacular effect on the coal rate, bringing it down from 1.072 pounds of coal per kilowatt-hour in 1946 to 0.814 pounds in 1955.

Engineers prefer to measure generating efficiency by the amount of heat energy required to produce a kilowatt-hour. The improved Southwark units, the first of the postwar installations, had a design heat rate of 11,560 Btu. Virtually all of the Company's newer units have shown a progressively better performance, with the two 1953 Delaware turbines rated at 9,100 Btu, and the big Schuylkill generator on order in 1955 designed for 8,990 Btu. Steam pressures rose from 850 pounds for Southwark to 2,400 for Schuylkill. Moreover, the Delaware, Cromby, Schuylkill, and subsequent generating units employed the reheat cycle, in which steam, after passing through the first stages of the turbine, is returned to the boiler and reheated before going the rest of the way through, thereby providing greater power per pound of steam. This process was an important forward step in generating efficiency, for it offset rising fuel and operating costs.

For a brief time after the war, Philadelphia Electric was threatened with a more serious worry than the rising price of coal. Several times, coal virtually disappeared from the market. Two severe coal strikes in 1946 stimulated the Company to consider other fuels. The coal crisis in the first half of the year brought on one of the worst tie-ups of its kind ever faced by American industry. Although Philadelphia Electric, the city's biggest coal user, was not forced to impose any mandatory curtailment in its load, the situation was tense. In a series of half-page newspaper advertisements it requested consumers to use electricity sparingly; the Company's industrial salesmen made personal calls on major customers, urging them to restrict their use of electricity to the bare necessities. A picture in *Time* showed Petty's Island swept bare of all its coal reserves.

Before this crisis, the only units equipped to burn oil were several at Schuylkill Station, but, during the emergency, oil conversion equipment was installed at Richmond, Deepwater, and Chester Stations. The second coal strike in November and December, 1946, was harrowing enough to bring on a "brown-out" order to conserve fuel. Fortunately, with the aid of its emergency oil-fired boilers and a huge coal storage pile built up by the coal bureau, the Company was again able to surmount the shortage.

Petty's Island, located in the Delaware River opposite Delaware Station, had been the principal storage yard since 1917. Its isolated position, its relatively outmoded coal handling equipment, and the fact that its convenience to Delaware Station was no longer of prime importance—with the passage of time Delaware had become one of the less efficient plants and was not used as much as before—were all factors influencing the decision to establish a new coalyard next to Richmond Station on the mainland. After this yard with its capacity of 1,000,000 tons was completed in 1952 at a cost of $2,500,000, Petty's Island was abandoned.

While coal remained the Company's chief fuel, other fuels were used whenever it was economical to do so. In 1952, a contract was made with the Atlantic Refining Company to provide for an increased oil burn at Schuylkill Station. Earlier, plans had been made to use natural gas to fire the new boilers at Chester and Barbadoes. The advent of natural gas was not actually to make much impact on the system's generating plants, but it was to have the profoundest influence on the development of the gas department.

The growth of the Company's gas business had been uneven. During the depression years, residential sales had fallen off considerably and industrial and commercial business had also suffered. In 1939, however, the manufactured gas business entered a period of increasing sales and peak loads that were due almost entirely to the war. Industrial use of gas increased fivefold. Federal and private housing projects mushroomed, many of them using gas for heating. Between 1939 and the winter of 1944–1945, the maximum gas send-out rose from 44,000,000 cubic feet a day to 74,000,000. Improvements in manufacture rather than large expenditures on plant were in part responsible for this increased capacity. Of course, the new coke oven battery at Chester did yeoman service. In addition, there was greater use of refinery oil for making reformed gas; butane and propane were also utilized in gas-manufacturing processes.

By the end of the war, thousands of people were clamoring for gas heat. All too vivid was the recollection that oil had been rationed, but gas had not. Unfortunately, the gas send-out necessary to take on this large new heating load was not available. In the summer of 1946, the Company had on hand 9,000 orders for gas installations. Customers had to wait their turn, with priorities being granted to hardship cases. It was true that in 1946 the Company's increase in house heating customers was the greatest in its history, more than twice the number connected in 1944, but, even so, this record came to only 1,721 installations and did little more than dent the service demand.

Some relief was provided in 1947, when additional gas manufacturing capacity of 10,000,000 cubic feet a day was built into the Chester reformed oil gas plant. But this increase fell short of satisfying area requirements. Meanwhile, Philadelphia Electric continued to supply non-area needs by transmitting gas to the Wilmington and Reading utilities under long-standing arrangements. Its ability to come abreast of the rapidly growing market, eventually to supply gas to all comers, was made possible when natural gas from Texas and Louisiana was piped into its plants.

During the war, the government had constructed the "Big Inch" and the "Little Big Inch" pipe lines, parallel pipes of 24-inch and 20-inch diameter, through which flowed the crude oil so urgently needed on the eastern seaboard. After the war, the government sold these lines to the Texas Eastern Transmission Corporation, which converted them to natural gas.

In July, 1947, Philadelphia Electric contracted for a daily delivery, starting in 1948, of 20,000,000 cubic feet of gas from Texas Eastern, to be used as a raw material in its gas-manufacturing processes, supplementing existing sources of supply. Natural gas, with its heating value of approximately 1,000 Btu, was highly desirable for processing into the Company's manufactured gas, which had a heating value of only 520 Btu. In the fall of 1948, when the initial deliveries were received at the Chester and West Conshohocken plants, Liversidge was encouraged to predict: "In view of the large number of customers applying for gas heating services, the supply of natural gas to Philadelphia Electric will permit it to increase its capacity and bring nearer the time when all applicants for gas services may be accepted and adequately supplied."

In January, 1951, with the completion of a new pipe line by the Transcontinental Gas Pipe Line Corporation,

Philadelphia Electric began to receive an additional 37,000,000 cubic feet of gas. Its supply, then totaling 57,000,000 cubic feet a day, was nearly three times the amount received in 1950, but was not nearly enough to warrant a complete changeover to natural gas.

Extensive research was undertaken to determine the best use the Company could make of its new gas supply so as to maintain economical production costs and to provide the most satisfactory service to customers. Laboratories were set up at two of the Company's plants to test the physical properties of various gas mixtures. Processed or manufactured gas proved best for the Company's area. However, to take advantage of natural gas, the heat content of the processed gas had to be increased from 520 to 801 Btu. This changeover to a higher heating value was made in 1951.

At Chester, a thermal reforming process was used in the manufacture of the new gas, while at West Conshohocken a bank of three catalytic reforming units, "Girdler Reformers," was installed, assisted at first by one and then by two U.G.I. Cyclic Reformers. The Girdler units, the only ones of their kind employed by a gas utility plant, convert natural gas into other gases by passing it through tubes filled with a catalyst (nickel). These gases are then mixed with more natural gas to make the type used in customers' appliances.

The changeover in the heating value to 801 Btu was one of the major developments in the history of the gas department; it called for adjustments to some 380,000 appliances owned by 170,000 customers. The complexity of the undertaking can be appreciated when it is realized that adjustments had to be made to more than 220 different types of gas ranges, to more than 160 different water heaters, and to more than 100 different house heaters, to say nothing of the various commercial and industrial gas appliances. This work was performed by a task force of four hundred men supplied by the John B. Shriver Company, specialists in gas changeover programs.

The higher Btu content of the gas did not produce a hotter flame, but it did provide that a smaller volume of mixed gas would produce the same amount of heat as before. Important economies in the changeover included the automatic increase in the capacity of existing transmission mains, and the need for less processing equipment. Many people asked why the Company went to 801 Btu instead of 800 Btu. Since the answer was rather technical, the facetious reason sometimes given out among the staff was the coincidence that the office number at Company headquarters of E. G. Boyer, manager of the gas department, was 801.

At times, particularly in the summer, and before the depleted gas wells in the Oakford area near Pittsburgh became available for gas storage in 1953, Philadelphia Electric had available greater quantities of natural gas than were necessary for its production requirements. This surplus gas was fed into two of its electric generating stations which had been equipped to use it as fuel. In 1952, a better market was obtained for "extra" gas—the bulk of it was sold to industrial users, the first customer being the giant Fairless Works. To supply Fairless, the Company built an eleven-mile eight-inch steel high-pressure gas main from the main artery of the Trans-continental Gas Pipe Line to the steel center.

As the years passed, Philadelphia Electric succeeded in obtaining larger contracts for natural gas from its two suppliers. By the heating season of 1954–1955, it was receiving 106,334,000 cubic feet a day. No longer was it necessary to buy coke oven gas at Conshohocken, which

Gas Turbine Generator. Capacity 20,500 Kilowatts
Designed for use during peak load periods

Eddystone, the World's Most Efficient Electric Generating Station, 1961
Designed Capacity, 650,000 Kilowatts

had cost $2,799,000 in 1954 and could now be replaced with lower-cost gas-making materials. On December 31, 1954, the contract with Alan Wood Steel Company (Rainey-Wood) was discontinued after having been in effect in one form or another since 1919.

With its gas supply enormously increased, Philadelphia Electric was able to take on a tremendous house heating load. It had only 3,085 house heating customers in 1940, only 13,589 in 1948. In 1949, when it enjoyed its first full year of natural gas supply, the Company added just under 8,000 customers. Each succeeding year brought substantial increases. In 1955, when a record of 10,763 new customers was tallied up, the total number of gas house heating users had risen to 76,708, eleven times the number served by the Company at the end of the war. Revenue from gas heating had shown an increase from $1,321,701 in 1945 to $17,461,342 in 1955, and represented more than sixty per cent of total revenues derived from gas sales. During the postwar decade, the Company's annual gas send-out had increased from 8,312,900,000 cubic feet to 21,730,200,000 cubic feet.

The gas department's construction program during these years was the largest it had ever known. Substantial sums had also been spent to enlarge the Company's steam heat business. Massive amounts of capital had gone into increasing the system's electric output and into extending and strengthening its transmission and distribution lines. Despite the retirement of about $65,000,000 in plant values, and adjustments reducing its actual legitimate costs, such as the Conowingo decision and the annual amortization of other write-offs, the net increase in the value of Philadelphia Electric's plant during the years 1946 through 1955 was $443,000,000.

To finance its construction, the Company relied in part on retained earnings and reserves, and in part on the sale of securities. Half a dozen bond issues were sold through competitive bidding:

1946	$30,000,000 in 2¾% bonds
1948	$25,000,000 in 2⅞% bonds
1952	$35,000,000 in 3¼% bonds
1953	$30,000,000 in 3⅞% bonds
1953	$20,000,000 in 3⅛% bonds
1955	$50,000,000 in 3⅛% bonds

Proceeds of the 1955 issue were used not only to provide new capital, but to refund the high-rate $30,000,000 issue of 1953. In addition to bond sales, preferred stock was offered on three occasions: in 1946, 300,000 shares of 3.8% preferred brought in approximately $30,000,000; in 1948, 150,000 shares of 4.3% preferred realized about $15,000,000; and in 1953, 150,000 shares of 4.68% preferred sold for another $15,000,000.

A sign that better times had arrived at last was the Company's sale of common stock in 1949, Philadelphia Electric's first common stock offering since 1930. Stockholders were given the opportunity to buy 972,624 shares on the basis of one share for each ten they owned. The price was twenty dollars a share. In this $19,000,000 sale, the stockholders purchased ninety-three per cent of the offering, and the Company's employees took up the rest with such enthusiasm that it was clear they wanted greater ownership in Philadelphia Electric.

Liversidge, accordingly, obtained the stockholders' approval for 300,000 shares of common to be set aside for occasional offerings to employees at discounts up to fifteen per cent of the market price. In June, 1953, 100,000 of these shares, enough, it was believed, to satisfy the current demand, were offered to the employees at a price of $26.50, market value being about $31.12. The purchase terms were attractive in other ways: there was no brokerage charge; payment could be made through payroll deductions; noninterest-bearing bank loans were available. Once again, employees and annuitants, nearly 3,000 of them, oversubscribed.

A second common stock offering was made in 1954, when 906,917 shares were priced at $34.00. The shareholders subscribed for ninety-seven per cent of these and, with the balance going to underwriters, $29,420,429 came into the treasury. In 1955, another 132,232 shares were sold to the employees on easy terms. Only 100,000 shares had been offered, but the large oversubscription by the 4,431 employees and annuitants who purchased was allowed. The proceeds to the Company came to $4,337,210.

Philadelphia Electric's common stock paid an annual dividend of $1.20, a discouraging comparison with the $1.80 rate it had paid from 1931 through 1940, to say nothing of the $2.00 rate and higher which had prevailed between 1923 and 1929. Earning ability was definitely shackled, caught between the upward spiral of inflationary costs and the controlled prices of utility services. Early in 1949, when it became apparent that earnings were not keeping pace with costs, the Public Utility Commission permitted the Company to raise its electric rates a flat ten per cent, with certain rates, such as sales to utilities and transportation companies, remaining unchanged. This was the first upward revision in its electric tariffs since 1922. Except for two increases for transportation companies, there has been no electric rate rise since.

The gas business had also been hard hit by inflation. Moreover, its rate structure was out of date. With plentiful capacity but a limited market, the company had adopted promotional rates in the 1930's. These rates were designed to keep equipment operating, but could not meet construction costs for new plants which became necessary after the war. In 1947, the Company filed for higher gas rates, noting that since 1939 the price of coal had gone up sixty per cent, oil forty-four per cent, by-product gas produced by refineries ninety per cent, but that there had been no increase in gas rates for twenty-five years. These rates could no longer cover the continually rising cost of labor and of raw materials used in gas manufacture. Through a rate increase of 12.8 per cent in 1948 on certain classes of business, and a 1953 increase of 11.6 per cent, primarily on house heating service, Philadelphia Electric was able to adjust the cost of gas to fit the times. The introduction of a fuel clause was of great advantage in enabling the gas department to adjust rates automatically with fuel costs.

With rates in better alignment, and with new and more efficient generators coming into operation, Philadelphia Electric began to show a healthier earnings potential. In 1950, its dividend rate went up from $1.20 to $1.35. By 1955, successive increases had restored it to its 1940 level of $1.80.

Postwar years brought not only upward readjustment in rates and in electric and gas capacity, but a forward movement in all lines of the Company's activity, particularly in personnel. With the return of many of its people from the armed services, nearly nine hundred workers were added to the payroll in 1946, bringing the total to 7,425. About four hundred more were gained in the next year, and from then on, growth in personnel, if not spectacular, was steady. By the end of 1955, Philadelphia Electric was employing 8,700 men and women.

Again, the International Brotherhood of Electrical Workers made efforts to organize the generating station employees, centering their first try on Schuylkill Station.

On October 1, 1946, some of its workers made application to the Pennsylvania State Labor Board for a union election. The election was held on December 18, when the union was rejected as an agent for collective bargaining by a vote of 174 to 80.

The second attempt to unionize Philadelphia Electric was more determined, for it lasted longer than five years. On July 28, 1949, a representative of the I.B.E.W. notified the Company that an organizing campaign was under way. Philadelphia Electric took the position that its workers did not require union protection. This stand was solidly endorsed by *Forbes*, the business magazine, in January, 1951: "Best labor relations records in the utility industry belong to Philadelphia Electric, Cleveland Electric Illuminating, Consolidated Edison, and Commonwealth Edison." Moreover, "Philadelphia Electric is one of those rarities among large corporations—a company which traditionally has had such a fine labor policy that unions have made scarcely a dent in organizing its employees. The company has had the reputation of being one of the best work-places in Philadelphia, has had a company-paid pension program since 1911, and had a pay review policy to adjust for cost-of-living rises before such provisions became common."

The I.B.E.W. increased its efforts, striking at paternalism, and warning that without a union contract workers were at the mercy of the "boss." In 1952, it intensified its campaign, meetings were held throughout the system, and much literature was distributed. From August, 1953, until the climactic election day of November 9, 1954, the union issued a special publication, *IBEW News for Philadelphia Electric Employees*.

It is doubtful that the organizers could have done more to bring the union issue squarely to the front. At last, satisfied that the time had come, I.B.E.W. leaders notified Philadelphia Electric in February, 1954, that the union now represented all of the power plant employees and was ready to engage in collective bargaining on their behalf. Liversidge refused to recognize this claim, and the controversy was referred to the National Labor Relations Board, which had replaced the Pennsylvania State Labor Board in jurisdiction over Philadelphia Electric. Unlike the Pennsylvania Board, the National Board would not permit elections for individual stations, ruling, instead, that the appropriate unit for collective bargaining was the total number of production and maintenance employees working in all the Company's generating stations. At the election which the National Labor Relations Board directed to be held, the workers again rejected the union by a vote of about two to one.

Labor unions make a strong appeal to an employee's sense of security. While it is important that he have a good, well-paid job, the most vital factor in his working life is having a job at all. In the contest just described, wages were not the compelling issue because at Philadelphia Electric they were near the top in the utility industry. Fringe benefits had also been greatly increased in the years just past and the Company was in a strong position in this respect.

During the war and for some time after, wages and retail prices had been virtually frozen under government regulation, but, despite these controls, living costs had mounted. Philadelphia Electric's first general postwar wage increase, a thirteen per cent raise, was made on March 1, 1946. Living costs rose so sharply that year that on October 1 another general increase was made. Inflation continued to lower the purchasing power of the dollar, but each time living costs threatened to pull away from wage rates an increase was made. During the first ten years after the war, the following twelve general salary raises were declared by the Company:

March 1, 1946	13%	October 1, 1950	6%
October 1, 1946	13¢ an hour	September 1, 1951	3%
August 1, 1947	4%	June 1, 1952	7½%
April 2, 1948	4%	August 1, 1953	6%
January 1, 1949	7%	August 1, 1954	4%
February 1, 1950	6%	August 1, 1955	3¼%

In terms of rising labor costs, these increases do not tell the entire story. Additional benefits in vacation time, insurance, pension, and other fringe areas added to the over-all amount paid out by Philadelphia Electric on behalf of its employees.

Inevitably, the postwar decade brought hundreds of changes in the personnel ranks, and a number of changes in officers. Vice-President Bernard P. Carey died in 1947, and was succeeded by Vincent P. McDevitt as general counsel in charge of the legal department. McDevitt, who had served as chief counsel of the Public Utility Commission, was elected vice-president and general counsel in 1949 on the same day that A. S. Corson, formerly a vice-president of U.G.I., was appointed comptroller of the Company.

In the meantime, other important changes had taken place. On June 24, 1947, Liversidge was elected chairman of the board, a position which relieved him of some of the Company routine and permitted him to concentrate his energy on matters of policy. It is customary for the president of a corporation to be its chief executive officer, but, in electing Liversidge chairman, the directors would not permit him to lay down the executive leadership. He retained it to the day of his death. Executive

Vice-President Bryans succeeded him as president, with N. E. Funk moving into the executive vice-presidency and a Company directorship. In the following year, 1948, K. M. Irwin was elected vice-president in charge of engineering, and H. N. Ramsey became vice-president in charge of purchases, insurance, and real estate.

On February 27, 1950, N. E. Funk resigned his positions, having served as a vice-president since 1929. He continued with the Company, however, as an engineering consultant. A man of forceful character, of impressive technical skill, Funk had demonstrated exceptional ability in training executives. It was he who had brought Irwin to Philadelphia Electric in 1931, and thereby provided a successor for himself in the engineering department. It was Funk also who helped develop R. G. Rincliffe, who now became executive vice-president and a director. Honors followed Funk into his semi-retirement. He was awarded the American Society of Mechanical Engineers' gold medal, and, in 1953, was cited by the Pennsylvania Society of Professional Engineers for "outstanding engineering achievements in the power generation field."

In February, 1952, President Bryans, who had passed the normal retirement age, decided to avail himself of the benefits of the Company's service annuity plan. He had spent nearly forty-five years in the utility business, and, like Funk, had been an officer of Philadelphia Electric since 1929. During his career, Bryans had attained to many posts of responsibility and prominence in the community and in his profession. He had served as president of The Union League of Philadelphia, the American Standards Association, the Pennsylvania Electric Association, and as vice-president of the Edison Electric Institute.

R. G. Rincliffe
Elected President, February 25, 1952

R. G. Rincliffe became Philadelphia Electric's new president. A number of attributes had brought him forward to the position. He learned quickly and retained what he learned. A Company way of indicating that someone was eager to learn was to say, "Why, he can ask as many questions as George Rincliffe." His ability had been demonstrated in the success he had made of every job he had tackled. Possessed of an analytical mind, an original thinker open to new ideas, his personality was aggressive and yet not disturbing. People did things for him because they wanted to.

Other changes at the executive level in this period included the election in 1952 of R. P. Liversidge as vice-president in charge of electric operations. Son of the chairman of the board, Liversidge had come to the Company in 1932, and, as superintendent successively of Barbadoes, Delaware, and Southwark Stations, had gained broad operating experience.

In 1954, when Edward Porter was advanced to the rank of senior vice-president, A. S. Corson was elected vice-president in charge of finance and accounting. Corson's career in public utility work extended back to 1906. Another executive change followed the death of Vincent A. Sommar in 1954, when Vincent J. Walsh succeeded him as secretary of the Company. Although never an officer, Charles M. Breitinger had served many years as the number two man in the financial department before his retirement in 1955. Typical of his important work was his role as principal witness at the hearings before the Federal Power Commission on the original cost of Conowingo.

Changes in directors were not numerous. The retirements of Funk and Bryans have been mentioned, as well as the election to the board of Rincliffe, who took Funk's place. Directors joining from the outside were Charles S. Redding, president of Leeds & Northrup (elected 1945), Albert A. Garthwaite, president of Lee Rubber & Tire Corporation (elected 1946), and Philip T. Sharples, chairman of the board of The Sharples Corporation (elected 1952). Only one director, Jeremiah J. Sullivan, Jr., died in office during these years. Elected in 1929, Sullivan was the senior director at the time of his death in 1954.

Philadelphia Electric's officers and directors reflected the personality of Horace P. Liversidge. Whether as president or chairman of the board, he ran the Company and took tremendous pride in it. Toward the end of 1955, he could look back on the completion of ten postwar years during which the Company had spent $1,000,000 a week in improvements. There had, of course, been problems, not the least of which was the Korean outbreak in June, 1950. Again the nation had shifted from a peacetime economy to one that bore a resemblance to that of World War II. Far-reaching security and defense plans for the Company's property were put into effect under the direction of Ralph V. H. Wood. Inflation took on renewed impetus, a large number of employees joined the service, matériel and manpower shortages developed.

No enemy action damaged Philadelphia Electric during this anxious time, but during the 1950's it was battered by storms as never before. A devastating storm in November, 1950, cut off current to 75,000 customers and blacked out 35,000 street lights. Within forty-eight hours, service was completely restored through the efforts of 2,500 employees who worked around the clock.

The 1950 storm was gentle compared with what nature had in store for the years ahead. On October 15, 1954,

Philadelphia was hit by the worst disaster so far in its history, "Hazel," a vicious tropical hurricane characterized by a sustained wind velocity of fifty to eighty miles an hour, with gusts up to ninety-four miles. Poles and wires were left a shambles, and nearly a third of the Company's 1,000,000 customers were without electricity. The giant task of restoring service was promptly undertaken by a small army of employees aided by an additional thousand tree-trimming experts, electric contracting personnel, and linemen from co-operating utilities who came in by airplane, train, and truck from Detroit, Pittsburgh, and New England. By October 18, all but about 19,000 customers in outlying areas were receiving current.

The cost of repairing the wreckage, $1,953,000, prompted Philadelphia Electric to take out an all-risk coverage to indemnify the Company for any single loss to the extent of $3,000,000 in excess of the first $500,000 of damage. This coverage was underwritten 77½ per cent by ten American companies and 22½ per cent by two English syndicates. It had not been long in effect when "Hurricane Diane" visited the area in August, 1955. Instead of wind, "Diane" brought a record-breaking rainfall which resulted in floods. To ward off the rising waters, riverside generating stations were bulkheaded with sand bags at all entrances. Fortunately, no extraordinary damage was incurred.

Of more potential danger to investor-owned utilities than acts of God was the growing trend toward public ownership of power plants. Public power advocates in Washington had discussed the establishment of additional valley authorities, similar to T.V.A., a plan which, if carried to its ultimate development, would virtually blanket the United States with government-owned generating stations and transmission lines. Should this happen, what would be the future of taxpaying utilities in competition with subsidized, nontaxpaying, government-owned systems?

The spread of government ownership was alarming to Liversidge and other public utility men. They noted that in 1935 only 1⅓ per cent of the electricity generated in the United States was manufactured by the Federal government, whereas in 1945 the amount had increased to fourteen per cent. By 1955, the government's output was to rise to 16.3 per cent, with other agencies—co-operatives, municipalities, and state power utility districts—contributing 6.2 per cent more of the national total.

Management believed it to be the Company's duty to support activities that opposed the nationalization of electric light and power, that promoted the free enterprise system against what appeared to be socialism. The chief agencies backed by Philadelphia Electric, and by the industry in general, were the Electric Companies Advertising Program, a medium for stressing the advantages and good work of private companies and for giving information on government ingress in the power business; the National Association of Electric Companies, which followed legislation in Washington affecting the industry; and the Public Information Program, which disseminated pertinent data.

Philadelphia Electric's official stand on government hydro developments was expressed in its 1949 annual report: "Your Company is not opposed to river valley developments by the government when there is justification for a sound flood control, irrigation, or reclamation project. It is opposed, however, to the sale of subsidized electric power produced by those hydro-electric developments and transmitted over government-owned transmission lines in direct competition with taxpaying utilities."

Worrisome though the government's favorable attitude toward public power had become, the nearest river valley authority was remote from Philadelphia Electric territory. If some industries had left Philadelphia to seek cheaper electric power in distant places, far more industries had recently established themselves in the Company's service area. Certainly, Philadelphia Electric's postwar growth had been impressive when viewed from the vantage point of 1955.

Impressive also was Liversidge's position in these years as the Company's "senior statesman." It would be difficult to imagine Philadelphia Electric without him. On May 25, 1948, the board made formal record that on that day he had completed fifty years of uninterrupted employment. Later, at a gathering of 3,000 employees, the anniversary was again observed. Liversidge was presented with a gold medal, and a biographical motion picture tracing his career was shown.

Civic honors attested to the high place he had earned for himself in the community. In 1951, he received from Mayor Bernard Samuel the first Powell Award "for meritorious service to the City of Philadelphia through untiring efforts in the promotion of its economic advancement and expansion." The check for $10,000 accompanying the award Liversidge signed over to the Drexel Institute of Technology, of which he had been the first alumnus to be chosen as a trustee, and of which he was to be the first trustee not connected with the Drexel family to serve as chairman of its board.

Less than a year after he received the Powell Award, the William Penn Award of the Chamber of Commerce of Greater Philadelphia—an award presented annually to an American who has contributed decisively through industry to the welfare of the people—was bestowed

335

upon him. Shortly before this was announced, *Forbes*, in rating the nation's twelve largest utilities on the basis of management, labor relations, public relations, community relations, and stockholder relations, ranked Philadelphia Electric first. Here was a mark in which Liversidge could take pride!

Other honors followed in course, several of them coming in the fall of 1955. In September, Liversidge and Rincliffe accepted on behalf of the Company an award from the Chamber of Commerce for its national advertising campaign. In making the presentation, the representative of the Chamber of Commerce said, "Today, there are many industries here that would not have been here but for Philadelphia Electric's far-sighted program." When the 1955 National Human Relations Award of the National Conference of Christians and Jews was given to him in October, Liversidge was praised for conducting his Company's affairs in such a way as to "merit for himself a place in the hall of fame of business."

As 1955 drew to its close, Liversidge had every confidence in Philadelphia Electric's future growth. Its current five-year plan called for an expansion program of $1,400,000 a week, for a total of $375,000,000 in new construction. Exciting days lay ahead. The Company was active in the research and development of atomic power, and was about to build a monumental and revolutionary new generating plant.

These were developments, however, whose culmination lay beyond the life span of Horace P. Liversidge. He died on December 8, 1955, having enjoyed good health to the very end, and having been at work as usual only two days before. In an eloquent memorial, the directors extolled his concept of public service, his integrity, courage, enthusiasm, progressiveness, judgment, and warmth of heart, his faith in Philadelphia: "We who had the privilege to know him well salute him as a great individual who enriched the life of myriads of others by an unselfish devotion to the highest type of useful public service."

For many years, Liversidge had imparted dynamic and inspiring leadership to Philadelphia Electric. His career recalls that of the man who had made him an officer, Joseph B. McCall. These two chief executives were responsible in large measure for instilling into the Company fundamental ideals of service, for imparting that certain spirit which lives on after them.

CHAPTER 20

Into the Future

Philadelphia electric's employees could draw inspiration from the leadership with which the Company had been provided from its very beginning, but the challenge of the times obscured past accomplishments. The emphasis, as always, was on the future, on the urgent necessity for improving performance. New concepts in the operation of many phases of the Company's work had to be developed and put into action.

For years, electric service prices had followed a declining trend. The spectacular growth of the industry had brought increasing customer density, concentration of load, and resultant operating efficiencies. Then, too, economies realized through the reduction of the unit fuel rate were instrumental not only in lowering the price of electricity, but in maintaining earnings in the face of inflation. Between 1948 and 1958, the system's coal rate had shown a twenty-three per cent improvement, having been reduced to 0.81 pounds per kilowatt-hour, with Cromby, the outstanding station, requiring only 0.70. Then, in July, 1958, the Company was strengthened by its 185,000-kilowatt unit at Schuylkill, which set efficiency records. A fuel oil pipe line, capable of pumping 39,000 gallons an hour into Schuylkill Station from the Atlantic Refining Company's Point Breeze works, reduced handling costs and enhanced operating dependa-

NUMBER ONE UNIT, EDDYSTONE STATION

This 325,000-kilowatt machine represents an advance to steam conditions in the supercritical range, higher than previously used in industry.

CONTROL ROOM, EDDYSTONE STATION

bility. Many impressive innovations were adopted into the system in post-World War II years—so many, in fact, that the question of how much more the Company's operations could be improved by conventional methods was becoming increasingly serious. Only through successful large-scale basic and applied research could substantial progress be made toward manufacturing electricity more cheaply.

When Rincliffe assumed the executive leadership following Liversidge's death, he created a research and development department under a new vice-president, L. R. Gaty, who had come to Philadelphia Electric as a cadet engineer in 1924. Through this department, Rincliffe hoped to strengthen and unify the Company's research endeavors, and keep it abreast of all improvements within the industry.

Gaty and his assistants worked on many promising long-range projects, including those related to atomic power applications, new methods of using electric power for heating, profitable uses and markets for fly-ash, the development of high-voltage underground transmission cables, the development of methods for using high pressures and high temperatures in power generation, and the development of gas appliances for year-round residential air conditioning. In co-operation with the engineering and operating departments, a study of electronic dispatch of power production and transmission was also undertaken. Specifications were worked out for an electronic computer to control automatically the system's electric generating units. Capable of continuously and instantaneously adjusting the output of individual generators to obtain maximum economy in over-all production, the machine was ordered for installation at Philadelphia Electric.

Although research and development existed as a separate department for only four years, it gave impetus to the

Company's interest in nuclear energy and other projects. Following the death on October 3, 1960, of K. M. Irwin, vice-president in charge of engineering, the two departments were merged, and Gaty was designated vice-president in charge of engineering and research. This step followed close on what was, undoubtedly, the Company's most sensational engineering achievement. Eddystone Station, which represented so notable an advance in the art of generating electricity, had some months earlier been placed in commercial operation.

Economies in the manufacture of electricity had been achieved by technological improvements involving the gradual increasing of operating pressures and temperatures to 2,400 pounds per square inch and 1,100 degrees Fahrenheit, with units of 150,000-kilowatt capacity and larger becoming both practicable and desirable. The decision of the American Electric Power Company in 1953 to install a 120,000-kilowatt supercritical unit at its Philo plant was a logical development in this line.

Spurred on by Rincliffe and Irwin, Philadelphia Electric management decided that it, too, would utilize supercritical pressures and temperatures at its proposed plant at Eddystone, a Delaware River section south of Philadelphia where the Company had purchased forty-five acres of water-front property in 1953. The plan, when announced in September, 1954, made headlines: Philadelphia Electric intended to build the world's greatest power plant. In it was to be installed the largest steam turbogenerator ever made, one which would operate at the hitherto unheard-of steam pressure of 5,000 pounds per square inch, the highest pressure ever used in a power station steam generator.

Eddystone Station, as it evolved through changing plans, contains two generating units, each rated at 325,000 kilowatts. Both operate in the supercritical range, although at different temperatures and pressures. Number 1 turbine, built by Westinghouse, was the one designed for main steam conditions of 5,000 pounds per square inch and 1,200 degrees Fahrenheit. The steam generator of the Sultzer Monotube type was built by Combustion Engineering, Inc. These two manufacturers, and several others, assumed that part of the developmental cost of the new equipment which represented the most advanced pioneering contribution. Number 2 unit is a more conventional machine, designed for 3,500 pounds per square inch and a temperature of 1,050 degrees.

There were no large supercritical generators in operation when Philadelphia Electric decided to build Eddystone. Consequently, the adoption of the supercritical principle was of benefit to the electric industry because it tested the promise held out by that concept. By way of explanation, "critical point" is that pressure and temperature of a substance at which the densities and other physical properties of the liquid and gaseous states are identical. Under these conditions, steam has the density of water. At supercritical pressures, water does not come to a boil. Instead, it passes directly into the supercritical state of steam with density equivalent to that of water. In so doing, it contains far more heat energy than ordinary steam, and produces more kilowatt-hours for each unit of fuel than was possible before. In fact, the Number 1 unit at Eddystone was designed to be fifteen per cent more efficient than Cromby, the Company's most economical station before Eddystone went on the lines. Its fuel rate was to be about 0.60 pounds of coal per kilowatt-hour.

The creation of this giant plant, with its generating capacity of one-fifth the system's total output, was the design and work of thousands of individuals, a few of whom carried the brunt of responsibility. Foremost among them was Vice-President Irwin, who died just as the project reached completion. Chief Mechanical Engineer Harlow supervised the mechanical end of the station and E. F. Sheehan was the general construction superintendent. Chief Electrical Engineer C. C. Farrell had charge of the electrical work until transferred to the research department, when E. B. Shew took his place. Roy Larsen served as consulting architect.

Unusual problems encountered in placing so large and advanced a station in operation slowed the construction timetable. Number 1 unit was placed in commercial operation on February 5, 1960, and, after a period of tests and corrective measures, was brought up to its rated capacity early in June. On October 7, unit Number 2 was declared in commercial use. Within a few weeks, it was producing its rated capacity and had handled loads up to 360,000 kilowatts. Thus, after six years of designing and building, Eddystone, the largest plant in the Philadelphia Electric system, came into its own at a cost of $162,000,000. Eddystone required the rebuilding of the transmission system; new substations and more than one hundred miles of transmission lines, costing $30,465,000, were erected.

While Eddystone exemplified the height of efficiency attainable from fossil fuels, Philadelphia Electric was mindful of atomic power and had taken steps to familiarize itself with nuclear energy as soon as the government had allowed private industry to do so. For some years, industry had been prohibited by the Atomic Energy Act of 1946 from producing or utilizing nuclear fuel. Atomic energy was a government monopoly. In 1950, however, the Atomic Energy Commission (A.E.C.) encouraged groups of companies to form study teams, and gave them the clearances needed for access to the closely guarded

342

information on atomic reactors. Philadelphia Electric became a member in 1952 of one of the four original groups, an organization of investor-owned utilities and manufacturing concerns ultimately known as the Atomic Power Development Associates, Inc. For several years, this group sought a feasible method of utilizing atomic fission as a source of economical electric power. Meanwhile, several Company engineers were assigned to other atomic projects. Prominent among those attached to these early developments in the atomic field were Robert F. Gilkeson and J. Lee Everett, III.

After nearly three years of investigation by groups like the one to which Philadelphia Electric belonged, it became clear that several different types of reactors were technically feasible and had attractive potential as sources of heat energy for the production of power. The preliminary studies had accomplished their purpose. It was now necessary to build and operate sizable plants to determine the economics of atomic power.

Late in 1953, industry's first opportunity to build such a plant came at the invitation of the A.E.C. Various companies submitted proposals. Philadelphia Electric and Pennsylvania Power & Light filed a joint offer, but Duquesne Light Company was awarded the project. Before long, construction was started at Shippingport, Pennsylvania, on the nation's first full-scale atomic plant.

In 1954, the atomic power field was broadened by a revision of the Atomic Energy Act of 1946. Private enterprise was now permitted to own and operate atomic power plants, but could not own atomic fuels; it was to pay rental to the government for fuel in inventory and be charged for fuel consumed. Furthermore, the licensing provisions in the 1954 Act gave the A.E.C. broad discretionary control over those seeking to construct and operate atomic facilities. Under the new law, the A.E.C.

343

in 1955 announced its first Power Demonstration Program, and invited industry to submit proposals to build large-scale atomic power plants. Later in the year, a second invitation was issued for building smaller atomic plants.

The Atomic Power Development Associates, Inc., which was supported by Philadelphia Electric, promptly formed a separate nonprofit group—Power Reactor Development Company—to design and build a 100,000-kilowatt fast-breeder reactor plant, the Enrico Fermi Atomic Power Plant, on the shores of Lake Erie at Lagoona Beach, Monroe, Michigan. On August 8, 1956, ground-breaking ceremonies for this project were held, with Admiral Lewis L. Strauss, chairman of the A.E.C., in attendance. R. G. Rincliffe, as executive vice-president of Power Reactor Development Company, gave an address, emphasizing the promise a fast-breeder reactor had of becoming commercially competitive: "It not only produces heat for generating electric energy, but it also breeds new fissionable fuel." This by-product fuel could be sold for use in other reactors.

Rincliffe and his associates foresaw the day when an atomic power plant would be built in Philadelphia Electric territory. Anticipating that time, the directors in September, 1955, decided to acquire an electric generating plant site suitable for that purpose. Three years later, when the opportunity came, Philadelphia Electric was ready.

On September 22, 1958, the A.E.C. announced that until November 21 it would receive proposals from private industry for the development, design, construction, and operation of a gas-cooled, graphite-moderated nuclear power plant of sufficient size to serve as a prototype for a future full-scale plant of similar design. To accept this welcome opportunity, an organization of

344

companies, Philadelphia Electric included, was formed; a West Coast utility agreed to serve as sponsor for the project and erect the plant in its service area. Shortly after Philadelphia Electric had committed $1,000,000 to this endeavor, the West Coast company withdrew its sponsorship, and it appeared that the investor-owned utility industry was not going to avail itself of the A.E.C. offer.

Rincliffe, who had recently returned from a tour of Russian power plants and atomic installations in Western Europe, discussed the situation with Gaty and Constantine Bary, economic analysis engineer, while flying out to Chicago. Convinced that private enterprise must play its part in atomic development, they decided in principle that Philadelphia Electric should step in as sponsor. A special meeting of the board of directors was called for November 13, the decision was made, and Gaty and his assistants then underwent a hectic eight days preparing the highly technical and lengthy proposals to be submitted to the A.E.C. Under McDevitt, the legal department, working against the same time limitations, negotiated and prepared the necessary legal documents. In the meantime, Robert E. Ginna, chairman of the board of Rochester Gas and Electric Corporation, and one of the country's leading advocates of the development of economic atomic power, successfully arranged the enrollment of fifty-three utilities as contributors to research and development associated with the design and construction of the plant. The Company's proposal arrived before the November 21 deadline and was accepted early in 1959.

According to the proposal the fifty-three utilities, members of High Temperature Reactor Development Associates, Inc. (see pages 392—394), agreed to contribute $16,500,000 toward research and development costs.

345

Philadelphia Electric pledged about $1,300,000 of this amount. In addition, since the Company was to own the plant, it was to furnish the site and to pay $8,000,000 toward its construction, a sum representing the cost of a conventional station of its size. The A.E.C., for its part, agreed to reimburse the General Dynamics Corporation $14,500,000 for research and development of the nuclear portion of the plant, and to waive a $2,000,000 fuel use charge for the first five years of operation by the Company.

Peach Bottom Atomic Power Station, as the plant was named, was to be located nine miles upstream from Conowingo Dam on the western bank of the Susquehanna River, a few miles north of the Maryland border. Its design and construction were entrusted to the Bechtel Corporation, an organization experienced through work on six other atomic power plants. Under subcontract to Bechtel, the General Atomic Division of General Dynamics Corporation was to provide the nuclear reactor and steam supply system. Actual construction of the 40,000-kilowatt station will start as soon as the A.E.C. issues a construction permit. Approximately twenty-seven months will be required to build the plant.

On August 27, 1959, when the contracts with the government for Peach Bottom were signed, spokesmen for the High Temperature Reactor Development Associates, Inc., stated: "For nuclear power to succeed in competition with conventional power sources, which normally use fossil fuels, we must set about the development of nuclear plants designed to conform to modern-day steam conditions in terms of working temperatures and pressures. Under the contracts signed today with the A.E.C., we will proceed to carry out this important developmental task with vigor and enthusiasm."

While spending millions of dollars on atomic research and development, Philadelphia Electric engineers real-

BOARD OF DIRECTORS JUNE, 1961

GARTHWAITE, DIEMAND, MCDEVITT, SCHUTT, FULLER, RAMSEY, PRESIDENT RINCLIFFE,
AMSTERDAM, CORSON, SHARPLES, STRAWBRIDGE, BRINLEY

ized that for many years to come the Company's main reliance would have to remain on conventional fuels. To obtain maximum efficiency, these fuels should be used in large, modern generators. Such considerations made the value of interconnections between electric systems greater than ever. Companies participating in interconnections benefit from the maximum use of the lowest-cost power in the combined systems. This makes possible the full use of the largest generating units available, and, because of the diversity in loads and outages, each member of the pool is enabled to operate with lower installed reserve capacity, thereby reducing operating costs and plant investment.

Since the late 1920's, Philadelphia Electric had been a pioneer in co-ordinated systems operations as a member of one of the first high-voltage interconnections. This tri-party Pennsylvania-New Jersey Interconnection was augmented on November 4, 1956, when Philadelphia Electric, together with the other original parties—Public Service Electric and Gas and Pennsylvania Power & Light—established the Pennsylvania-New Jersey-Maryland Interconnection by bringing into it Baltimore Gas and Electric and four companies of General Public Utilities which operated in New Jersey and Pennsylvania. Through other contractual arrangements, the system operations of Atlantic City Electric, Delaware Power & Light, Luzerne Electric Division of U.G.I., and Potomac Electric Power were co-ordinated with the Interconnection. This power pool serves an area of about 50,000 square miles and a population of about 17,000,000 people. Its generating capacity amounts to more than ten per cent of the total capacity of the nation's investor-owned electric companies.

Once set up, the Interconnection required strengthening as changes took place within individual systems.

347

On November 1, 1960, for example, a new 220,000-kilowatt transmission line connecting Philadelphia Electric with Baltimore Gas and Electric was placed in service. This line was also designed to tie in the Peach Bottom atomic station. The next month, another tie to New Jersey was completed, but in this case the connection was made primarily to solve a serious transmission problem and not solely for the benefit of the Interconnection.

Major transmission capacity had to be provided to link Eddystone with lower Bucks County and the northeastern section of Philadelphia, two of the system's most rapidly expanding load areas. To firm up the supply to this general area, two 138,000-volt lines of approximately 200,000 kilowatts each were required between Eddystone and the area contiguous to Richmond Station. However, only one channel for aerial transmission was available through this densely developed section—the right-of-way of the New York-Washington line of the Pennsylvania Railroad. Arrangements were made with the railroad for joint use of the space over the tracks, but in order to minimize the possibility of trouble simultaneously involving both lines from Eddystone, only one of them was installed on this aerial route. It appeared that much of the second line would necessitate expensive underground construction.

Fortunately, such a program was avoided by a coordinated plan which solved the power development of the Delaware River areas not only of Philadelphia Electric, but also of Public Service Electric and Gas of New Jersey, and Atlantic City Electric. This plan provided the three systems collective benefits which would have cost them substantially more had they sought them independently.

The joint economy was achieved by constructing a Philadelphia Electric-Atlantic City Electric-Public Service tie line extending from Chichester Substation near Eddystone across the Delaware River and through Atlantic City territory to Public Service's new Gloucester substation. At this point the transmission line benefited Public Service by strengthening electric supply in its Gloucester load area. Meanwhile, by a tap to Mickleton substation of Atlantic City Electric, that company secured additional reliability and capacity for its northern area.

As for Philadelphia Electric, the extension of the line from Public Service's Gloucester substation to its Camden substation brought Eddystone power up to the tie lines constructed between Camden and Richmond Station in 1951 and between Burlington and Emilie Substation in 1952. These lines served as the remaining links in the second circuit between Eddystone and Philadelphia Electric's northeastern area. Visually, the most spectacular aspects of this project are the two towers which carry the transmission cables over the Delaware from a point near Chester Station.

The necessity for building an enormous station like Eddystone, for investigating atomic power possibilities, for strengthening the Interconnection and extending transmission lines, reflected national factors—a growing economy and the "population explosion." In the years following 1955, the utility industry increased its capacity rapidly, despite several business recessions. Thousands of new customers were connected to the Company's lines each year, and electric operating revenues rose from $187,600,000 in 1956 to $224,382,000 in 1960.

Relatively speaking, Philadelphia Electric's suburban gas business showed an even steeper rate of climb as gas house heating became ever more popular. On October 6, 1959, the 100,000th gas house heating customer was added to the system. Residential sales accounted for two thirds of the total gas revenue. By 1961, half the homes using Philadelphia Electric gas service were being heated by gas.

To meet the increased demand, the Company secured greater supplies of natural gas from the Texas Eastern Transmission and the Transcontinental Gas Pipe Line Corporations. Deliveries were increased from the original 20,000,000 cubic feet a day in 1948 to 219,000,000 cubic feet a day in the fall of 1961. Early in 1961, a contract was signed with Sun Oil Company for the storage of liquid propane in its underground cavern at Marcus Hook. This storage will provide sufficient peak fuel to supply the Company's requirements until the fall of 1964. Philadelphia Electric also increased its manufacturing capacity by 60,000,000 cubic feet a day in 1957 when it built a $2,000,000 catalytic reforming unit at the West Conshohocken plant. Since more transmission and distribution capacity was needed, the system converted from 801 Btu gas to 900 Btu gas in 1958. The ultimate was in sight—conversion to approximately pure natural gas.

On January 1, 1958, the manager of gas operations retired. E. G. Boyer had served the system for more than forty-six years and had won wide recognition as an authority on gas technology. During his career, he had been a director of the American Gas Association, president of the Pennsylvania Gas Association, and president of the Society of Gas Lighting. A hard worker, aggressive and creative, ever searching for better methods, Boyer made many contributions to the Company. His successor was J. Henry Long, whose entire professional career, beginning in 1927, had been spent with the system. In 1959, Long was promoted to vice-president.

With natural gas playing a predominant role in the Company's supply, the coke oven plant at Chester was shut down in the spring of 1961. These Koppers ovens were no longer economical because the closing of local steel plants had dried up the coke market. The men who had worked at the plant were reassigned to other jobs.

If the increase in gas sales was relatively greater than the increase in electric sales during 1956–1961, the increase in steam operations was, again relatively speaking, even greater than the growth of the gas business. By 1959, Philadelphia Electric's volume of steam heat sales was the third largest in the nation. Many new office buildings, stores, and hotels in central city were being added to the load, including the large structures in Penn Center. Moreover, in the fall of 1959, the Company took on the extensive steam heat needs of the University of Pennsylvania. Downtown, in the heart of the old city, large new mains supplied both modern buildings and such historic monuments as the Independence Hall group, and the Pennsylvania Hospital, oldest in the nation.

Since 1950, when a twenty-four-inch steam main had been constructed from Schuylkill Station, that plant had been providing the base load in central city. This was the Company's most economic supply. Willow Station, however, remained an important source for central city heat, and was supplemented by steam purchased from the Pennsylvania Railroad's big steam plant, which had been interconnected with the system. To provide increased reliability of service and to care for peak loads, Philadelphia Electric in 1958 erected a handsome plant at 908 Sansom Street, adjoining its Edison Building and on the site of Professor Marks's old Edison Station. The Edison Steam Plant was designed to house four oil-fired boilers capable of producing 720,000 pounds of steam an hour, two of which have been installed.

At a cost of $4,000,000, the Edison plant represented a large investment in the steam system and helped to swell total construction costs, which came to $67,000,000 in 1956, $94,000,000 in 1957, $118,000,000 in, 1958

$109,000,000 in 1959, and $75,000,000 in 1960. A member of the exclusive billion-dollar corporation group, with a value in plant at original cost and in other assets amounting to $1,075,000,000 at the end of 1960, Philadelphia Electric has maintained its position as one of the largest electric and gas utilities in the United States.

While much of the money needed for construction came from the Company's own reserves, a certain amount was raised by the sale of stocks and bonds. Stockholders were offered rights to subscribe to 609,815 shares in 1957, and an additional 640,306 shares in 1959. Between 1957 and 1959, four bond sales totaling $180,000,000 were marketed. The endless construction program and its attendant financing were accompanied by increased earnings which permitted larger dividends. In 1957, the dividend rate was raised from $1.80 to $2.00; in 1959, it went to $2.24; and in 1961, the stock was split two for one, with the dividend on the new stock set at $1.20.

The growth of electric, gas, and steam heat sales were, of course, the reason necessitating the construction program. To a degree, it could be taken for granted that these sales would rise, that every year thousands of new customers would apply for utility services. Census figures show that during the 1950's the Company's suburban areas grew amazingly. The population of Bucks County went up one hundred and twelve per cent, Chester County thirty per cent, Delaware County thirty-three per cent, and Montgomery County forty-six per cent. On the other hand, the Philadelphia County figure declined three per cent, following the trend of other large cities which suffered from the population shift to the suburbs. Wilmington, for example, lost fifteen per cent of its residents during this decade; its population fell below 100,000 for the first time in half a century.

Sales grew not only because there were more customers to be served, but because people were using more and more heavy-duty appliances in their homes. Thus, in a period which was generally prosperous and wholly inflationary, it was to be expected that the call on Philadelphia Electric would become increasingly great. In 1950, gross sales of electricity, gas, and steam were $155,537,000; in 1955, they had climbed to $209,909,000; in 1960, they amounted to $273,050,000. This progression led to the belief that the Company would double in size every thirteen years.

Sales department personnel bridled at the thought that such a growth rate was virtually automatic. In their estimation, it had to be constantly stimulated by a variety of promotional activities, such as the national "Housepower" campaign, and the local "100-A" program.

This latter program, instituted in 1954, a year before the "Housepower" campaign, was designed to install house wiring that could handle the heavy loads imposed by modern appliances. Most homes wired before 1950 needed increased wire capacity. In 1955, it was estimated that four out of five houses in the Company's service area were not properly wired. Out of 1,000,000 residential customers, 360,000 had only two-wire 30-ampere service, which could not run an air conditioner, range, or water heater. The Company had tried to strengthen residential wiring back in 1947, when it had required all new homes to have at least a 60-ampere service. This endeavor was a forerunner of the "100-A" program, set up by Philadelphia Electric and the Electrical Association of Philadelphia. Through the combined efforts of these two organizations and with the co-operation of contractors, builders, and dealers in the area, notable gains were made in modernizing wiring. The Company's contribution in

353

this thrust toward better living was recognized in 1956 by *Look* magazine, which presented Philadelphia Electric with its Community Service Award for its effectiveness in developing acceptance of better wiring.

On July 1, 1956, several months after the sales department had concentrated its scattered forces on four floors of the Pennsylvania Lumbermen's Mutual Insurance Company Building (formerly the Ritz-Carlton Hotel) at 211 South Broad Street, Vice-President George E. Whitwell retired. The sustained contribution he had made to the Company was recognized by the directors, who resolved that "the board hereby recognizes and acknowledges that during the past twenty-five years Mr. Whitwell has conducted the duties of his office with outstanding energy, loyalty, and intelligence, and has rendered valuable services not only to this Company but also to the community at large." Milton I. Allen, general sales manager and a member of the sales force since 1928, was elected vice-president to succeed Whitwell.

Under Allen, old and new promotional endeavors were pushed as vigorously as ever. By the end of 1959, when the Company completed the first five years of its adequate home wiring program, approximately 90,000 "100-A" installations had been made, including 13,000 under the Company's home wiring financing plan. By this time, 99.2 per cent of new residential construction enjoyed "100-A" service, thereby permitting the fuller exploitation of yet another program—"Live Better Electrically." At its Modern Living Center, which featured an attractive all-electric kitchen, laundry, and living room, the sales department presented public demonstrations on subjects relating to kitchen and home planning.

Good results were also shown by the Company's planned-lighting program, which encouraged the trend toward increased use of built-in and permanent lighting

Chichester-Gloucester River Crossing, Energized in 1961

AIR CIRCUIT BREAKERS AT NOTTINGHAM SUBSTATION
First all-aluminum 220,000-volt substation in the country

fixtures in new homes. Builders co-operating in this activity took advantage of advanced ideas in wall lighting, ceiling fixtures, kitchen work-surface illumination, and outdoor lighting. Meanwhile, efforts to stimulate industrial sales produced an unprecedented volume of business.

Area development continued to be an important part of the sales department's responsibility. Not only were efforts made to attract new industry to the Company's service area, but strenuous attempts were made to improve the industrial climate of the area, thereby discouraging businesses from moving away. Local industry was sold on the advantages of staying put. In tasks of this nature, the Company worked closely with the Philadelphia Industrial Development Corporation, which was backed by the city and by the Chamber of Commerce. Philadelphia Electric had done much to encourage the concept of such an agency and to bring about its formation.

While the Company fostered modernization of wiring and the greater use of electric, gas, and steam heat services, the city of Philadelphia continued its own modernization programs. The effect of these projects was impressed on Philadelphia Electric in various ways. For one, the redevelopment of slum and blighted sections and the construction of large shopping centers were responsible for a decrease in its commercial customers in the city, a loss which was partially offset by an increase in the suburbs. The razing of many small stores and multiple residences in such areas as the Independence Hall malls and the Vine Street and Roosevelt Boulevard extensions accelerated this trend.

New highways like these necessitated a relocation of electric and gas facilities. The board learned in May, 1957, that the Northeastern and Delaware River extensions of the Pennsylvania Turnpike had required the shifting of transmission and distribution lines at 118 locations, costing $743,000, which, after lengthy negotiations, the Turnpike Commission had agreed to pay. However, with respect to other highway projects, the Company was faced with the common law rule that utilities located in highways must pay their own relocation costs. To contend against liability for such costs, the Company took the stand that the Public Utility Law had changed the rule by giving the Public Utility Commission discretion in matters of reimbursement. But on September 29, 1958, the Pennsylvania Supreme Court overruled previous findings of the state Superior Court and the Public Utility Commission, and declared that the common law rule had not been changed—public utilities must bear the costs of relocating their facilities to make way for bridges and superhighways. In this suit, which had been brought by the Delaware River Port Authority over the cost of relocating Philadelphia Electric lines at the approaches of the Walt Whitman Bridge, the court reasoned that non-transportation utilities occupy public highways under a rent-free license, and hence may be ordered to move their facilities at their own expense by any competent state or municipal authority.

Another factor of interest to the Company in the changing scene was the gradual substitution of buses for trolleys. In September, 1956, Willow Grove Substation was shut down. The replacement of the trolleys and the Park changeover to alternating current meant that the substation was no longer necessary. With various other trolley lines giving way to buses, revenue from the Philadelphia Transportation Company declined $529,000, or sixteen per cent, in 1956.

If trolleys appeared doomed, Philadelphia's gaslight era actually came to an end, after having spanned a period of one hundred and twenty-three years. Once, the soft glow of 39,000 gaslights had illuminated the city's streets and alleys, but on April 15, 1959, Mayor Richardson Dilworth extinguished the last one. Its ornamental standard was donated as a permanent exhibit to the Franklin Institute. Indeed, such standards had already become coveted antiques; wired for electricity, they were to be seen lighting the drives of many a private residence.

Progress went hand in hand with obsolescence. The Schuylkill Expressway, twenty-two miles of multilane divided highway completed at a cost of $90,000,000 in 1958, was declared inadequate in 1960. This superhighway, which connects the Valley Forge interchange of the Pennsylvania Turnpike with the Walt Whitman Bridge, was already handling more traffic than engineers had thought it would carry by 1970. Eighteen deaths occurred on the crowded expressway in the first ten months of 1960, and Philadelphians began to refer to it as the "Surekill Crawlway."

Projects which had failed or had been disappointing were fortunately overshadowed by the magnitude of other plans and accomplishments. Buildings which could not stand the test of time were torn down to make room for new improvements. On November 1, 1960, the Reading Railroad shut its North Broad Street Station. When built in 1929, Reading officials believed that the area surrounding it was ripe for extensive apartment house development. Moreover, the station was located opposite the Phillies' ball park. But the apartment projects never materialized, and the ball park closed. Few passengers used the station, and so it was abandoned. In 1961 came the announcement that it would be razed to make way for a combination office building and motel. Although old buildings were constantly being pulled down and new ones erected all over the city, few sections experienced as much change as West Philadelphia, where the University

357

of Pennsylvania and Drexel Institute of Technology were transforming their campuses. A great redevelopment project was afoot for the creation of a "University City" in this area.

The ability of Philadelphia Electric to anticipate the ever-changing needs of its service area reflected in large measure both the technical proficiency and the high quality and dedication of its employees. Employee loyalty was nurtured by policies of long standing, and was well recognized in the community. In 1956, the Company received the Industrial Relations Award of the Chamber of Commerce of Greater Philadelphia because of its "development and maintenance of an effective employer-employee relations program." It was noted that Philadelphia Electric wages and working conditions were among the best in the utility business. Its safety record was outstanding; its labor turnover exceedingly low. More than ever, Philadelphia Electric was "a good place to work." Certainly its employees think so. More than half of them have expressed their faith in Philadelphia Electric by purchasing shares of its stock. Membership in the Company's Quarter Century Club is shared (1961) by nearly 1,000 service annuitants and by more than 2,200 employees.

Mention has already been made of salary increases granted in the years 1946–1955. These were followed by general pay raises of five per cent in 1956; five per cent in 1957; 4.76 per cent in 1958; five per cent in 1959; 4.75 per cent in 1960; and four per cent in 1961, the eighteenth since January, 1946. Philadelphia Electric ranks high not only in its wage scales but in its supplementary benefits, which in 1957 were estimated as costing the Company $1,500 a year for each employee over and above his wages. This cost covers such benefits as group life insurance, service annuities, disability insurance, sick leave, absent time allowances, and longer vacations.

To a vital degree, employee morale is heightened by a policy aimed at selecting the right person for the right job, of choosing men and women who have the ability to move ahead in the organization. This selectivity is one of the best ways of promoting the happiness of the worker and of ensuring his effectiveness and welfare in the Company. It avoids unnecessary transfers from job to job and the heartbreaking disappointment of not making good.

Much has been said about the Company's interest in improving the efficiency of its equipment. More needs to be said about the Company's interest in improving the fitness and training of the workers to whom the equipment is entrusted. Years ago, realizing the human factor as a variable in the maintenance of uninterrupted service, Edison had prophesied: "Problems in human engineering will receive during the coming years the same genius and attention which the nineteenth century gave to the more material forms of engineering."

In Philadelphia Electric, this movement had its genesis in an effort to lower the number of errors made by substation operators. A switching error by an operator can result in a serious service interruption with costly results to customers, or it may produce crippling damage to expensive equipment, to say nothing of injury and loss of life. In 1927, E. O. Macferran, superintendent of substation operations, suggested that it might be possible to improve performance by setting up psychological tests to determine the fitness of operators. His superior, N. E. Funk, endorsed the idea and also the plan of calling in Dr. Morris S. Viteles, a professor of psychology at the University of Pennsylvania who had experience in industrial psychology and who had helped several local companies.

After study, Dr. Viteles decided that the outlook was promising for the development of tests to determine how an operator would react in an emergency, as well as how accurately he would perform under normal conditions. Such tests, he believed, would eliminate, prior to employment, those men who had a predisposition to error, and would make possible the selection of those who were highly competent to carry on the job accurately and expeditiously. Funk was intrigued, but asked him if he could guarantee the success of such a program. No, said Dr. Viteles, he would not guarantee the outcome of the experiment. "Good," replied Funk. "Had you done so, I would not be interested."

In 1928, tests were begun for the selection of electric substation operators, Philadelphia Electric being the first company of its kind to institute studies for such testing. The procedure was strengthened several years later when an intensive program was undertaken to improve the training of new operators and to retrain old operators. Under the impact of the new psychological and training methods, operating errors plummeted. Whereas in the mid-1920's they had averaged thirty-six a year, they were soon down to twelve. During the period 1959–1960, with Philadelphia Electric many times larger than it was when Dr. Viteles began his program, operating errors were occurring at a rate of but six a year.

Although Dr. Viteles continued at the University of Pennsylvania as professor of psychology and director of its vocational guidance clinic, the Company appointed him director of personnel research and training in 1930. The success of his work with substation operators having been established, Liversidge encouraged similar testing and training programs throughout the Company. Today, few people obtain jobs at Philadelphia Electric without first passing an aptitude test. From then on, they are trained on the job, so that they can do their work properly and also be in line for promotion. Virtually all vacancies or other opportunities, save that of a basic, untrained "entry job," are filled by the promotion of Company personnel.

When Rincliffe was vice-president in charge of operations, he and Vice-President Conover extended the testing procedure to include qualifying examinations for promotions, a system unparalleled in the utility industry where seniority reigns. While seniority is given its place, people selected for promotion must be qualified for the higher job, and must demonstrate their knowledge and skill in an examination. Qualifying tests are now general throughout the Company for all promotions below the supervisory level. Thus, Philadelphia Electric has devised job descriptions, set up tests to determine the applicant's fitness for a particular job, has formulated programs to train the men and women who are hired, and has seen to it that advancements are merited. Under Dr. Viteles' supervision, the Company has done remarkable work in "human engineering." Its personnel is competent to handle not only the day-by-day routine, but the extraordinary problems which arise during a major emergency.

The ability of Philadelphia Electric workers to stand up under severe pressure was never better illustrated than during the greatest disaster ever experienced by the Company, a catastrophe heralded by heavy, wet snow which began to fall at dusk on Wednesday, March 19, 1958. Throughout the night and on into Thursday, the snow came down. It had a peculiar quality which enabled it to cling to wires. This packing of snow on the lines soon thickened to an unbearable weight. High winds came up, and heavily laden trees began to fall or lose their limbs.

Buffeted by the storm and weighed down by the enormous fall of clinging snow, wooden poles which had withstood hurricanes yielded to the elements, wires came down, modern steel towers were twisted into crumpled heaps, one of Conowingo's transmission lines collapsed. Four hundred thousand Philadelphia Electric customers found themselves without electricity.

Forming a valiant army, the Company's employees battled to restore service. By March 23, about eighty-six per cent of the outages had been cared for. By March 29, everything was back in service except for some street lighting. Philadelphia's City Council, under the presidency of James H. J. Tate, paid high tribute to the more than 9,000 men and women of Philadelphia Electric who had made this recovery possible. Many of these workers had averaged sixteen hours of toil a day, much of it of a hazardous nature. Praise was given to the Company for flying in line crews from New York, Ohio, Michigan, the Carolinas, and other parts of the country to help handle the unprecedented repair load, and for pressing helicopters into service to fly men and materials over impassable terrain. In expressing its appreciation to the employees "for their indomitable spirit of unselfish public service," City Council added: "Every employee of Philadelphia Electric Company combined his or her talents and efforts for the common good in superhuman striving to mitigate the disastrous effects of the snowstorm and to alleviate human sufferings."

This storm did $6,646,223 damage to the system, $3,000,000 of which was covered by catastrophe insurance taken out in 1955 after "Hurricane Hazel." When the insurance came up for renewal in the same amount later in the year, the insurance companies were more wary. The new policy provided that the Company assume the first $1,000,000 in catastrophe costs, instead of

THE PRESIDENT'S STAFF JUNE, 1961

Clockwise, PRESIDENT RINCLIFFE (*standing*), RAMSEY, VANANTWERP, CONOVER, FETTER, GATY, LIVERSIDGE, ALLEN, WATSON, LONG, JONES, McDEVITT, CORSON

the $500,000 stipulated in the earlier contract. Moreover, the premium for the policy was increased from $150,000 to $400,000.

The great snow did have one bright aspect—while it meted out several times the damage of "Hurricane Hazel," it took no longer to restore service. The reason lay in a carefully planned emergency procedure. For many years, the Company had had one form or another of emergency procedure, but nothing geared to a storm of hurricane size. A few days after "Hazel's" visit in October, 1954, Rincliffe called in J. A. English, general superintendent of the gas department, told him he wanted procedures developed that would cut outage time in half in the event of another disaster, and appointed him manager of emergency procedures.

English studied the former plans and found them too general. One of his first steps was to assign direct responsibilities to given individuals; in the event of a storm, each person would know exactly what to do. Lessons learned from "Hazel" were numerous. Most important, perhaps, was realization of the difficulty in determining damage, once the storm was over. Falling trees in suburban areas pulled down wires and cut communications. Consequently, reports on necessary repair work could not come through promptly. Without adequate knowledge of the extent of damage, it was impossible to assess the man-hours of repair work, and the Company could not tell how much outside labor it should call to its aid.

English overcame this problem by organizing a volunteer group from the nonoperating employees, those workers who would not normally be called on for aid in service restoration. The volunteers were assigned routes and were required to familiarize themselves thoroughly with their territories. In the event of a storm, they were to go out on patrol, noting all damage to the Company's 4,000-

volt primary distribution system, and, when possible, damage to the secondary lines leading to customers' premises. Their reports would enable the Company to evaluate damages within a short time, and to take the necessary action to restore service.

Arrangements were made with many electric utilities east of the Mississippi for prompt, mutual aid, so that repair crews could be imported in bulk from other systems if needed. Within Philadelphia Electric, English conducted drills, recruited volunteer telephone operators, wrote emergency manuals, and prepared plans for feeding and housing emergency workers, as well as for equipping and transporting them. In short, provision was made for all the extraordinary problems that arise during a disaster, to the extent, at least, that they could be foreseen.

Although the gas department had not suffered from nature's onslaughts, emergency procedures were also prepared for it in case a major gas outage should occur. Volunteers were recruited to go from house to house, turning off gas appliances. Not only were they instructed in the technique of turning off service, they received training in how to turn it on again.

And then, in March, 1958, came the big snow to test these procedures under the severest of emergency conditions. Without question, they met the goal that Rincliffe had set for English. Nevertheless, the magnitude of the disaster revealed certain weaknesses, and the procedures were revised in part. The principal change was the decentralization of repair work. Because the large forces of men brought into the area to help out had overtaxed service facilities, steps were taken to avoid such congestion in the future. In addition, the dispatching system, which directed repair crews to their work, was also decentralized.

Another lesson learned from the snow crisis was that certain standards of construction and equipment were no longer satisfactory. In September, 1958, the board approved a stormproofing program to be completed in five years at a cost of $28,000,000. Wires, poles, and auxiliary equipment which equaled or even exceeded the standards set by the National Electric Safety Code were to be replaced with larger and stronger facilities designed to withstand abnormal weather conditions. Many outside line crews were engaged to assist in this project; in December, 1959, there were forty-two contract crews supplementing the regular forces in stormproofing and line extension work. "Hurricane Donna" obligingly tested the progress of this program on September 12, 1960. While this violent storm brought down many trees and branches, and caused service interruptions to 100,000 customers, those parts of the system which had been reinforced withstood damage extremely well. A major step forward in the concept of high service reliability was thus built into the Company.

Philadelphia Electric is often asked why it does not protect its wires by placing them all underground. The answer is simple—the exorbitant cost of doing so would double the rates. Moreover, underground wires are more difficult to repair and are subject to breakage when trees are uprooted, or when excavations are made for streets, sewers, or water mains. They are also subject to damage from high water or inadequate drainage.

Considering nature's petulance, Philadelphia Electric did everything it could during the late 1950's to safeguard the continuity of its service, and to provide for future demands. Responsibility for the formulation of these programs, as well as for various other activities, was shouldered by a number of officers and other personnel who have been mentioned. There were, however, several changes in management during these years which have yet to be recorded.

On Liversidge's death in December, 1955, Vice-President Corson was elected to the vacant directorship, and, in the following month, the office of chairman of the board was eliminated, the function of chief executive being vested in the president. When Senior Vice-President Porter resigned as a director, his place was taken by Vice-President Ramsey, who was also elected executive vice-president and appointed to the executive committee.

Ramsey was particularly well equipped for his new position. Having served as president of several U.G.I. subsidiaries, he had more top managerial experience than the other officers. His sound grasp of the business aspects of Philadelphia Electric, so well demonstrated by his work in its purchasing department, had focused attention on him. W. H. Jones, a Philadelphia Electric man since 1926 and purchasing agent since 1949, was promoted to the vice-presidency vacated by Ramsey.

Subsequent top-level changes have not been numerous. In September, 1956, Senior Vice-President Porter retired after more than sixty-two years of service with U.G.I. and Philadelphia Electric. It was also in 1956 that Allan G. Mitchell, who had been with the Company since 1931, was appointed comptroller. Clifford Winner, treasurer for twenty-two years and an employee for nearly forty-nine, retired in 1959, being succeeded by George W. Miller. The next year, C. W. Watson, whose thirty years with the Company had been chiefly in the electric station operating department, was elected to the new office of vice-president in charge of general administration.

As for the most recent changes on the board, Samuel Lloyd Irving, the senior director, resigned in 1957, his place being filled by Edwin K. Daly, president of Horn &

Hardart. On Charles S. Redding's death in 1959, G. Stockton Strawbridge, president and general manager of Strawbridge & Clothier, was elected a director. In 1960, Daly died and Vice-President McDevitt was elevated to the board. Later in the year, Gustave G. Amsterdam, chairman of the board and president of Bankers Securities Corporation, was also added to the directorate.

In times of unparalleled and bewildering change, the responsibility of these men in furnishing leadership was a heavy one. With the atomic age yet in its infancy, the Russians on October 4, 1957, put "Sputnik I" into orbit around the world. Less than four months later, the United States followed suit with its "Explorer." Men everywhere, searching the evening skies for a glimpse of these twirling miracles, were seized with a dawning consciousness that they were not living in the atomic age after all, but in the space age. Before long, men themselves were being launched into space.

While experiments in space were as yet beyond the Company's horizons, it eagerly accepted the most modern concepts and methods. In 1959, after extended study, Philadelphia Electric ordered an electronic data processing system representing a $1,750,000 investment. When installed, the system will handle the large volume of data processing required in the Company's accounting and financial operations. This will include billing and related accounting for nearly 1,400,000 electric, gas, and steam customers, maintaining records for more than 100,000 stockholders, handling payrolls for more than 9,000 employees, and processing many other accounting records and reports. The electronic system will also be used for a growing volume of economic and technical engineering studies.

Experiments in "peak shaving" generators were undertaken in 1959 with the installation at Plymouth Meeting

Substation of a 6,000-kilowatt diesel-driven unit. The concept of "peak shaving," originally suggested by Constantine Bary, embraces the utilization of small, strategically placed, unattended, low-cost generating units. Through their ability to take on peak loads, to shave the peak requirements otherwise supplied by conventional means, they defer construction of an additional large-scale generating station. While the operating cost of this equipment is high, it actually runs only a few hours a year, and the cost is more than offset by its low fixed charges.

The "peak shaving" program was extended in 1961 with the erection of two experimental gas turbine electric generating units at Barbadoes Station. These units, the largest of their type, have design capacities of 20,500 and 22,000 kilowatts respectively, and are capable of being turned on or off as needed. Their economy in initial operations for short intervals will be studied.

With respect to peaks, the changing pattern of electric demand brought a new high of 2,317,000 kilowatts on June 18, 1957. This was the first time that a summer peak was higher than that of the preceding winter in the Philadelphia Electric system, a revolution caused by the increase in cooling and refrigeration loads. Again, on June 30, 1959, the Company experienced its second record peak in summertime—2,543,000 kilowatts; on August 30, 1960, that record was shattered by a peak of 2,628,000; and on September 5, 1961, a hot, sunny day, another high of 2,826,000 kilowatts was reached.

According to the Edison Electric Institute in 1960, such growth was in line with its prediction that the electric industry would have to double its capacity in the 1960's and again in the 1970's. Electric demand in 1980 would be four times that of 1960! The use of heavy-duty appliances, the Institute pointed out, was far from the satura-

BURHOLME SUBSTATION

Typical landscaping designed to blend such an installation with its surroundings

PROPOSED PEACH BOTTOM ATOMIC POWER STATION

tion point. Electricity for house heating was to be the next enormous market. A burgeoning population would require these conveniences.

How was Philadelphia Electric to keep up with such a demand, to quadruple its electric output in twenty years? For the moment, in 1961, it was protected by the large block of capacity at Eddystone, which represented the growth requirements of approximately a four-year period. After considering nine plans culled from twenty-five proposed, the Company decided late in 1960 to install additional units at Conowingo.

Conowingo's original installation comprised seven generating units, each with a rating of 36,000 kilowatts, but space had been provided for four additional units, should they be needed. Their need would be conditioned by certain economic factors. Conowingo's total capacity cannot be operated continuously when the river is low, but a maximum firm capacity can be obtained for peak use to an extent which depends upon minimum river flow and the peaking characteristics of the load being served. By 1960, the load character of the Pennsylvania-New Jersey-Maryland Interconnection was such that it could firm not only Conowingo's original capacity, but also the capacity of the projected four new units. The time had come when it was economically justifiable to enlarge the hydroelectric plant.

Modern technology played an important role in the Conowingo decision. Recent developments in the art of hydrogeneration make possible the installation of 60,000-kilowatt units in each of the spaces originally planned for 36,000-kilowatt units. Thus, by 1965 the four new units will add 240,000 kilowatts to Conowingo's capacity, an increase of ninety-five per cent.

Future years will see the enlarging of old plants, the building of new ones, the utilization of atomic power. Invention will create new uses for electricity, stimulating increased demands on the system's capacity. The Company's service area, already identified as part of a "super-metropolis" stretching from New Hampshire to Virginia, will experience growth requirements difficult to visualize. It is abundantly clear, however, that the territory served by Philadelphia Electric is a dynamic one, an area in a transitional state of accelerating change. Every assurance is evident that the Company will take a notable part in the expansion of the area's economy, that in the years ahead Philadelphia Electric will continue to grow in stature and service.

Turning from the challenge of the future to the achievements of the past, the history of the Company's growth is reflected in the plans and work of Dolan, Professor Marks, Maloney, McCall, Eglin, Liversidge, Rincliffe, and a host of others. This growth, to be sure, was not in itself a phenomenon. It was a part of the rapid rise of the entire industry; it was a response to the insistent demand of an increasing population. How typical Philadelphia Electric's development has been is a matter for conjecture, but it is certain that it has developed with a minimum of public controversy and with a maximum of public acceptance. It has built soundly, serves well, and has reason to face the future with confidence.

APPENDICES

DIRECTORS AND OFFICERS
1899–1961

CHAIRMEN OF THE BOARD

JOSEPH B. McCALL	1924–1926
ARTHUR W. THOMPSON	1928–1929
JOHN E. ZIMMERMANN	1929–1938
WILLIAM H. TAYLOR	1938–1940
JOHN E. ZIMMERMANN	1940–1943
HORACE P. LIVERSIDGE	1947–1955
R. G. RINCLIFFE	1955–1956

CHAIRMEN OF EXECUTIVE COMMITTEE

JOSEPH B. McCALL	1904–1908
HORATIO G. LLOYD	1927–1928
JOHN E. ZIMMERMANN	1928–1940
WILLIAM W. BODINE	1940–1943
HAROLD S. SCHUTT	1943 to date

MEMBERS OF EXECUTIVE COMMITTEE

THOMAS DOLAN	1904–1908
WILLIAM F. HARRITY	1904–1908
JOSEPH B. McCALL	1904–1908
HORATIO G. LLOYD	1927–1928
CHARLES E. INGERSOLL	1927–1928
JOHN T. WINDRIM	1927–1928
WALTER H. JOHNSON	1927–1928
THOMAS N. McCARTER	1928–1938
THOMAS NEWHALL	1928–1932
WILLIAM H. TAYLOR	1928–1940
JOHN E. ZIMMERMANN	1928–1943
EDWARD HOPKINSON, JR.	1932–1939
WILLIAM W. BODINE	1938–1943
HORACE P. LIVERSIDGE	1938–1955
JEREMIAH J. SULLIVAN, JR.	1939–1954
HAROLD S. SCHUTT	1942 to date

373

CHARLES E. BRINLEY	1943 to date
JOHN A. DIEMAND	1946 to date
HENRY B. BRYANS	1947–1952
R. G. RINCLIFFE	1952 to date
H. N. RAMSEY	1956 to date

DIRECTORS

WILLIAM L. ELKINS	1899–1903
P. A. B. WIDENER	1899–1902
THOMAS DOLAN	1899–1914
JEREMIAH J. SULLIVAN	1899–1928
WILLIAM F. HARRITY	1899–1912
JOHN M. MACK	1899–1903
JOSEPH B. McCALL	1899–1926
ALLEN B. RORKE	1899–1899
A. V. R. COE	1899–1928
JOHN V. SHOEMAKER	1900–1910
CHARLES M. SWAIN	1902–1904
WILLIAM P. CONOVER, JR.	1903–1911
CHARLES E. INGERSOLL	1904–1931
J. R. McALLISTER	1905–1928
EDWARD D. TOLAND	1911–1915
JOHN T. WINDRIM	1912–1934
WALTER H. JOHNSON	1913–1928
SIDNEY F. TYLER	1914–1935
MARTIN V. BERGEN	1915–1941
WILLIAM A. LAW	1922–1936
HORATIO G. LLOYD	1922–1937
MORRIS R. BOCKIUS	1926–1936
THOMAS NEWHALL	1927–1932
W. C. L. EGLIN	1927–1928
ARTHUR W. THOMPSON	1928–1929
SAMUEL T. BODINE	1928–1932
WILLIAM H. TAYLOR	1928–1940
THOMAS N. McCARTER	1928–1938
JOHN E. ZIMMERMANN	1928–1943
JEREMIAH J. SULLIVAN, JR.	1929–1954

EDWARD B. ROBINETTE	1929–1936
MORRIS W. STROUD	1929–1937
EDWARD HOPKINSON, JR.	1932–1939
WILLIAM W. BODINE	1932–1943
HORACE P. LIVERSIDGE	1936–1955
SAMUEL LLOYD IRVING	1936–1957
CHARLES E. BRINLEY	1938 to date
WALTER E. LONG	1939–1943
HENRY B. BRYANS	1940–1952
HAROLD S. SCHUTT	1941 to date
JOHN A. DIEMAND	1943 to date
WALTER D. FULLER	1943 to date
EDWARD PORTER	1943–1956
CHARLES S. REDDING	1945–1959
ALBERT A. GARTHWAITE	1946 to date
N. E. FUNK	1947–1950
R. G. RINCLIFFE	1950 to date
PHILIP T. SHARPLES	1952 to date
A. S. CORSON	1955 to date
H. N. RAMSEY	1956 to date
EDWIN K. DALY	1957–1960
G. STOCKTON STRAWBRIDGE	1959 to date
VINCENT P. MCDEVITT	1960 to date
GUSTAVE G. AMSTERDAM	1960 to date

PRESIDENTS

JOSEPH B. MCCALL	1899–1924
WALTER H. JOHNSON	1924–1928
WILLIAM H. TAYLOR	1928–1938
HORACE P. LIVERSIDGE	1938–1947
HENRY B. BRYANS	1947–1952
R. G. RINCLIFFE	1952 to date

EXECUTIVE VICE-PRESIDENTS

HENRY B. BRYANS	1938–1947
N. E. FUNK	1947–1950
R. G. RINCLIFFE	1950–1952
H. N. RAMSEY	1956 to date

VICE-PRESIDENTS

WILLIAM F. HARRITY	1899–1912
WALTER H. JOHNSON	1907–1924
W. C. L. EGLIN	1912–1917
ARTHUR B. HUEY	1922–1939
CHARLES J. RUSSELL	1922–1936
W. C. L. EGLIN	1922–1928
HORACE P. LIVERSIDGE	1924–1938
WALTER E. LONG	1926–1928
EDWARD PORTER	1929–1956
N. E. FUNK	1929–1947
STUART COOPER	1929–1929
HENRY B. BRYANS	1929–1938
GEORGE E. WHITWELL	1931–1956
L. B. EICHENGREEN	1937–1940
BERNARD P. CAREY	1943–1947
GEORGE R. CONOVER	1944 to date
R. G. RINCLIFFE	1945–1950
K. M. IRWIN	1948–1960
H. N. RAMSEY	1948–1956
VINCENT P. McDEVITT	1949 to date
R. P. LIVERSIDGE	1952 to date
A. S. CORSON	1954 to date
W. H. JONES	1956 to date
L. R. GATY	1956–1961
MILTON I. ALLEN	1956 to date
J. HENRY LONG	1959 to date
C. W. WATSON	1960 to date

SECRETARIES

A. V. R. COE	1899–1937
VINCENT A. SOMMAR	1937–1954
VINCENT J. WALSH	1954 to date

TREASURERS

WILLIAM P. CONOVER, JR.	1899–1911
H. C. LUCAS	1911–1937
CLIFFORD WINNER	1937–1959
GEORGE W. MILLER	1959 to date

History Highlights

April 1, 1852   The West Chester Gas Company incorporated, first gas utility to operate in territory now served by Philadelphia Electric Company.

December 26, 1878   First store in Philadelphia to be illuminated by electricity was John Wanamaker's Grand Depot at Thirteenth and Market Streets, where arc lights were installed and supplied from a plant in the building.

March 31, 1881   The Brush Electric Light Company of Philadelphia incorporated.

December 3, 1881   First electric utility service in Philadelphia furnished with the arc lighting of Chestnut Street between the Delaware and Schuylkill Rivers by The Brush Electric Light Company of Philadelphia.

September 2, 1884   International Electrical Exhibition, sponsored by the Franklin Institute, opened in Philadelphia.

December 13, 1886   The Edison Electric Light Company of Philadelphia incorporated.

March 5, 1889   Edison Station placed in operation at 908 Sansom Street, first building in the country specifically constructed as an Edison generating station.

October 20, 1892   Tilghman Street Gas Plant, Chester, began operation, producing carbureted water gas.

December 15, 1892   First electric trolley operated in Philadelphia on Catharine and Bainbridge Streets.

February 4, 1898   Pennsylvania Manufacturing Light and Power Company incorporated. Its bonds registered as "Philadelphia Electric Gold Trust Certificates."

November 27, 1898   Callowhill Station, at Twenty-sixth and Callowhill Streets, originally designed to supply direct current to Hestonville, Mantua and Fairmount Passenger Railway Company, began operation as an alternating current station.

November 27, 1898   Two 400-kilowatt, 250-volt, 60-cycle rotary converters, first of their type, installed at Edison Station.

October 5, 1899   National Electric Company and Pennsylvania Manufacturing Light and Power Company consolidated into Philadelphia Electric Company (of New Jersey).

January 7, 1900   Columbia Substation, 1622 North Eighteenth Street, first alternating current substation in Philadelphia, placed in operation.

September 26, 1900   Philadelphia Society of Electric Metermen, later Philadelphia Electric Society of Metermen, organized.

October 27, 1902   The Philadelphia Electric Company (of Pennsylvania) incorporated.

November 14, 1902   Battery of forty Semet-Solvay ovens built at Highland Avenue, Chester, for production of coke oven gas.

September 28, 1903   Schuylkill Station, at Christian Street and Schuylkill River, began operation.

November 23, 1903 "Number 2," a 5,000-kilowatt Allis-Chalmers horizontal-vertical cross-compound Corliss unit, largest of its kind ever built, placed in service at Schuylkill Station.

September 15, 1904 A 500-kilowatt, 2,400-volt, two-phase, 60-cycle, vertical turbogenerator, first on the system, placed in operation at Tacony Station.

January 4, 1906 First turbogenerator at Schuylkill Station, a 5,000-kilowatt, 6,000-volt, two-phase, 60-cycle General Electric vertical unit, installed.

April 7, 1907 Company offices moved from the rented building on the northeast corner of Tenth and Sansom Streets and other locations to new central office building at 1000 Chestnut Street.

March 9, 1909 Philadelphia Electric Company Employees Association organized under the name "Philadelphia Electric Company Section of the National Electric Light Association."

March 19, 1909 Taylor automatic stokers placed in service at Schuylkill Station.

April 17, 1909 The first interdepartmental baseball games were played under the auspices of the newly organized Philadelphia Electric Company Athletic Association on the leased grounds of the old Tacony Athletic Association at State Road and Unruh Street, Tacony.

April, 1909 *Current News*, an employees magazine, first published as a medium for printing technical papers.

April 12, 1911 Company-financed service annuity plan adopted.

May 6, 1911   A serious fire in the Edison Station caused a service interruption of from four to twelve hours to a majority of customers in the central district of Philadelphia.

November 1, 1911   A new substation was erected in the record time of four months in the Schuylkill Station yard to convert 60-cycle current to the 25 cycles required by the Philadelphia Rapid Transit Company.

April 23, 1912   Athletic field, originally known as "Kelly's Lane" (later Howard McCall Field and now designated as Philadelphia Electric Country Club), leased from the Pennsylvania Railroad by Philadelphia Electric for a term of three years and subsequently purchased and enlarged.

October 23, 1913   First 15,000-kilowatt, 13,200-volt, three-phase, 25-cycle General Electric turbogenerator placed in service at Schuylkill Station.

March 18, 1915   Paoli branch of Pennsylvania Railroad supplied with 25-cycle service from Schuylkill Substation, marking the first time an electrified railroad received public utility service. Chestnut Hill branch was electrified in 1918.

March 18, 1916   At Schuylkill Station a 35,000-kilowatt, 13,200-volt, three-phase, 60-cycle horizontal turbogenerator, largest of its kind at that time, was placed in service.

September 10, 1916   First of two General Electric 5,000-kilowatt, 25-cycle phase converter sets (only ones ever made) placed in service at Schuylkill Station to balance Pennsylvania Railroad single-phase load on the three-phase system.

November 8, 1917   The 66,000-volt transmission line between Schuylkill and Chester Stations energized.

October 1, 1918   First turbogenerator installed at Chester Station.

October 5, 1919   Addition to central office building at 1000 Chestnut Street completed, and offices occupied.

December 10, 1919   Original West Conshohocken Gas Plant built for handling and distribution of coke oven gas purchased from Rainey-Wood Coke Company.

October 31, 1920   Delaware Station, at Beach and Palmer Streets, placed in service.

July 28, 1921   Last of Edison bi-polar dynamos at Edison Station taken out of service.

September 3, 1921   Unit Number 8, a 30,000-kilowatt turbogenerator at Schuylkill Station, was wrecked when a low-pressure turbine wheel broke.

July 19, 1923   Interconnection with Public Service Electric and Gas Company of New Jersey at Camden completed with installation of four 26,000-volt submarine circuits under Delaware River.

October 15, 1923   Twelve 2,300-volt A-C feeders installed at Ludlow Substation in preparation for D-C—A-C changeover.

January 2, 1924   First customer changed over from D-C to A-C service.

November 24, 1925   Richmond Station, at Delaware Avenue and Lewis Street, placed in service.

1925   Carbureted water gas sets installed at West Conshohocken Gas Plant to supplement coke oven gas sendout.

February 20, 1926   Federal Power Commission issued license to The Susquehanna Power Company and Philadelphia Electric Power Company to develop Conowingo hydroelectric project.

March 20, 1926 First 66,000-volt underground cable on the system, installed between Richmond Station and D and Luzerne Streets for the interconnection with Public Service Electric and Gas Company at Trenton.

May 1, 1926 One of this area's first waterless-type gas holders, with a capacity of 5,000,000 cubic feet, was completed at Long Lane and Marshall Road, Upper Darby Township.

September 16, 1927 Agreement signed for 220,000-volt interconnection between Philadelphia Electric, Public Service Electric and Gas Company, and Pennsylvania Power & Light Company, forming the Pennsylvania-New Jersey Interconnection.

October 15, 1927 Willow Steam Heating Plant, first station specifically constructed by Philadelphia Electric to supply steam heat service, placed in operation.

February 14, 1928 Control of The Philadelphia Electric Company acquired by U.G.I.

March 1, 1928 Conowingo placed in operation with the delivery of power at 220,000 volts to Plymouth Meeting Substation.

August 1, 1929 Thermal reforming of refinery oil gas introduced for first time in history of gas utility industry at Tilghman Street, with replacement of retorts by reformed oil gas sets.

October 31, 1929 The Philadelphia Electric Company and Philadelphia Suburban-Counties Gas and Electric Company merged to form Philadelphia Electric Company.

February 2, 1930 One of the largest gas holders in this section of the country, with a capacity of 10,000,000 cubic feet, erected at West Conshohocken Gas Plant.

April 1, 1930   The 66,000-volt interconnection with Delaware Power & Light Company energized.

May 12, 1930   Philadelphia Electric acquired a half-interest in the Deepwater Station at Pennsgrove, New Jersey, from U.G.I.

July 14, 1930   Edison Station shut down.

November 19, 1932   Two 30,000-kilowatt, single-phase frequency changers installed at Richmond Station for the electrification of the Pennsylvania Railroad from Philadelphia to New York.

October 1, 1934   Steam heating system interconnected with the Pennsylvania Railroad steam plant.

July 26, 1935   Pulverized fuel and electrical fly ash collectors used for first time by the Company at Richmond Station.

September 1, 1935   World's largest tandem-compound unit on a single shaft, a 165,000-kilowatt Westinghouse turbogenerator, placed in commercial operation at Richmond Station.

October 4, 1935   D-C service from Cherry Substation to City Hall disconnected, final customer to be changed over to A-C.

April 4, 1937   While trying to clear a local fault at Plymouth Meeting Substation, a 66,000-volt circuit breaker exploded, causing a complete system shutdown for eight minutes and partial shutdown for twenty-one minutes.

September 14, 1938   First hydrogen-cooled generator on the system, a 50,000-kilowatt "topping unit," placed in service at Schuylkill Station.

December 22, 1942   U.G.I. filed application with the S.E.C. for approval of a plan for divesting itself of its stockholding of Philadelphia Electric. This was approved and stock was distributed August 20, 1943, on the basis of one-third share of Philadelphia Electric common stock for each share of U.G.I. common stock held on record date of June 15, 1943.

January 22, 1947   Rupture of high-pressure gas main in compressor room at West Conshohocken Gas Plant caused a serious fire, lasting two and a half hours, with extensive damage to plant but no injury to personnel. The Norristown area was without gas service for approximately twenty-four hours, and other suburban areas were affected for shorter periods.

July 31, 1947   First turbogenerator placed in service at Southwark Station.

August 25, 1947   A 66,000-volt "oil-o-static" cable (cable in steel pipe under high oil pressure) linking Southwark, Delaware, and Westmoreland Stations placed in operation.

September 17, 1948   First delivery of natural gas made to Tilghman Street Gas Plant by Texas Eastern Transmission Corporation, for use in reforming and enriching sendout mixture.

July 24, 1950   The Company's half-interest in Deepwater Station sold to Atlantic City Electric Company.

November 7, 1950   First steam supplied to steam heating system from Schuylkill Station.

December 15, 1950   First large-scale demineralization system for boiler water purification (600,000 pounds of water per hour) placed in service at Schuylkill Station.

1950   Philadelphia Electric entered atomic energy field: first, by participation in industrial group program of A.E.C.;

later, by taking active part in development of Enrico Fermi fast-breeder reactor at Monroe, Michigan.

January 12, 1951   Catalytic reforming of natural gas utilized for first time in history of gas utility industry with installation of first of three Girdler continuous catalytic units at West Conshohocken Gas Plant.

March 10, 1951   Btu content of gas per cubic foot raised from 520 to 801.

July 23, 1954   First turbogenerator placed in service at Cromby Station.

September 27, 1954   Broken rotor on Cromby Number 1 unit damaged generator beyond repair. Entire generator replaced and in operation by late December.

October 15, 1954   More than 300,000 customers suffered service interruptions as a result of "Hurricane Hazel."

November 4, 1956   Eight companies joined in a new and enlarged interconnection agreement known as the Pennsylvania-New Jersey-Maryland Interconnection. In addition to the original three companies of the Pennsylvania-New Jersey Interconnection—Philadelphia Electric, Public Service Electric and Gas Company, and Pennsylvania Power & Light Company—the agreement included Baltimore Gas and Electric Company, Pennsylvania Electric Company, Metropolitan Edison Company, New Jersey Power & Light Company, and Jersey Central Power & Light Company.

February 18, 1958   Edison Steam Plant placed in service.

March 19–20, 1958   More than 400,000 customers suffered service interruptions from the most damaging snow storm in the history of the Company. The monumental task of restoring service to customers and repairing damage to electric transmission and distribution facilities was termed "Operation Snowdrop."

April 19, 1958   Btu content per cubic foot of gas increased from 801 to 900.

August 27, 1959   Contracts signed with A.E.C. for construction and operation of a 40,000-kilowatt, helium-cooled atomic power station at Peach Bottom, Pennsylvania.

February 5, 1960   First unit, a 325,000-kilowatt, supercritical pressure (5,000 pounds) cross-compound turbogenerator, placed in service at Eddystone Station.

September 12, 1960   "Hurricane Donna" tested the adequacy of the Company's stormproofing program. While fallen trees caused service interruptions to 100,000 customers, parts of the system that had been reinforced withstood damage.

October 7, 1960   Second unit, a 325,000-kilowatt, supercritical pressure (3,500 pounds) cross-compound turbogenerator, placed in service at Eddystone Station.

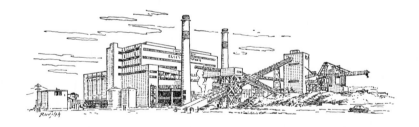

PHILADELPHIA ELECTRIC COMPANY

Consolidated Income Statement

Thousand $

	1902	1910	1920	1930	1940	1950	1960
Operating Revenues:							
Electric	$3,148	$ 5,663	$19,734	$57,770	$67,914	$135,926	$224,382
Gas	—	—	—	6,977	6,765	16,497	42,022
Steam	8	18	58	534	1,116	3,114	6,646
Total	3,156	5,681	19,792	65,281	75,795	155,537	273,050
Operating Expenses:							
Operation and Maintenance	—	—	—	24,730	28,215	77,003	138,206
Depreciation	—	—	—	5,768	6,444	14,669	34,920
Taxes	—	—	—	4,802	12,353	29,648	43,898
Total	1,669	3,453	16,276	35,300	47,012	121,320	217,024
Operating Income	1,487	2,228	3,516	29,981	28,783	34,217	56,026
Other Income	266	264	1,789	488	287	898	886
Gross Income	1,753	2,492	5,305	30,469	29,070	35,115	56,912
Income Deductions:							
Bond Interest	—	—	—	8,237	6,372	6,582	17,680
Interest Charged to Construction	—	—	—	—	(138)	(55)	(3,877)
Other Deductions—Net	—	—	—	688	720	30	839
Total Income Deductions	1,299	1,276	2,262	8,925	6,954	6,557	14,642
Net Income	454	1,216	3,043	21,544	22,116	28,558	42,270
Preferred Stock Dividends	—	—	231	1,624	2,360	3,797	3,927
Common Stock Earnings	454	1,216	2,812	19,920	19,756	24,761	38,343
Common Stock Dividends	338	877	2,100	17,346	18,953	14,444	30,155
Balance Retained For Use in Business	$116	$339	$712	$2,574	$803	$10,317	$8,188
Earnings Per Share	$0.45	$1.22	$2.26	$1.92	$1.88	$2.31	$2.84
Dividends Per Share	$0.34	$0.8775	$1.75	$1.65	$1.80	$1.35	$2.24
Shares of Common Stock Outstanding (000's)	100	100	1,200	10,349	10,529	10,699	13,509

PHILADELPHIA ELECTRIC COMPANY

History of Capital Investment

Thousand $

	1902	1910	1920	1930	1940	1950	1960
Long Term Debt							
Bonds	$28,277	$28,277	$72,800	$159,377	$162,437	$235,000	$509,165
Serial Notes	—	—	—	—	—	6,000	—
Real Estate Mortgage	—	—	—	230	—	—	—
Subsidiary Co. Purchase Money Mortgage	—	—	—	—	1,000	—	—
Total Long Term Debt	28,277	28,277	72,800	159,607	163,437	241,000	509,165
Preferred Stock	—	—	5,994	25,211	39,608	72,472	87,472
Common Stock Equity							
Common Stock	24,988	24,988	30,000	135,116	137,816	157,268	248,275
Premium on Preferred Stock	—	—	—	—	—	1,169	1,214
Retained Earnings	563	623	4,920	15,858	16,237	44,048	123,290
Total Common Stock Equity	25,551	25,611	34,920	150,974	154,053	202,485	372,779
Total Capitalization	$53,828	$53,888	$113,714	$335,792	$357,098	$515,957	$969,416

PHILADELPHIA ELECTRIC COMPANY

Miscellaneous Statistics

	1902	1910	1920	1930	1940	1950	1960
Number of Customers							
Electric—Thousands	12	33	158	631	722	872	1,073
Gas—Thousands	—	—	—	127	134	171	230
Steam	—	—	—	813	1,078	1,070	1,069
Number of Employees	—	1,778	4,205	8,314	7,161	8,027	9,370
Number of Common Stockholders	—	—	12,731	—	—	94,002	95,524
Taxes—Thousand $							
Federal	—	—	—	2,405	7,699	24,077	33,077
State and Local	—	—	—	2,397	4,654	5,571	10,844
Total Taxes Per Cent of Operating Revenue	—	—	—	7.4%	16.3%	19.1%	16.1%
Electric Output—Thousand Kwh							
Steam	54,089	125,633	910,065	2,076,224	3,728,544	6,919,642	12,196,160
Hydro	—	—	—	982,258	1,235,443	1,655,010	1,327,050
Internal Combustion	—	—	—	—	—	—	2,226
Purchased and Net Interchange—Other Utilities	—	—	265	32,751	(309,618)	271,887	97,503
Total Output	54,089	125,633	910,330	3,091,233	4,654,369	8,846,539	13,622,939
Electric System Peak Load—Kw	19,101	42,246	203,624	691,000	978,000	1,678,000	2,628,000
Electric System Generating Capacity—Kw	22,778	56,244	257,200	902,315	1,092,415	1,879,250	3,439,250
Gas Sendout—Thousand cubic feet at 900 Btu	—	—	—	4,301,134	5,763,614	13,537,957	30,562,728
Maximum Daily Sendout—Thousand cubic feet	—	—	—	19,917	24,290	78,948	208,329
Steam Output—Thousand lbs	—	—	327,034	806,170	1,780,884	2,928,746	5,767,902

389

PHILADELPHIA ELECTRIC COMPANY

Residential Electric Service

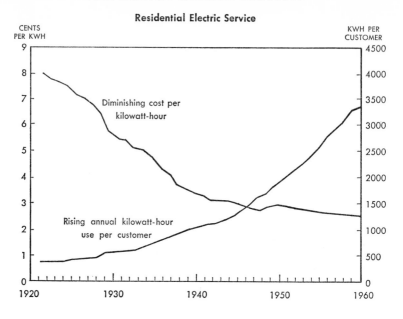

CENTS PER KWH

KWH PER CUSTOMER

Diminishing cost per kilowatt-hour

Rising annual kilowatt-hour use per customer

Gas Sales

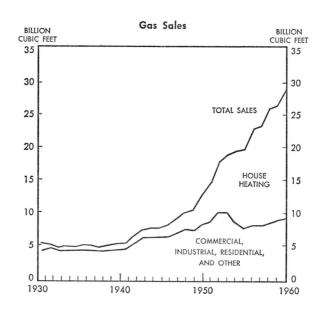

BILLION CUBIC FEET

BILLION CUBIC FEET

TOTAL SALES

HOUSE HEATING

COMMERCIAL, INDUSTRIAL, RESIDENTIAL, AND OTHER

PHILADELPHIA ELECTRIC COMPANY

How Improved Efficiency Has Lowered
the Coal and Heat Rates

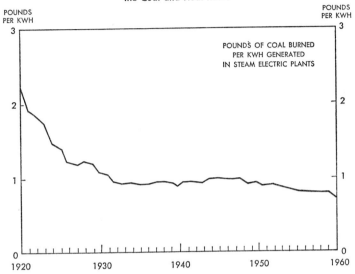

POUNDS
PER KWH

POUNDS
PER KWH

POUNDS OF COAL BURNED
PER KWH GENERATED
IN STEAM ELECTRIC PLANTS

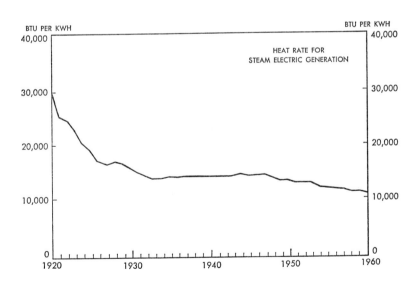

BTU PER KWH

BTU PER KWH

HEAT RATE FOR
STEAM ELECTRIC GENERATION

Companies Comprising
High Temperature Reactor
Development Associates

High Temperature Reactor Development Associates, Inc., was incorporated as a nonprofit Delaware corporation on November 13, 1958. It was organized for scientific and educational purposes, including research and development activities looking toward the utilization of nuclear material for the generation of usable energy and for other commercial and industrial applications as may appear of practical value. The fifty-three utility companies associated with HTRDA are:

Alabama Power Company
Arizona Public Service Company
Arkansas Power & Light Company
Atlantic City Electric Company
Baltimore Gas and Electric Company
California Electric Power Company
Central Illinois Electric and Gas Co.
Central Illinois Light Company
Central Illinois Public Service Company
Central Louisiana Electric Company
Central Power and Light Company
The Cincinnati Gas & Electric Company

The Cleveland Electric Illuminating Company
Delaware Power & Light Company
The Detroit Edison Company
Gulf Power Company
Gulf States Utilities Company
The Hawaiian Electric Company, Ltd.
Idaho Power Company
Illinois Power Company
Iowa Public Service Company
Kansas City Power & Light Company
The Kansas Power and Light Company
Kentucky Utilities Company
Louisiana Power & Light Company
Mississippi Power & Light Company
Mississippi Power Company
Missouri Public Service Company
The Montana Power Company
New Orleans Public Service, Inc.
New York State Electric & Gas Corporation
Niagara Mohawk Power Corporation
Pacific Gas and Electric Company
Pacific Power & Light Company
Pennsylvania Power & Light Company
Philadelphia Electric Company
Portland General Electric Company
Potomac Electric Power Company
Public Service Company of Colorado
Public Service Company of New Mexico
Public Service Company of Oklahoma
Public Service Electric and Gas Company

Puget Sound Power & Light Company
Rochester Gas and Electric Corporation
St. Joseph Light & Power Company
San Diego Gas & Electric Company
Sierra Pacific Power Company
Southern California Edison Company
Southwestern Electric Power Company
The United Illuminating Company
Utah Power & Light Company
The Washington Water Power Company
West Texas Utilities Company

INDEX

Index

397

399

405

Philadelphia Trades League, 90–91
Philadelphia Transportation Company, 356
Philipsburg, 25
Philler, George R., 55
Phoenixville, 213, 293, 313
Pigeon Point, Del., 215
Pinchot, Gov. Gifford, 175, 232, 245, 246; attacks PE, 225, 226; attacks Public Service Commission, 224, 225, 226–227; attacks utilities, 224–227; and "giant power," 198–199, 225
Pittsburgh, 24, 25, 61, 207, 322, 333; steel strike, 143
Pittsburgh Publishing Company, 24–25
Pocono Mountains, 279
Point Breeze Track, 83
Politics. See City Councils; Government; Pennsylvania
Population, 349, 369; of Phila. (1880), 1; suburban growth, 1, 5–7, 11, 306, 352, 355; of Wilmington, 352
Port of Philadelphia, 307–308
Port Richmond piers, 153, 154
Porter, Charles, A., 27–28, 29, 59
Porter, Edward, 216, 272, 276, 366
Porter-Allen steam engines, 18
Potomac Electric Power Company, 347
Pottstown, 25, 214
Pottstown Gas Company, 278
Pottsville, 279
Powelton Electric Company, 27, 59
Power Reactor Development Company, 344
Prices: of coal, 131, 155, 156, 326; during World War I, 131; ferry (1880), 5; of meals (1915), 129; of milk, 114, 131; of oil, 326; P.R.T. fares, 107–108, 144, 175, 176; of culm, 51; water rental (1888), 40. See also Rates
Printing presses, 22, 41
Prohibition, 143–144, 187–188
Public Information Program, 334
Public Ledger, viii, 87, 217, 235
Public Service Commission (Md.), and Conowingo, 173–177 passim
Public Service Commission (Pa.), 114, 138, 219, 245; and Conowingo, 173–177 passim; grants rate increases, 136, 155; PE rate cases before, 114, 116–121, 174; Pinchot attack on, 224–227 passim; reduces rates, 246–247. See also Public Utility Commission
Public Service Corporation of N. J., 139, 220, 244; buys PE power, 150, 211; cuts dividend, 136, 144; U.G.I. interest in, 136, 209, 258, 269, 271
Public Service Electric and Gas Company, 215, 293; Burlington station, 132, 316, 349; Camden substation, 349; co-ordinates with PE system, 316, 348–349, 381, 382; Gloucester substation, 150, 349. See also Pa.-N.J. Interconnection
Public Utility Commission (Pa.), 329, 356; allows rate increase, 325; policy on utility earnings (1943), 289; reduces electric rates, 247, 288
Public Utility Holding Company Act (1935), 249–250, 260, 265, 269–273 passim
Public Utility Law, 356
Public Works Administration (P.W.A.), 241–242, 244, 245

Quay, Matthew S., 10, 24, 27, 59, 61

Racing. See Auto racing; Boating; Horse racing
Racquet Club, 274
Radios, 186, 198, 232, 252, 282; PE broadcasts, 196; reception, 197
Railroads, 2, 153; coal car shortage, 153, 154, 155; electric trains, 22; freight costs, 155, 156; operated by government, 139, 154; strikes, 153. See also Baltimore & Ohio Railroad; Pennsylvania Railroad; Reading Railroad
Rainey-Wood Coke Company, 214, 279, 323, 381
Ramsey, H. W., 277, 330, 366
Ranges: coal, 2, 99; electric, 99, 101, 149, 235, 240, 252, 266, 300, 304; gas, 99, 231; wood, 2. See also Kitchens
Rates: 34–35, 49, 64; of arc lights, 20, 34; of Edison Co., 43; gas (U.G.I.), 89, 114; and holding companies, 221; Maloney reduces, 56–57; political attacks on, 224–229 passim,

413

with Brush Electric Light Co., 24–
25, 31, *see also* Electric Trust
United States Shipping Board, 133,
140, 218
United States Steel Corporation, 250;
Fairless Works, 306, 307, 315, 322
University of Pennsylvania, 37, 351,
357–358, 359, 360
Utilities: and atomic power, 342–346;
federal investigation of, 222; political attack on, 224–229; public ownership of, 199, 228, 240, 243, 244–
245, 248, 251, 333–335; regulation,
119; strike of, 291. *See also various
utilities;* Holding companies

Vacuum cleaners, 78, 99, 101, 148,
149, 196
Vail, J. H., 39, 55
Vare, William S., 113–114
Vauclain, Samuel, 188
Villard, Henry, 43
Vine Street, 310, 355
Virginia, 370
Viteles, Dr. Morris S., 359–360, 361
Volta, Alessandro, 14

Wagner, Herbert A., 183
Wagner, Gen. Louis, 40
Walnut Street, lighting on, 102
Walsh, Vincent J., 331
Walt Whitman Bridge, 308, 356, 357
Wanamaker, John, 13, 15, 17, 83
Wanamaker Grand Depot, 13, 15, 18,
20, 377; Chestnut St. store, 98
War Industries Board, 138, 139
War Manpower Commission, 295
War Production Board, 283, 284, 286,
287, 290, 295, 299
Warden, William G., 9, 11, 12, 24, 25,
31, 32, 259
Warden, Frew and Company, 11
Warwick, Mayor Charles F., 58
Washing machines, 101, 148, 149, 196,
305, 306
Washington, D. C., 286
Water heating: electric, 252, 300; gas,
321
Water supply, 2, 40, 132
Watson, C. W., 366
Weaver, Mayor John, 88

Weeks, Ada Mae, 160
Welfare Federation, 231
Welsbach mantle, 12
Welsbach Street Lighting Company,
113
Welsh, John, 17
Welsh, John Lowber, 17, 23, 31, 32, 55
West Chester, 192
West Chester Gas Company, 278, 377
West End Electric Company, 57, 59, 72
West End Hotel, 18
West Philadelphia, 315, 357; elevated
line, 84, 92
West Virginia, 143, 154
Westinghouse, Henry H., 30
Westinghouse Electric Manufacturing
Company, 30–31; equipment, 237–
238, 281, 285, 341, 383
Westmoreland, 182
Weston arc light, 15
Weston Electric Lighting Company, 24
Wetherill engine, 73
Wharton, William, Jr., 7
Wheeler, Burton K., 248
Wheeler-Rayburn bills, 248, 249. *See
also* Public Utility Holding Com-
pany Act
White Hall, 5
Whitemarsh Hall, 144
Whitwell, George, vii, 264, 277, 307,
309, 354; and Edison Electric Insti-
tute, 239–240, 253; honors, 297;
sales campaigns, 234–235, 254; vice-
president, 234, 276
Widener, P. A. B., 9, 46; biog. sketch,
10; electric company interests, 24,
25, 29, 31, 62; PE director, 66, 84;
traction interests, 11, 25, 45, 83, 84,
87, 108; and U.G.I., 12, 85
Widener Building, 98
Wilkes-Barre, 25, 277
Williamson, Isaiah V., 16–17
Willow Grove, 109, 232
Willow Grove Park, 46–47, 356
Wilmington, Del., 5, 192, 214, 320, 352
Wilson, Alex, 128, 276
Wilson, S. Davis, 245
Wilson, Woodrow, 133
Windmill Island, 46
Windrim, John T., 73, 78, 95, 105,
127, 131, 137, 190, 204
Winner, Clifford, 276, 290, 366
Wires, 3; follow railroad right of
way, 182, 348; overhead, ordinance

Text letterpress printed by The Winchell Company, Philadelphia, in 12-point Baskerville on 70 lb. Sonata Text paper made by the Hopper Paper Company, Reading, Pa. Illustrations photo-offset by The Winchell Company on 80 lb. Sonata Text. Binding by William Marley Company, Philadelphia. Cover and dust jacket designed by Harry J. Oshiver; pen and ink illustrations by Norman Guthrie Rudolph.

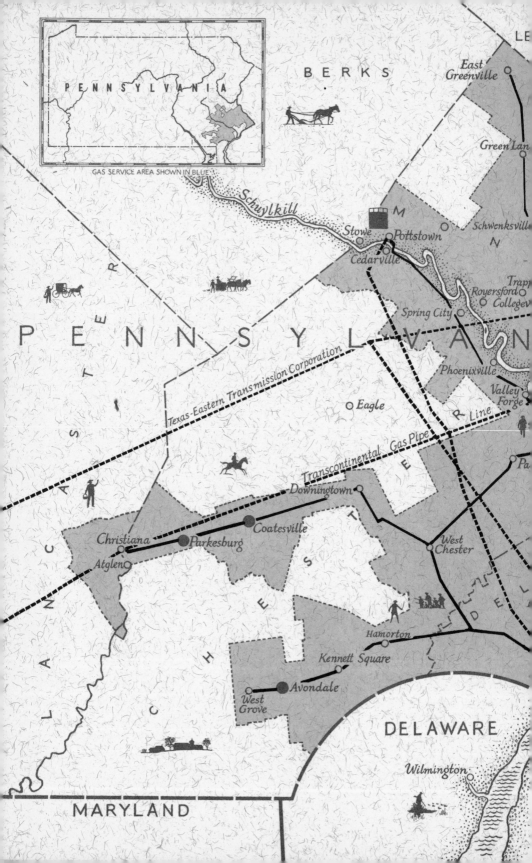

PENNSYLVANIA

GAS SERVICE AREA SHOWN IN BLUE

BERKS

East
Greenville

Green Lan

Schwenksville

Schuylkill

Stowe

Pottstown

Cedarville

M

N

Trapp
Royersford
Collegev

Spring City

PENNSYLVANIA

Phoenixville

Valley
Forge

Texas-Eastern Transmission Corporation

R Line

Eagle

E

Transcontinental Gas Pipe

Pa

Downingtown

Christiana

Parkesburg

Coatesville

West
Chester

Atglen

C

H

E

S

T

E

R

D

E

L

Hamorton

Kennett Square

West
Grove

Avondale

DELAWARE

Wilmington

MARYLAND

LE

L A N C A S T E R